POLISH SAUSAGES
AUTHENTIC RECIPES AND INSTRUCTIONS

STANLEY MARIANSKI, ADAM MARIANSKI
MIROSLAW GEBAROWSKI

Bookmagic, LLC.
Seminole, Florida.

Polish Sausages, Authentic Recipes And Instructions.
Stanley Marianski, Adam Marianski, Miroslaw Gebarowski.

ISBN: 978-0-9824267-2-2
Library of Congress Control Number: 2009905129
First edition 2007. Second edition 2009. Third edition 2015.

Bookmagic, LLC.
www.bookmagic.com

Printed in the United States of America.

Contents

Introduction

In November 2004, a Pole, Miroslaw Gebarowski, became so dissatisfied with the deteriorating state of Polish meat products that he decided to do something about it. He started a Polish forum on the Internet dedicated to the proper methods of meat preparation and the idea took off like a roller coaster. At that time Stanley Marianski lived in the USA and one day at a party he was arguing with his friends over some Polish sausage recipes. He jumped on the Internet and started to look for more information but the information he found in English was far from satisfactory. Finally in desperation he formed the question in Polish and imagine the surprise when he found his answer on the newly created forum.

That started the relationship that continues to this day. The Forum became so popular that in February 2005 its web presence was established www.wedlinydomowe.pl (Polish version) and the English site www.wedlinydomowe.com (presently www.meatsandsausages.com) soon followed. At present, with 30,000 members, the Polish site is the biggest site of its kind in the world. The explanation for this incredible popularity of the site was the general dissatisfaction with the steady decline in quality, of once great meat products which can be traced to the collapse of the communist system in Poland and joining the European Common Market. The country opened up to Western Europe and this introduced new chemicals and preparation procedures which were designed to produce products in the fastest and cheapest way. Unfortunately, those changes resulted in processed meats of lower quality.

The home based sausage maker does not face those problems and for him the quality of his sausage is of the utmost importance, after all he and his family will eat it. Besides, for most people sausage making is a hobby from which they derive pleasure and the time spent is not a limiting factor. Having unlimited time and putting his heart into the process, he can create a product that is superior to the one available in the supermarket. In the pages that follow you will find everything about the production of sausages, covering topics like meat technology, curing, home style smoking, and even some old-fashioned tips and advice.

By carefully reading the material presented in this book and making different sausages, one can become an accomplished sausage maker in no time at all. He will be able to produce superior quality sausages and they will be made without chemicals. We can proudly say that this book represents over 500 years of sausage making, as well as all Polish sausage recipes. The following recipes are not just another invention of someone who likes to drink beer and make sausages. They are time proven recipes compiled, checked and enforced by the Polish Government Standards as applied to making meat products after World War II. With their vast resources and university educated meat professionals, the government became the final authority on the subject and took control of enforcing the standards.

Why did the Polish Government Regulate Sausages

The answer is as old as the world itself: the money. When the war ended Communism was forced on Poland which had been a free country before. That isolated the government from the rest of the world and prevented Poland from receiving any assistance from the West. The country was in ruin, some cities were 80 % damaged, every fifth person in the family was dead and the Polish currency "zloty" was not convertible. In other terms, nobody in the free world would accept that currency. The government was not able to purchase goods from other countries nor obtain loans or credits. That forced the country to go back in time and start selling natural resources like coal, vodka, fruits and meat products. Those products had to be of an exceptional quality if they were to be accepted in the West and the Government spared no effort.

The Communistic doctrine says that everything belongs to the state and all independent meat plants were nationalized (became the property of the state). That also applied to sausage making plants and here is where the government excelled. The party members run the meat plants now and they spent half of their time drinking vodka and eating well. Being generally smart, well educated and opportunistic people they could easily determine which sausages tasted the best and they became good judges of quality. The Department of Meat Industry *(Centralny Zarząd Przemysłu Mięsnego)* was established and those creative people came up with the great idea of standardizing Polish meat products. College educated meat technologists wrote great guides about making meat products which covered processes like meat aging, meat curing, smoking and cooking in great detail. The first 300 page long manual was written in 1958 and contained step by step instructions for making meat products and 70 sausages. The guide was for internal use only and the general public had no access to it. But at least the meat plant managers now had a set of instructions for making quality meat products and those norms were rigidly enforced by the government meat inspectors. This set of regulations was revised in 1964, 1974, 1978 and the years that followed. Even today the Polish Government publishes standards for making Polish sausages.

Unfortunately the latest norms are just a shadow of the detailed instructions from the past and basically they list the meat type and the list of ingredients that should go into a particular product. Today the meat industry consists of hundreds of independent plants and as there is no enforcement from the government, the standards are loosely obeyed. The present products are just echoes from the past.

Some may argue that today's products are healthier. Well, we agree with that but this is not a diet book. This is a book about making the best tasting products possible. Imitation butter is also healthier than butter but no respectable chef will take a risk of making creamy sauce with an imitation butter. He will be out of the door in a minute as there is no way to replace butter's great flavor. The same applies to mayonnaise, cream cheese, milk and other products. There is a choice to be made between eating well and eating healthy.

During the war Mr. Goebels, the German Minister of Propaganda used to say that if the lie is repeated often enough it would become the truth. If you and your wife will start repeating every day that imitation mayonnaise or lean meat sausage taste better because it is healthy, most likely you will eventually and sincerely believe in it and for you it will become the truth. But your friends will hold a different opinion. We are not claiming that the sausages must always be made the way our recipes call for. We are simply offering those recipes with detailed instructions on making them so they will never be forgotten.

Why Did We Make Better Sausages Before?

The general consensus in Poland is that Polish meat products were absolutely the best in the years 1950 - 1990 and that statement will probably hold true for other European countries as well. We have the utmost respect for the latest in science and computers but we do think that making meat products might be an isolated case where the technology has lowered the taste of the product. Sausage making has been a dying art and there is almost no way to obtain quality products unless they are home made.

That does not mean that our meat plants are not capable of making quality products. After all, in 1969 we put a man on the moon, the Internet has been running for 40 years, and computers allow us to change the very rules of nature. So why can't we make a decent sausage? We can't because everything is controlled by the dollar, including sausages. They must be made in the most efficient manner, and that means cheap and fast. As long as supermarkets keep on renewing orders, and the Food and Drug Administration does not object to the ingredients, quality plays a secondary role. The job of the FDA is to regulate what chemicals can be added into a product and in what quantities they can be safely used when added to meat. The FDA was not created to judge products according to taste and flavor.

Well, we understand that you cannot change the latest technology as it follows the commands of economics which in turn follows the laws of finance. And those laws dictate that money must be made as this is the nature of business. There are hundreds of marketers that would explain why we produce foods differently today and they will all argue that it is done for the good of the consumer. We also know that there is a growing number of people who don't care what's good for the consumer, they care about what's good for them and that is why they make their own products.

How Our Book Differs From Others

1. Factory procedures. This is probably the only written book on sausages that provides factory floor step by step instructions on making different products. It is like revealing the most treasured internal secrets and recipes to the world at large. And this is exactly what we have done: we have revealed sausage recipes and instructions on their making which have been strictly guarded for generations. Go to any sausage making plant and ask the manager for the recipe and detailed instructions of the products his company makes. You will be shown the door.

Just by studying those recipes and instructions one can develop a good feel of the subject. You will see how every part of the animal was utilized to make different types of sausages. *And these are not recipes that were copied from a neighbor or found somewhere on the Internet.* These are recipes and production processes of the products that have been made in Poland for centuries and those products were distributed all over the nation for the public to consume. Studying this material a newcomer to the business can easily open his own commercial sausage kitchen and even experienced people will fine tune their skills by just reading this book.

2. Meat Curing for Sausages. This book introduces the concept of meat curing for sausages as it has always been practiced in Poland by the general population and the meat plants. This extra processing step improves the looks, texture, taste and the flavor of the product. And this is not a secret, everybody in Poland knows that meat for sausages must be cured. This is something that is almost sacred and not even open for discussion. Even if you decide to continue making sausages without curing meat first, it would be nice to know how it should be done properly.

Yes, meat plants cure hams, butts, loins, bacon and other large pieces of meat. And we have million dollar machines that inject those meats with commercially prepared solutions. But if one opens a sausage book he finds that there is total silence on curing meats for sausages. And curing meats for sausages is not limited to Poland but is practiced in Russia and Germany, both countries famous for their meat products and sausages.

3. "Whys". You will find many books that provide valuable information like: remove visible air pockets by pricking casings with a needle, shower smoked products with cold water, boil some sausages and bake others, stuff casings firmly or stuff them loosely, etc. We provide this general information as well but at the same time we go into extreme detail to explain to the reader why it is done that way and not the other. And all those "whys" are what will help you fully understand and master the art of sausage making.

For Whom is This Book Written

Anybody that makes or intends to make Polish sausages or any kind of sausage will greatly benefit from this book. Even Polish butchers that make sausages all over the world should make it a point of reference. We have a label from the popular Polish Kabanosy meat stick made by a butcher plant in New York that calls for beef in addition to pork. For 200 years Kabanosy was always made with pure pork so why mess up the 200 year old recipe?

For centuries sausage recipes were not publicized. They were passed from the father to the son, but otherwise kept closely guarded. The government compiled all known recipes together and established manufacturing rules and instructions. They were, however, reserved for internal use only. In other words they were classified. Butchers who were licenced by the Official Trade Associations were issued those detailed sausage standards but to limit competition they kept them strictly to themselves.

We at Wedliny Domowe have every publication that was written on the subject by the long gone government and we have decided to open up this treasure chest of sausage recipes. There are Polish families living all over the world and kids are definitely introduced to sausages at an early age. One day when older, they will not be able to get the answer from their parents who will not be around forever. And if they decide to make their own Polish sausage this book will be of invaluable help.

There are many so called Polish sausage recipes floating on the Internet and many originate on some huge sites that employ who write well. This is what they do for a living, they fish for recipes and they place them in a particular category. They did not get the job because they studied meat science, they got the job because they write well. How many do you think have ever made a blood sausage, head cheese or cold smoked salmon?

A hard working mother of four does her shopping in a supermarket and buys sliced turkey breast and some sausages. The price is the main factor she's concerned with. After a few days her kid says: "look Ma, this sliced turkey breast is still juicy". And Ma acting in her best intentions will reply: "yeah, this is good stuff." Little she knows that the phosphates and other ingredients have finally lost their binding power and all this juice (slime) is nothing else than the water that was injected with chemicals into the meat during production. Her ignorance is of an innocent kind because she simply does not know any better, but what is tragic is that there are generations of young people who will never find out what the real ham or smoked turkey should taste like. To sell mass produced and passable quality products to a hard working mother of four, all the supermarket has to do is to say: "save money" and "buy one get one free." That is why we have all those flyers and manufacturer's coupons.

This book is written for those people, to wake them up so they can realize that a pork loin, ham or a sausage can have a completely different taste to the one they have been accustomed to. They could order it by mail from some specialty suppliers, or they could buy it from some ethnic butcher stores if still present in the area they live in, or *they could make it themselves.* Our task is to preserve the legacy of those wonderful products, uncover original and authentic recipes and provide instructions on how to make them. That way they will not become a forgotten thing of the past but will live forever.

Our group consists of hundreds of professional and home based sausage makers who have been making those Polish products all their lives. They know how they were made and how they tasted 50 years ago and they can see the difference when they buy the product today. And they all agree as to the authenticity of the following recipes. Fortunately more and more people start making sausages and this book was written for them. Another reason is to preserve the centuries of knowledge and tradition that were instrumental for the development of so many wonderful products.

For the novice some recipes may at first look somewhat intimidating as they are loaded with technical information and detailed instructions for their making. We believe the real strength of this book lies exactly in those instructions and by just reading them one can develop a great feel for what sausage making is about. In this chapter we intend to simplify some of the steps used in the production process and make them more acceptable to the average sausage maker. This way he will be able to make any sausage from this book and the key is understanding the basic sausage making steps.

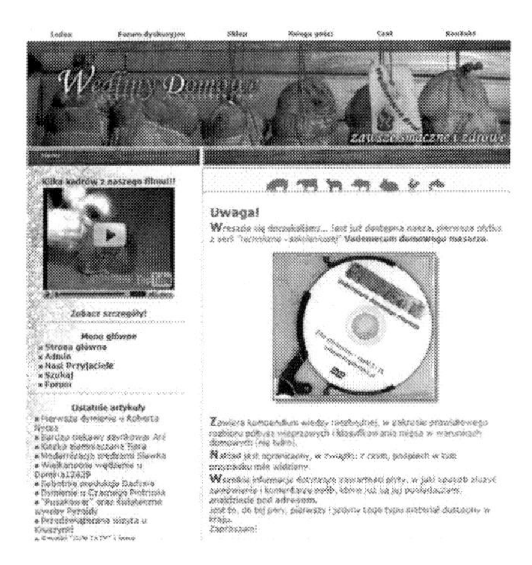

www.wedlinydomowe.pl

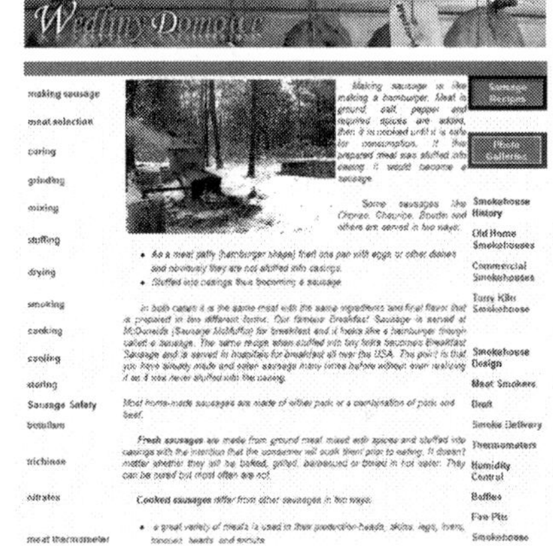

www.wedlinydomowe.com
www.meatsandsausages.com

Chapter 1

History of Polish Sausages

Even today in countries like Poland or Germany smoked meats and sausages account for about 60% of all meat products sold to a consumer. For comparison it is estimated that in the USA smoked meats account for about 30% of meats sold. And hot dogs constitute the largest portion of this number, though few people ever think of them as a smoked product. A meat department in an American supermarket pales in comparison with its counterpart in Poland or Germany where in addition to fresh and smoked meats there are dozens of different sausages and all kinds of smoked fish such as eel, herring, mackerel and others. The popularity of pork in smoked products can be attributed to a few reasons:

- Pork meat was most popular among the masses. Unlike pragmatic animals like cows and horses, pigs were not of much practical benefit besides the fact that they were the first sanitation system. In ancient Rome they roamed the streets at nightfall and ate any leftover garbage. In early Europe, there was a strong sentiment towards cows. They produced milk which was processed into butter, cheese and cream. They were also used for labor, pulling ploughs and performing other chores. Upon death they were buried, not eaten. On the other hand, pigs were not of much practical use, but they tasted good and were prepared in hundreds of different ways. The pigs were smart: when the times were hard they ran away to the forest where they ate nuts, acorns and berries. When the danger passed they would return to villages where they would roam around and eat whatever was available.
- Pigs reproduced rapidly and ate everything.
- Pork meat was the best meat for curing and smoking.
- Pigs felt much safer living next to humans and became one of the first animals domesticated by man.

Countries in Northern Europe smoked meats well before America was discovered. In 1493 Christopher Columbus took 8 pigs into new territories and they were released in Cuba. Then in 1539 Hernando de Soto landed with 13 pigs in Tampa Bay, Florida and he deserves to be called the king of the pork industry in the USA. By that time the art of making sausages was in full swing in Europe.

The Importance of Christmas and Easter Holidays

When Poland became a Catholic nation in 966, it affected the ways people ate and behaved. There was an unusually large number of days when people had to fast and of course on those days meat consumption was not allowed. Even today most Catholics do not eat meat on Friday. But there were two periods when people were allowed to celebrate and eat to their hearts content, and that was Christmas and Easter.

A pig would be slaughtered and processed a few weeks before Christmas or Easter, and the noble cuts of meat like ham, butt, and loins would be cured and smoked. Remaining scraps of meat such as the liver, tongue, heart, skins and blood were reserved for headcheeses, liver and blood sausages. Bacon and fatback would be smoked, some of the back fat would be rendered to make lard. A pig is a very unique animal where nothing is wasted. Even the bones will be used to make soup stock. Those products had to last over the winter and often until summer when it was time to gather crops and the ready to eat sausages would become food and snacks out in the field. For a common person eating meat was still limited to holidays or family occasions like weddings. Even relatively well off people would eat meat only on Sundays.

Photo 1.1 As every year Dziadek (Grandpa in Polish) starts Christmas production. He makes it all: smoked hams, loins, sausages, liver, blood sausages, and head cheeses and when he is done not a single scrap of meat remains.

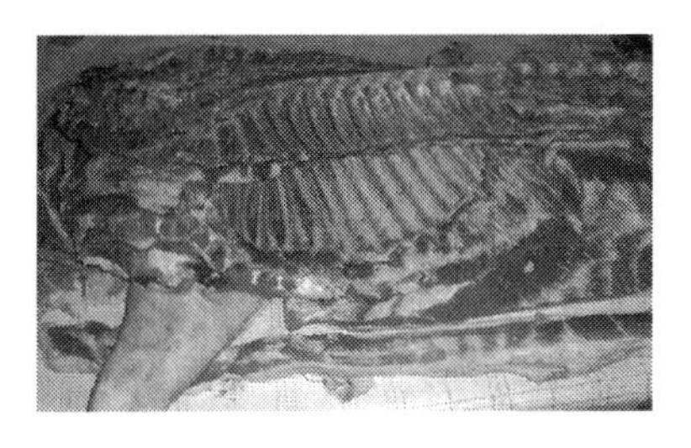

Photo 1.2 This is what separates sausage makers like "Dziadek" from others. He can do it all.

Photo 1.3 Finished sausages.

They might land a good paying job in a large factory taking care of some department, but to make it from A-Z by yourself is a different matter. Pig slaughter was not just a kill, it was a long awaited event, a kind of social gathering where in addition to the host and his family, his friends and neighbors were also invited.

Christmas Eve dinner traditionally would be served after sunset, then many people would attend Midnight Mass. The table would be set up close to the beautifully ornamented Christmas tree and the gifts would be placed under it. People would walk to one another, break a little part of holy wafer and make wishes for the new year. Then the dinner was served although no meat was allowed. Fish was fine and the carp was traditionally prepared in different ways. But on the first day of Christmas all restrictions would be lifted and people would try to make up for all those days of rigid fasting. This is when some serious eating took place and meat products and sausages played an important part.

During Easter Holidays meat products became the most important item on the menu. For those that did not witness it first hand, it is hard to imagine hundreds of people standing in a line that began outside of the meat store and waiting their turn to get the provisions they need. And that continued non-stop for 12 hours a day. This is how Christmas and Easter have been celebrated in Poland for a thousand years and these holidays definitely sustained the popularity of sausages until today.

In Poland people eat sausages all the time, most of them smoked. The commonly eaten "White Sausage" is a not smoked fresh sausage which is traditionally served with soup called "żurek" at Easter time.

Photo 1.4 Leaving church.

A day earlier people prepared a wicker gift basket that contained items like bread, eggs, horseradish and of course sausages.

This basket was taken to the nearest church where it was blessed by the priest during a short mass. This blessed food was arranged on the breakfast table among hams, bacon, and countless varieties of sausages.

A holy wafer was used to make wishes at Christmas and sliced egg was used to make wishes at Easter. People walked to one another and shared a piece of quartered egg exchanging wishes.

Photo 1.5 The Catholic priest blessing food in Brooklyn, New York City.

Photo 1.6 & **Photo 1.7** Large and small family tables. On Easter Day the sausages are everywhere.

History of Polish Sausages - the Middle Ages

Until the late 900's when Poland became a unified country, there were no written records on Polish customs or everyday life. We do know from archeological sites that trade merchants from Rome and other countries visited Polish territories reaching as far north as the Baltic Sea as early as 500 B.C. They followed what was known as the Amber Route to get amber (thousands of years old crystallized tree resin or sap) that was held in high esteem and was washed ashore by the Baltic Sea. Besides valuable amber the local tribes provided merchants with fine furs.

On the other hand the merchants displayed manufactured goods such as gold and silver jewelry, silver and bronze dishes and drinking cups, gold medallions with the likenesses of Roman nobles and coins. In addition they brought swords, knives, spices and dry sausages. Romans liked pork and made the whole assortment of sausages. Without a doubt the art of making sausages had originated in Rome and reached other areas by trade merchants and Roman military legions.

The ties between Poland and Rome strengthened when Poland accepted Christianity as a nation in 966. In 1000 Otto III, a highly educated Holy Roman Emperor and a fervent Christian, travelled to Poland where he became friends with Polish King Boleslaw I the Brave (Boleslaw Chrobry). Both nobles exchanged gifts and dined for three days. Contacts of this kind were helpful in learning social customs and culinary arts between different countries and new ways of meat preparation were of great interest to all. The Catholic Church required many days of fasting and that influenced the way people dined. On many days not only meat, but even eggs, butter or milk were prohibited and the penalties were severe. Adding to it the fact that meat was very expensive and beyond the reach of an average peasant, we can conclude that sausages were mainly consumed by the privileged class and clergy. The monasteries were cultural centers where most of the science research was conducted and those places were familiar with methods of meat preservation or beer and wine making.

In the second part of the Middle Ages (X - XVI century) the individual castles or large households were the centers of cultural life and culinary arts. Of course they were owned by noblemen who also owned entire villages. All of them were self-reliant on food. The peasants that lived in a particular village were also self-reliant and they prospered quite well. It was not unusual when some of them owned cattle or horses. Polish cuisine of that era was simple and based on meats, sausages, fish, bread, grouts, vegetables, fruits and honey that was commonly used in place of an expensive sugar. The food warehouse or kitchen pantries were stocked with items like wheat and rye, flour, bread, buckwheat and barley groats, peas and beans, vegetable oils, dry and pickled mushrooms, sauerkraut, salted and smoked meats, sausages, salted and smoked fish, cheeses, butter, eggs, wooden barrels with beer, honey and fruit wines. The most popular vegetables were cabbage, onion, garlic, cucumbers, carrots, parsley and caraway. The dishes were simple but the plate had to be large and full of food.

In the Middle Ages as the cities grew larger in size and the food markets developed, this culinary exchange of ideas progressed even further and people got acquainted with new dishes and recipes. Some regions became well known for the type of sausage they made and many sausages of today still carry those original names. Those independent households gave origin to the regionally prepared foods and sausages were no exception.

In 1646 Polish King Mieczyslaw IV married French Ludwika Maria Gonzaga, the daughter of Prince Charles Gonzaga and that brought sophisticated French cuisine into Poland. Liver sausages and pâtés became popular and not the size of a meal, but its looks and presentation became more important.

The next 50 years were very turbulent as the country was invaded by the Swedish, Russians and Turks and had to deal with mutiny by Cossacks. Although Poland repelled those invasions, it emerged from those wars terribly ruined and depopulated. The wars were accompanied by plagues and famine. The population which before 1645 amounted to some 10 million, decreased to 6 million at the end of the century. Trade shrank, currency lost in value and economic reconstruction was slow.

In XVIII century we find first mention of the word *"kielbasa"*. It describes a thick sausage, dark in color (heavily smoked) and a few feet long. This sausage was an ever present item on the tables of noblemen and better off knights. Merchants would carry it during their long travels, knights would be seen riding horses and carrying sausages at the belt. In those times the favorite hobby of the royalty was hunting and venison with wild birds was served regularly on the menu. So it comes as no surprise that wild boar, deer or rabbit meat was often combined with pork and new spices were introduced, thus creating new sausage varieties. In time the kielbasa diversified into regional brands and new recipes were created. Copying customs of the rich households, the peasants in villages started to make sausages, first for their own enjoyment, then for the trade and sale.

Lithuanian Products

There was a region in the Northeastern part of Poland that we have to mention as it produced magnificent products. This region known today as Lithuania was once a part of Poland. It became famous for its smoked products that would last for 2 years at room temperature (76°F, 25°C) without apparent loss of flavor. The meat was carefully chosen from 12-15 month old pigs that were fed mainly rye, barley and potatoes. In some cases the pig was fed exclusively with flour. Different methods of slaughter were employed; the pig was killed by inserting a knife into its heart and the wound would be immediately closed with a wooden plug. That prevented blood loss and imparted a dark-red color to the meat. For the same reason the pig was not hung but lay stomach down. To remove the hair, the pig was not scalded with hot water as this would have made skin and meat too soft. Instead the pig was burned all over its body with burning hay and then the hair was scraped with knives. Then the entrails would be removed and the pig would be carved into pieces.

Large meat cuts would be cold smoked for 2-3 weeks and smaller products for 10-12 days. Unusually tall smokehouses with a free standing source of smoke were employed to produce cold smoke. Then the finished products were covered with a 2-3 mm (0.1") layer of wax to prevent drying. What must be mentioned is that juniper twigs ("juniperus"-gives gin its characteristic flavor) were commonly added to wood logs during smoking to create a specific flavor. Sometimes juniper berries would be added but those most often would be added directly to meat, either in whole or ground form. Juniper sausage ("jałowcowa") had been made in Poland for as long as anybody can remember.

In those times sausages were originally made by cutting meat into smaller pieces and stuffing them into casings through a suitable funnel, often called a stuffing horn. Most old-timers are familiar with the "Finger Sausage" (Palcówka), that derives its name from the word fingers (palce) which were used to stuff the sausage.

There were continuous wars in XVII, XVIII and XIX centuries and only after the end of WWI in 1918 we see making sausages becoming an art. The country was a capitalistic state now and many great sausage making businesses opened up and flourished. The first books on regional cooking and sausage making started to appear.

Between the Wars Period - 1918-1939

After the first World War ended in 1918 there was no centrally organized meat industry. There were hundreds of small meat plants and butcher shops across the country which made products in a slow traditional way using primitive equipment. The city owned slaughter houses provided services to individual butcher shops. Large slaughter houses had some cooling facilities but smaller houses located in little towns did not.

The Czerniewice Meat Plant was one of the first large industrial meat plants and started working in 1912 exporting bacon to England. The plant would buy pigs from local farmers and process meat into finished products. Another known plant located in Motycz specialized mainly in the production of bacon. Bacon would go to England, hams to America and canned hams and dry sausages to Africa. That was a typical method of operation for about two thousand Polish plants in the years 1930-1938. From 1932 and on, more and more factories started to make canned hams and butts for export although the production was still taking place in little plants.

World War II - 1939-1945

Due to Polands's very unique geographical location (the East meets the West) there were always wars taking place on its territory. Always problems with the Russians and the Germans. When Napolean tried to conquer Russia his armies marched through Poland on the way to Moscow and when he retreated the Russians chased him again through Poland. The same happened during WWII, the war did not stop in Poland for a second and either Germans were chasing Russians, or the Russians were chasing Germans with Poles fighting them both. Poland was the buffer zone, a boiling pot where fighting never seemed to stop. When the war ended 20% of the Polish population (6.5 million) was dead and some cities were completely destroyed.

The horses and cattle were decimated but the pigs escaped to the forests and returned back when it was safer. As there was no industry and no farm machinery the agriculture had to be rebuilt using horses and cattle. Pork was the meat of the necessary choice and the products had to be cured and smoked to be preserved for later use as there was no refrigeration. During the war Germany took over Czerniewice meat plant to produce meats for its military. In 1950 the plant was back in Polish hands and it resumed its meat production. Better equipment was installed and the plant started producing the whole assortment of meats and sausages for export and for the local market. In the 1990's after the fall of the government the plant was in deep trouble and declared bankruptcy in 2000. A year later the plant was taken over by the Polish company "Mat" and has been continuing its operations until today.

The Glory Years (1945-1989)

During WWII (1939 - 1945) most meat plants were destroyed and the re-birth was very slow. In 1948 only about 600 slaughter houses were in operation. Creating a new, modern and prospering meat industry became a necessity for the government. The country's currency "zloty" was not convertible, the government needed hard currency and the only way to get it was to export raw (coal) materials or finished goods (vodka, meat products). The government spared no effort to create the best meat industry. A peculiar characteristic of the new regime was its fondness for long-term planning:

- 3-year plan (1947-1949) - re-building war damages and re-growth of animal herds.
- 6-year plan (1950-1955) - modernization and development of the meat industry. Mechanical methods of slaughter were introduced, new plants were built and older ones were modernized. More types of meats, sausages and canned products were produced, both for export and for local needs.
- 5-year plan (1956-1960) - further modernization and development of the meat industry. Specifically designed machines were introduced to facilitate faster and more economical cutting and carving of animals and newer methods of production were implemented. Huge diversification of meat products was visible. Assembly line production concept was introduced. *Meat technology manuals with manufacturing instructions and detailed recipes were written to be used in meat plants in order to produce a consistent and high quality product.* That was the beginning of the Golden Era of Polish Sausages.

Until 1945 a sausage of the same name had many variants and although the basic recipe remained the same, different regions used different spices which led to different flavors of the product. The typical example was the sausage known as Kabanosy that in 1920-1930 started to appear in all areas of the country. In 1945 someone in the newly organized government came up with a brilliant idea of standardizing Polish meat products using traditional time proven recipes.

The official list of products was drawn and the Department of the Meat Industry started to work out details. In 1959 the first official guide for making meat products and sausages was issued. The publication was known as *# 16 Collection of Recipes and Instructions for Making Meat Products and Sausages* and it was reserved for internal use only. At three hundred pages long it had sections on meat curing, making brines, grinding and emulsifying, cooking, methods of smoking, the whole factory process was described in details. It covered 31 smoked products (hams, butts, loins, bacon, 46 sausages, 11 head cheeses and 13 liver and blood sausages. In 1960 the *# 17 version* was issued which was a slightly revised version of # 16. Then in 1964 the Polish Government issued an expanded version called *# 21 Collection of Recipes and Instructions for Making Meat Products and Sausages*. It was 760 pages long and included: 39 smoked products (hams, loins, bacon, ribs), 119 sausages, 12 headcheeses, 19 liver and blood sausages and 11 pâtés and meat loaves. In total 200 meat products were covered and ONLY ONE chemical was used.

The additive was potassium nitrate which had been used for centuries and is still used today although it has been replaced by its easier to administer cousin - "sodium nitrite." In fifty years millions of pounds of meat products and sausages were made without the use of chemicals. Just quality meats and spices. Those government manuals helped to create the best meat industry that ever existed anywhere though its life was only about 50 years. Those manuals were not written by restaurant cooks or college students, but by the best professionals in meat science the country had.

The sausage recipes presented in this book come from these manuals and they were never published before. The project was government funded and no effort or money was spared. This standardization allowed Poland to produce sausages of high and *consistent* quality. Moreover it taught people what to expect from a particular sausage as its taste, texture, color and flavor were basically the same in all areas of the country. All meat plants and retail stores belonged to the government and meat inspectors rigidly enforced the regulations. Suddenly the Kabanosy or Krakowska Sausage tasted exactly the same even when produced in different regions of the country. In 1948 Kabanosy were officially approved as the product name that would be sold in Polish meat stores. In 1954 production instructions were worked out and in 1964 taking under consideration the traditional recipes of the product, the Polish Government adopted the standard recipe that became a legally binding document that could not be changed.

Although those products were of such high quality, their recognition and popularity was mainly limited to Poland. The country was behind the Iron Curtain, its communist system was the worst evil the world has ever known, there was always a possibility of a new war and the Polish currency was not convertible. Those were not helpful conditions for trading sausages between countries of opposite political systems. From that time until the collapse of the system in 1989 Kabanosy and other meat products were always made the same way. This uniform quality enforced by the government meat inspectors made them very famous Polish sausages. Some sausage makers were lucky and rich enough to bribe their way out to getting a passport, others simply defected crossing the border between Yugoslavia and Italy, those people brought the taste of Polish sausages to the USA and other countries.

The war damage and general poverty did not provide the right conditions for fast rebuilding of agriculture. Farmers raised pigs in traditional ways, feeding them with potatoes, grains and kitchen leftovers. The chemical industry was in its infancy, there were no fertilizers so cow's manure was used and this made all products organic and healthy. Those were not conditions that would favor the growth of the economy but *they were the ideal conditions for raising animals of the highest quality meat possible.* Those high quality meats, great recipes without chemicals and proper manufacturing practices allowed the production of great products. Those government manuals covered not only sausages but also hams, bacon, loins, butts, ribs, picnics and all meats that could be boiled, baked, smoked or dried. There are still master butchers and sausage makers from that era and they have been holding on to those publications all their lives. We are very fortunate to have them as members of our site www.wedlinydomowe.pl and our discussion forum. Those people are walking encyclopedias of sausage making knowledge and to them we are deeply indebted.

The Polish ham "Krakus" brand became the best ham in the world and the sausages that were exported had to conform to the highest standards. At that period, between the end of the war and collapse of the communist system Polish meat products were made the best ever. The decline in Polish meat products is synonymous with the fall of the Berlin Wall and the subsequent collapse of communism. This opened Polish borders to the free trade with the West and created new business ventures between Poland and other European countries.

Poland became a new undeveloped market and capital started to flow in. European standards for making meat products were more relaxed than those in Poland and some countries feared competition from Poland once it became the member of the group. As we mentioned the only chemical used in Polish meats and sausages was potassium nitrate even though the list of food additives allowed in Europe was long and impressive. It starts at E 100-Curcumin and ends at E1518-Glyceryl Triacetate. In total 1418 different ingredients can be introduced to the food we consume.

The story goes that when Poland was invited to join the European Common Market it was granted an exception and was permitted to use any quantities of food additives to its sausages. Kind of a catch up game: "jump on the waggon guys and start putting chemicals in your products." Soon many meat processors established joint ventures loaded with capital and new partners. That allowed them to bring the latest technology meat machines and the products were made faster and cheaper. Factory prepared curing solutions were injected into meat to shorten curing time and to increase gain of the product. This peaceful revolution came so suddenly that the new government was not able to control all that was happening. The meat industry imported the latest machinery and chemicals from other European countries and started to follow the same standards of production.

Unfortunately those standards were much lower than the high quality sausage standards that were enforced by the former Polish regime. When Poland officially joined the Common Market in 2004 the situation deteriorated even further. Now the country had to conform to new European regulations and that did not make sausages any better. For example in the 1900's the Polish government allowed 1.5 mg (150 parts per million) of phosphates to be added to 1 kg of meat (phosphates increase meat's water holding capacity). New standards allowed 5 mg of phosphates and of course manufacturers loved the idea as it amounted to higher profits. On the other hand now an average Polish consumer had to swallow three times more chemicals than before and was buying a product with more water in it.

Common Market policies have affected other countries as well. For instance, Germany never allowed the use of liquid smoke in its products. When Germany became a member of the European Common Market it had to conform to new regulations and liquid smoke was added to meat products.

Unfortunately, hundreds of smaller sausage makers who made wonderful products, could not compete with larger companies and went out of business. Very few managed to survive by charging higher prices for their superior products and catering to a more demanding consumer.

Trade Associations *(Cechy)*

In XIII-XVIII century Poland there were trade associations *(cechy)* which enlisted highly trained and experienced members in their particular field. Membership was highly sought as those organizations provided many benefits to their members who in turn gained financial wealth. They also performed the following functions:

- Provided exclusive rights to supply and sell products in a particular city or geographical area.
- Enforced proper manufacturing methods to make sure that their products were of the highest quality.
- Enforced that delivered meat conformed to standards.
- Estimated market demand and accordingly controlled supply.
- Provided specialized training to new would-be members.

The trade organizations structure remained basically the same. What varied was the amount of power they held. Originally they were very strong monopolistic organizations that protected interests and markets of their members. This type of structure continues to this day though it may be called a worker's or trade union. The first sausage making trade organizations were established in XIII century in Kalisz and Torun (birthplace of Nicolaus Copernicus), then in XIV century in Wroclaw and Szczecin. In XV century such organizations prospered in every larger city. At the end of XV century the trade unions made it very difficult for new members to join it. The apprenticeship was made longer, membership fees were higher and no new seats were created. That was done to limit competition and to stabilize prices at the same level. Unfortunately this course of action largely backfired as more people got involved in the sausage making trade by by-passing trade unions.

Photo 1.9 Crest of the City of Belchatow Trade Association.

Photo 1.8 Sausage Makers Trade Association still functions inside Belchatow City Chamber of Commerce building. It was re-established after the war and its first function was to work on new government standards for sausages.

Then came centuries of very turbulent history and trade unions lost much of their enforcing power. Eventually they became training centers and issuers of the trade licences. Although they could not control the market the way they once did, they provided a great service by educating and licensing people who chose sausage making as a career. All individually owned businesses had to belong to the regional trade association that held jurisdiction over that area. Only there they could sign up for new courses, take exams and become members of the group. That allowed them to buy materials that were not available at the market at large, but were centrally distributed by the government to licenced establishments. They were also issued new recipes and only they were authorized to make those sausages. For the struggling economy, materials like fuel, meats and sausages were of utmost importance for the country's survival. The meat industry and its distribution were centralized and so important for the government that any deviation in the recipe or adding food additives not called for was punishable by law. There were few larger affairs where dishonest operators introduced cheap meat substitutions to increase profits and we know of two cases where those responsible were sentenced to death and executed. The Polish Government still issues latest guidelines for making processed meats and sausages. However, they include all chemicals and additives as permissible by the European Common Market Law.

Which Way Are We Going?

There is an enormous interest in the traditional methods of food preparation. A customer is well aware of the present state of the meat industry and expects his products to be healthy. There is a universal dislike towards chemicals and people want to know what goes inside. And they start to make those products at home if only once or twice a year. After just one year our organization Wedliny Domowe has grown so much that its First National Convention took place in August 2006. In addition to hundreds of attendees a number of professional courses and demonstrations were offered. This three day gathering became so popular that it became a yearly celebrated event. Our 8th National Convention took place in August 2013.

Due to many requests from our members in February 2009 we have established our own sausage making school in Lazy. The main objective is to preserve traditional ways of sausage making and save traditional recipes from becoming extinct. These 3 day hands-on experience courses have become a popular event and are offered every month. There are also advanced sausage making, salami making, processing wild game and cheese making courses.

Photo 1.10 Wedliny Domowe First National Convention in 2006.
Left-a woman meat technologist discusses a freshly made sausage.
Middle- a young sausage maker tries to figure it out.

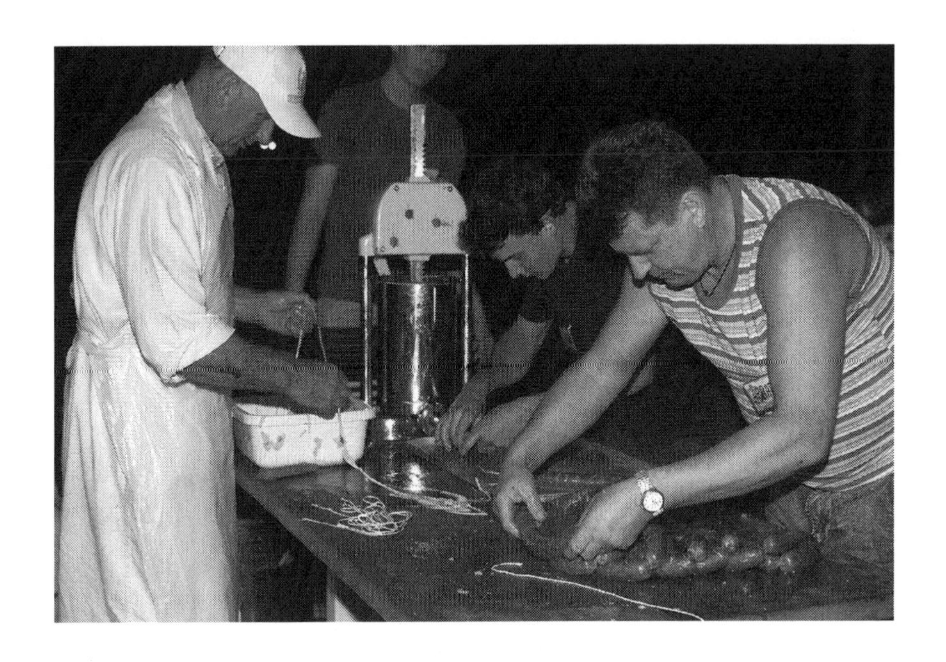

Photo 1.11 Wedliny Domowe 8th National Convention in 2013.
Photo 1.12 A young sausage maker learning trade under supervision.

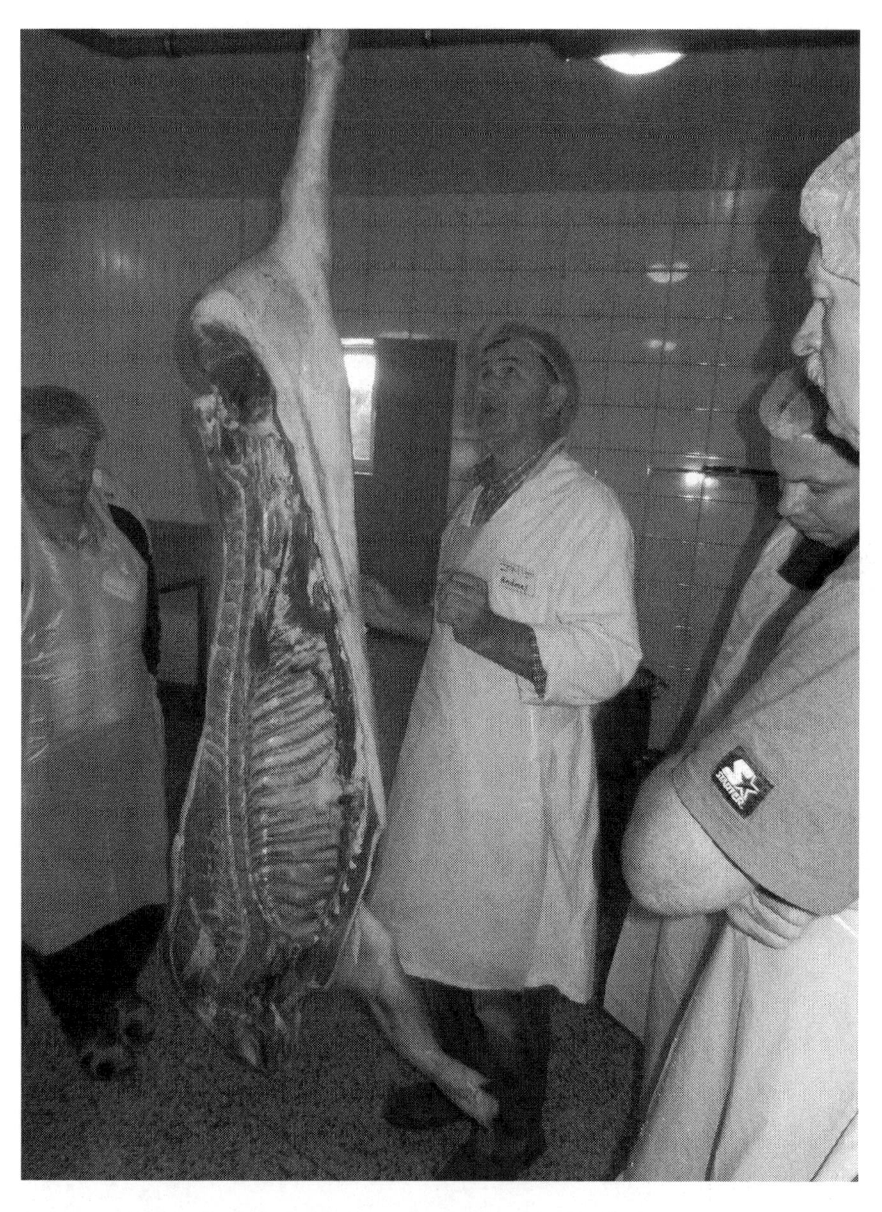

Photo 1.13 The beginning of a sausage making course.

The Mystery of Polish Sausage - What is Kielbasa?

Without a doubt the word "Kielbasa" has worldwide recognition yet it is just one of many wonderful meat products that have been produced for centuries in Poland. It is also often misunderstood. Kielbasa is the Polish general name for "a sausage." You cannot walk into a Polish store and say: "please give me a pound of kielbasa." The sales lady surrounded by 50 different types of kielbasa will inevitably reply: "yes, but which one"? It is like going into a deli and asking for a cheese. Sure, but which one: American, Provolone, Swiss, Gorgonzola, Gouda, Muenster - you have to provide some details.

As the most popular Polish sausage is without a doubt Polish Smoked Sausage, *(Polska Kielbasa Wędzona)* we are willing to speculate that this is what people have in mind. This is probably what the first immigrants brought with them to America. The little problem we face here is that you can find Polish Sausage in almost every supermarket in the USA and no two are made the same way.

Many books were written about sausages and each one provides some Polish sausage recipes. And they are all wrong but.... one book had it right. The book, considered a classic today, was *The Great Sausage Recipes and Meat Curing*, written in 1976 by a Pole, Rytek Kutas from Buffalo. Later Mr. Kutas created the Sausage Maker Inc, the biggest mail order (now also selling online) company specializing in sausage making equipment and supplies.

Photo 1.14 Rytek Kutas. *Photo courtesy The Sausage Maker Inc, Buffalo, N.Y.*

The Polish Smoked Sausage has been well defined for centuries and almost everybody in Poland knows what goes inside.

We do not intend to become the judges in this matter and instead *we are going to rely on* Polish Government Standards for Polish Smoked Sausage as those rules have remained unchanged for the last 60 years. *This way if any reader does not agree with our recipes,* he is welcome to contact the Polish Meat Industry in Warsaw, which still publishes the latest standards for meat products and sausages through the Polish Bureau of Standards *(Polish Komitet Normalizacyjny).*

Before we anger many people who have been making Polish Smoked Sausage in their own way for many years, let's clarify something further. If you add an ingredient that you or your children like into your sausage it is fine and you have the full right to say that you have made a better sausage than the famous Polish Smoked Sausage. You may say that your grandfather who came from Poland made the best Polish sausage in the world and we honor that. Maybe he used chicken stock instead of water or maybe he added something else. What we are trying to say is that he was making *his own version* of the known classic or some other Polish sausage and it could have tasted better for you and your family. We do not dispute that fact. You can of course add anything you like to your sausage, but it will no longer be the original Polish Smoked Sausage *(Polska Kielbasa Wędzona)* or another name brand sausage. Once you start changing ingredients, you create your own recipe and you may as well come up with your own name. Let's unravel some of the mystery:

1. For centuries Polish Smoked Sausage was made entirely of pork. Then in 1964 the Polish Government introduced a second version of the sausage that was made of 80% pork and 20% beef. All other ingredients: *salt, pepper, sugar, garlic*, and marjoram remain the same in both recipes. The marjoram is optional but the garlic is a must.

2. The meat is cured before it is mixed with spices.

3. The sausage is stuffed into a large hog casing: 36 - 38 mm.

4. The traditional way was to cold smoke it for 1 to 1.5 days (it had to last for long time).

5. In most cases it is hot smoked and cooked in water today.

For curiosity let's see how large American manufacturers make Polish Smoked Sausage. Four sausages called Polish Kielbasa were bought at the local American supermarket in Florida and each of them were produced by a large and well known meat plant. Let's see how they compare with the original Polish recipe.

Name	Meat used	Ingredients
Authentic Polish Smoked Sausage	Pork	salt, pepper, sugar, garlic, marjoram, ***sodium nitrite***
Authentic Polish Smoked Sausage version 2	Pork 80% and beef 20%	salt, pepper, sugar, garlic, marjoram, ***sodium nitrite***
Polish Sausage Natural Hardwood Smoked	Pork, beef, turkey	salt, water, corn syrup, 2% or less dextrose, *flavorings,* ground yellow mustard, autolyzed yeast, hydrolyzed whey protein, monosodium glutamate, potassium and sodium lactate, sodium diacetate, ***sodium nitrite***, starch, (modified food, potato starch), Vitamin C (Ascorbic Acid, Contains: milk.
Polish Sausage *Natural Smoke Flavoring Added*	pork, turkey, beef (2% or less)	salt, turkey broth, water, corn syrup, starch (potato, modified starch), dextrose, hydrolyzed milk protein, *smoke flavoring,* Vitamin C (Ascorbic Acid), autolyzed yeast, gelatin, sodium phosphate, sodium diaceteate, ***sodium nitrite***, potassium lactate, potassium chloride, granulated garlic, oleoresin of paprika, *flavorings,* ingredients not found in or in excess of amount permitted in regular smoked sausage, Contains: milk.
Polish Sausage Naturally Hickory Smoked	Pork, beef	salt, water, dextrose, *natural spices,* garlic powder, paprika, monosodium glutamate, sodium erythorbate, ***sodium nitrite.***
Polska Kielbasa Fully Cooked	Beef	salt, water, corn syrup, 2% or less of: natural spices, natural flavors, dextrose, monosodium glutamate, isolated soy protein, Vitamin C (Ascorbic Acid), sodium phosphates, ***sodium nitrite***, Contains: soy.

Looking at the above sausage recipes we tried to come up with a name of an equivalent Polish sausage that might fit the description but we couldn't. It becomes quite clear that different manufacturers put different ingredients inside of the casing and the name Polish Kielbasa is used just for credibility and to gain the trust of the consumer. It seems that for some manufacturers any sausage that is smoked and stuffed in a 36 mm casing will qualify to be called the Polish Smoked Sausage or Polish Kielbasa. With all due respect to the Polish meat industry we can say that *although the recipes remain basically correct, binders, fillers and chemicals are widely used in order to improve yield and profits.* That is why there is such an interest in home made products as people want the old quality and taste. It is not realistic to expect that a person will make sausages all the time, but it is feasible that he might do it once for Christmas and another time for Easter, exactly as it was done 100 years ago.

Although we do love the latest achievements in science and technology, we feel that the simple time proven methods of sausage manufacturing will still create higher quality products. It may not last as long on the shelf or in a refrigerator, it may lose its pink color sooner, *but it will definitely taste better.* I do not care much how pretty and plump they are, as they will not hang on the wall among my paintings and photographs. I am going to eat my sausages and I want them to be good.

As mentioned before the best quality sausages were made in Poland until the collapse of the Berlin Wall in 1989. Then in 2004 Poland joined the European Common Market and the situation deteriorated even further. Joining an organization of this kind is like living in a community controlled apartment complex. You lose your freedom and decision making and have to submit to regulations that are forced on you, be it the height of the grass on your lawn, the amount of guests you can accommodate overnight, or until what time you can make noise.

Why Would Sausages Made 50 Years Ago Be Better Than Those of Today?

Well, there are three answers to this question and the one can be found already in the first step of sausage making-*the meat selection process.* Good meat cuts make good meat products, everybody knows that.

1. Meat quality. The flavor of the meat, especially the pig, depends on its diet. If the animal eats a lot of barley *(jęczmień)* its meat is firm and fat. If the same pig will be fed with corn, its meat will be softer and fatter. Meat of pigs that were fed with kitchen meal leftovers or fed mainly with potatoes or beets, will contain more water in it. Famous Spanish Serrano ham even today is still made from pigs that graze freely on grass and eat a lot of oak acorns. Change that diet and you will change the quality of the ham. Old sausage makers were well aware of those factors and for them meat was quality food and they strived for the best. Today all pork tastes the same as it is mass produced, growth hormones and antibiotics are added, the pigs movement is restricted in order for the animals to grow as fast as possible. An average meat of today is not a quality food, it is just a product for sustaining our bodily functions. Living in large metropolitan centers, there is little we can do about choosing our meat. That large piece of meat that we buy from a supermarket will be most likely already individually packed and injected with liquid. If you read the label it will say: "up to 12% of patented solution was added to improve tenderness and juiciness." And the ingredients are listed on the label: potassium lactate, sodium phosphates, salt, sodium diacetate. Pig meat was perfect for thousands of years and now suddenly we need to improve it? Well, the truth is that this patented solution was added to improve meat's shelf keeping qualities and preserve color, but that does not sound as nice as saying: to improve "tenderness and juiciness." Another factor which is completely beyond our control is that the pigs of today are fed a specially prepared diet to make their meat much leaner. You have to take that under consideration because the fat is what makes sausages succulent and those meats used in old recipes were much fatter. You may not agree with me, but when I eat my hamburger I want it to be good and juicy, and I intend to compensate for my cholesterol in another way.

2. Adding water. It seems that today's meat technology is obsessed with adding the maximum amount of water that the meat can hold inside. Entire labs with college educated scientists are working on better and more efficient ways of trapping water inside. Check out any meat equipment supplier and you will see that half of all equipment manufactured today is related to injecting meat with curing solutions and shaking it in tumblers to uniformly distribute this liquid. You can shake it all your life and it still will not distribute the solution so evenly as immersing a ham for 30 days in a container. And the final result? Of course more juiciness, after all you are eating more water now. But what happened to the original meat flavor? Well, it's gone now so you have to use all kinds of flavor enhancements to compensate for it. Here is a simple example to follow. Let's assume that for many years you have been drinking your favorite Earl Grey tea and you have always used one tea bag per cup of water. What will happen if you still will use one tea bag but add 50% more water to your tea? *Will it taste the same or will it taste weaker?* The answer is self-explanatory. The same happens to the quality of meat, it may be juicier but it will have a watered-down flavor. Commercially prepared curing solutions allow the introduction of up to 80% of the solution into the meat. In simpler terms you can add 8 lbs of solution (water, salt and chemicals) into 10 lbs of meat. After cooking, smoking and other processes the finished product will weigh 13 lbs what constitutes 30% gain in relation to the original weight of meat.

As a curiosity matter Soviet hams were: salted, cured, soaked, air-cured for 10 days at 12-18° C (54-64° F) and the relative humidity not exceeding 80%. Then they were smoked for 3 days at 30-35° C (86-95° F) or for 15 days at 18-20° C (64-68° F) and dried for 10 days. The yield of the finished product was 70% of the original meat weight. Hams that are smoked today *after losing moisture* during smoking and cooking still weigh the same as what the original weight was. This miracle is due to the water that is injected into the meat and held there by phosphates. The present day ham may be juicier (extra water) than those old European products but its flavor does not even come close.

3. Extra ingredients. Looking at the original recipes you will see how little spice was needed to impart a required flavor to a particular sausage. And this is how they were made and they were great. No binders, fillers or chemicals were used, *only meat, salt, pepper, sugar and spices.* The only chemical that was used was potassium nitrate and that ingredient was mandated by law in Poland and everywhere else in the world. Nitrates are still used in every country, although in its different form called nitrite. All those extra ingredients that are added to meat today have a certain cumulative value and will distort the flavor of the sausage. To compensate for that we have to increase the amount of spices and use flavor enhancers. We are not picking on meat plants that make those products as we understand that they have to walk a very thin line between profits and quality. Our aim is to convince you that you can make those sausages at home the way they were once made.

To stress the point that you can make a superior product without adding chemicals let's show the example of the famous Polish ham "Krakus" brand that was made during the Communism era. The main reason Polish Ham "Krakus" brand was the best ham in the world was that it was produced from carefully selected young hogs and no water was added. The consumer enjoyed full taste and flavor. The ham was cured in water, salt and nitrate only. Nothing else was added. This cure (1.5 - 7 %) was injected into an artery and then the ham was immersed in cure for 10 days. Then it was rinsed, dried, smoked and cooked. The ham was canned, it had its own certificate of authenticity and its own serial number. It was so good it grabbed 30 % of the American market share and was displayed in every supermarket. The Krakus brand still exists but is now produced by Polish company "Animex" which is owned by American Smithfield Foods. In 2014 Smithfield Foods was purchased by China. We have no details about how this ham is manufactured today.

Chapter 2

Making Sausages

This is not a beginners book about making sausages. We do provide detailed information on curing and smoking as those steps play such an important role in making sausages, but we assume that a reader is familiar with the basic sausage making process. More space is dedicated to a special group of sausages such as head cheeses, liver and blood sausages as these products require slightly different production methods and there is little written information on the subject of their making.

Making sausages is like making hamburger: meat is ground, salt, pepper and the required spices are added, and then it is cooked until it is safe for consumption. If this prepared meat were stuffed into casings it would become a sausage. While various recipes usually get the spotlight the technical know-how behind preparing sausages is far more important.

The basic sausage making process:

1. Meat selection.
2. Curing.
3. Grinding/emulsifying.
4. Mixing.
5. Stuffing.
6. Conditioning.
7. Smoking/if needed.
8. Cooking/if needed.
9. Cooling.
10. Storing.

Meat Selection

All cuts of good meat make good sausages. The trick is to know when and how to use them. Trim out all gristle, sinew, (discard glands and blood clots), excess fat, silver screen and any connective tissue and save them. Those visually unappealing trimmings are very important. They are used for regular sausages, but are an absolute must for making emulsified products like hot dogs or bologna. Once they are ground 2 times through a fine plate or emulsified in a food processor they become a paste that will bind larger particles of meat together.

If you use only lean cuts of meat, your sausage will definitely be healthier but its texture will be poor and you will miss out on the taste. Fat carries flavor and provides a pleasant mouth feel. Our palate likes this mouth feel and that is why we love fatty foods such as ice cream, chocolate, butter, mayonnaise, cream and so on. To make a low fat sausage we have to cheat our senses by introducing more water and chemical agents like phosphates (bind water), hydrocolloids (gums that bind water) and commercially prepared fat replacers, for example micro cellulose. This book deals with traditionally made high quality sausages that are made without those additives.

Most sausages are made of either pure pork, or a combination with other meats, mainly with beef (about 20%). Sausage made entirely from beef will be drier with a harder texture. People living in off beaten track areas, for example Alaska might use wild game meats like moose, bear, elk, reindeer, or rabbit. However, it is still recommended to mix these lean meats with pork to achieve better texture and flavor. When it comes to selecting pork meat for sausages, the majority of books and recipes mention the same word: "use a pork butt." Sure, it has the right lean meat to fat ratio of 70/30 and the sausage will be fine. What about someone with a big family who buys the whole hog - there are only two pork butts but what to do with the rest of the meat? He should have nothing left, some meat like ribs, chops and loins will be eaten right away and the rest can be processed to make all kinds of meat products such as smoked hams, butts, Canadian Bacon, smoked bacon, back fat, blood sausage, liverwurst, head cheese and dozens of different sausages.

There is a unique meat classification system in the USA:

1. Acceptable grade - the only fresh pork sold in supermarkets.
2. Utility grade - used in processed products and not available in supermarkets for purchase

Pork is divided into five prime areas:

1. Shoulder butt (Boston butt).
2. Shoulder picnic.
3. Loin.
4. Ham.
5. Side (belly, ribs).

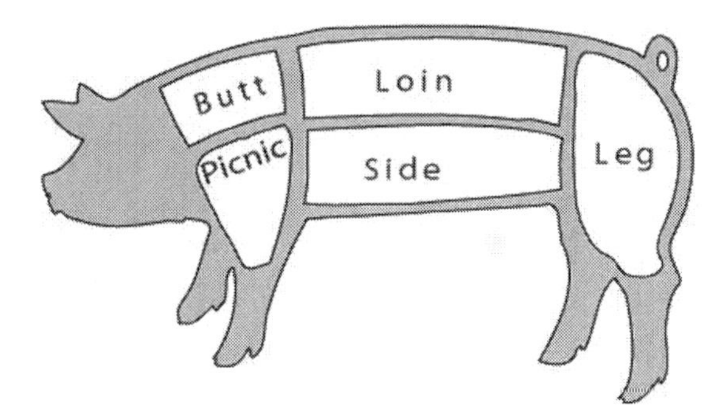

Photo 2.1 Pork prime cuts.

Those main cuts are further broken down to additional parts. They all have unique names and numbers and they are listed in a trade catalog. These five primary cuts are the meat that a home sausage maker will be able to purchase in a supermarket. There are many meat products and known sausages that require meats from other parts of the hog's body. Special sausages such head cheeses and as liver and blood sausages use offal meat such as head meat, jowls, brains, kidneys, hearts, back fat, lungs, tripes, etc. To make head cheese you need head, shank (hocks), jowls and skins. These parts are rich in collagen and will form a gelatin which will hold meat ingredients together. Blood is needed for blood sausages. Meat processors dealing with slaughter houses have access to those meats and they do use them to manufacture different sausages. A person living on a farm will be able to obtain a hog without much difficulty, a person living in a large city will need to visit Vietnamese, Thai or other ethnic stores.

Meat Classes

Once the pig is gutted and the hairs are removed, it is split into two halves and processed into individual cuts. Imagine a butcher cutting hog into pieces until nothing is left on the table. Before he can carve out a ham from the leg he has to separate it from the body, then cut off the lower leg, remove the bones, tendons, gristle, sinews, skin, pieces of fat, silver screen and other connective tissue. To get a clean piece of meat like a ham, butt or pork loin a lot of work has to be performed first that leaves scraps of meat which can not be sold in one piece. Keep in mind that the meat plant was established to bring profits to its owners, and every little piece of meat, fat, and even blood is money.

Photo 2.2 A half of pig can weigh 100 pounds so this is a lot of meat. Wojtek can process a half of a pig in 40 minutes all by himself.

Photo 2.3 and 2.4 Pig is cut into main parts such as ham, butt, loin, belly, back fat, picnic and hocks. Trimmings are graded into classes.

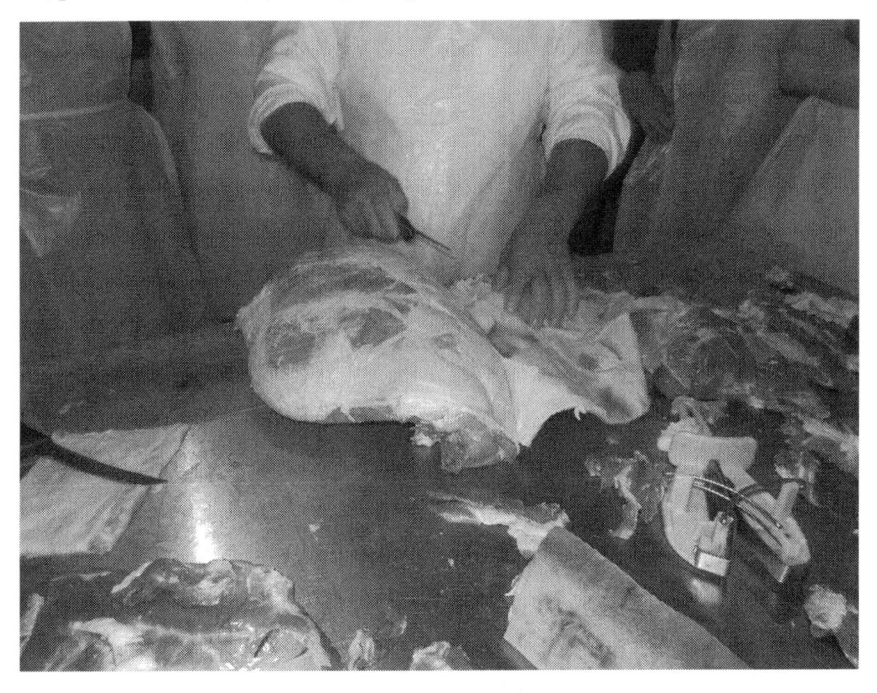

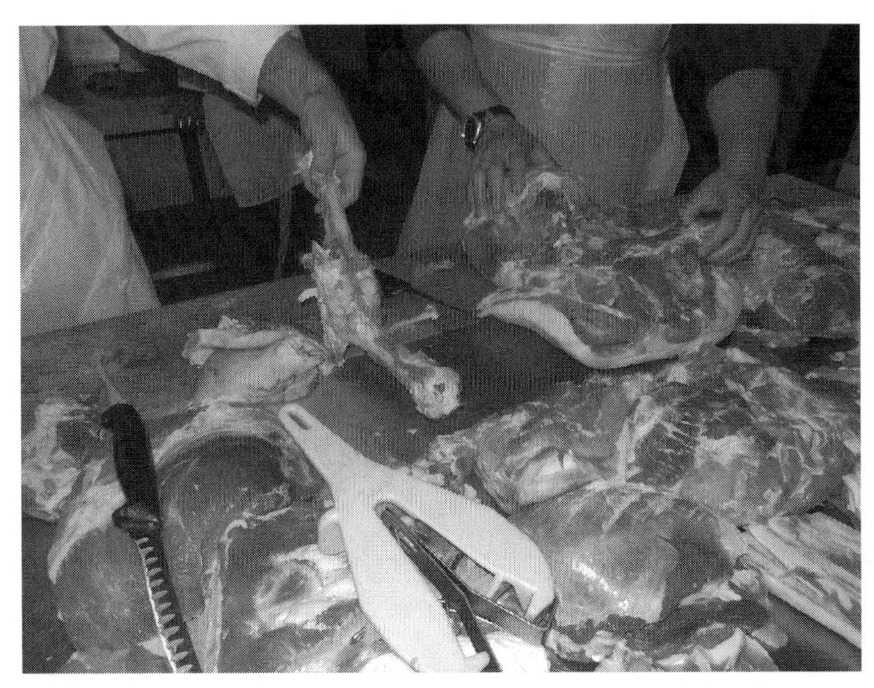

Photo 2.5 and 2.6 A lot of meat scraps are left over and they will be used for making sausages.

Photo 2.7 and 2.8 At first the task may look confusing, but there is always someone who has done it before.

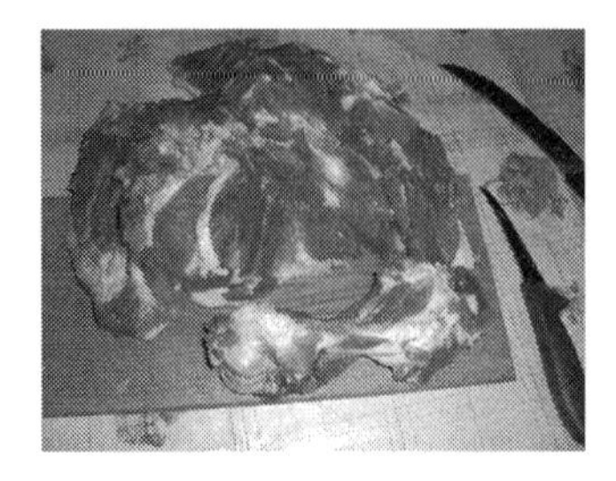

Photo 2.9 Removing bone.

Photo 2.10 Leftovers.

Photo 2.11 Final cuts.

Only *after meat trimmings are used up*, can a meat plant resort to using noble parts like ham or loin for sausages.

The bones with attached remaining meat are saved and will be boiled to make head cheeses.

Photo 2.12. As the butcher carves the meat he separates meat trimmings into different classes and places them in separate containers.

Pork Meat Classes

It matters little how a meat cut is called, what matters is how it looks.

Try not to think of how a particular cut is called, but rather look at its structure. Is it lean or fat, where the fat is located, is the fat hard or soft, is the skin present and how much connective tissue it contains.

Photo 2.13 Pork class I.

Photo 2.14 Pork class IIA.

Photo 2.15 Pork class IIB.

Photo 2.16 Pork class III.

Photo 2.17 Pork class IV.

Photos courtesy Andrzej Piątek "Bagno"

With time you will not have to think into which meat class a particular cut belongs. It will come naturally, remember it will not matter much if you mix some of pork class I with II. Make sure you get enough class III. Looking at meat class III that contains a lot of sinews one can develop the feeling that it is a poor kind of a meat scrap. After all who wants to chew meat with sinews. The truth is that *this is a very important meat class as it contains a lot of collagen* which is necessary for creating gelatin and binding meat particles together. It also binds water very well making products juicier.

Knowing meat classes will also help you immensely when shopping for better deals at large supermarkets. You will see what quality meat you will be buying, regardless of what's on the label. When trimming pork chops, loins or hams for roasting, save the skin and those meat trimmings and store them in a freezer. You can use them to make sausages at a later date. Or when making sausages from pork butt, save the skin and fat for later use in a head cheese or liver sausage. When carving ham or butt you will get *all* meat classes, of course in different proportions. Picnic which is mainly class III, will also provide class II or even a piece of meat class I. It is a good substitute for pork head meat.

Pork Class I	Market Equivalent
No bone, lean, no connective tissue. Fat between muscles up to 2 mm. No more than 15% fat.	**Ham** (rear pork leg). *You can obtain all meat grades from pork leg.*

Pork Class II A	Market Equivalent
No bone, medium fat, little connective tissue. Fat between muscles up to 10 mm. No more than 30% fat.	**Pork butt.** *You can obtain all meat grades from pork shoulder.*

Definition of connective tissue covers collagen rich trimmings such as tendons, gristle, sinews, and silver screen. We regularly consume those parts by eating hot dogs where those trimmings are are hidden in the form of an emulsified paste.

Pork Class II B	Market Equivalent
No bone, little connective tissue. Fat between muscles up to 10 mm. No more than 45% fat.	Pork picnic (pork shoulder). Other cuts.

Pork Class III	Market Equivalent
Lean or medium lean, ***a lot of connective tissue***. No more than 25 % fat.	Pork picnic, legs. Other cuts.

Above photos **P2.18-22** *courtesy "Dziadek"*

Pork Class IV	Market Equivalent
No bone, traces of blood, tendons, glands. No more than 36% fat. Other criteria not defined. Lowest quality pork meat.	Pork picnic, legs. Other cuts.

Pork Fat Classes

There are different types of fat and they will all be used but for a different purpose. There are hard, medium and soft fats and they have a different texture and different melting point. There is a: belly fat, back fat, dewlap fat, jowl fat, kidney and casings fat.

Many head cheese, emulsified and blood sausage recipes call for jowl fat that may be hard to obtain. Sliced jowl looks like belly, however, belly has little connective tissue. Belly is a soft fat and jowl is a hard fat with a lot of connective tissue. Pork belly is not a good replacement for jowl. Fatter cuts from a pork butt are a good choice as they contain hard fat and meat (class II B).

You have to use your own judgement, for example trimmed pork loin is a very lean cut of meat and definitely class I. It is also expensive and most of us would not use it for making a sausage. In addition such a sausage will have a very dry texture unless some fat was added.

Photo 2.23
Belly.

Photo 2.24
Jowl fat.

Photo 2.25
Back fat I.

Photo 2.26
Back fat II.

Beef Meat Classes

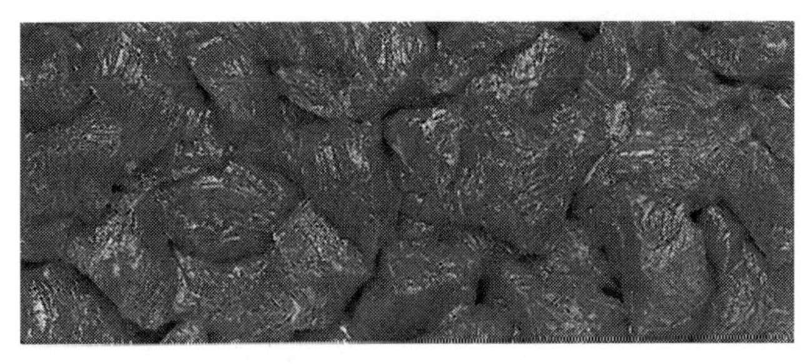

Class I, no bone, lean, no tendons. Fat between muscles - none. No more than 7% fat.

Photo 2.27 Beef class I *(Short loin, sirloin, round, flank).*

Class II, no bone, lean, some tendons. Fat between muscles up to 2 mm. No more than 16% fat.

Photo 2.28 Beef class II *(Chuck, rib).*

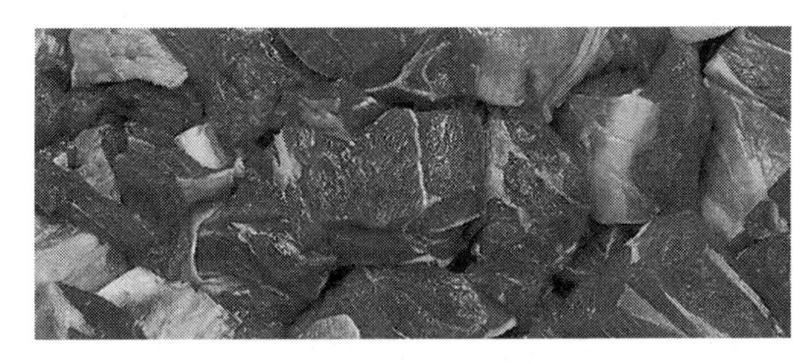

Class III, fat beef. Fat between muscles up to 10 mm. No more than 45% fat.

Photo 2.29 Beef class III *(Chuch, brisket, shank).*

Class IV, no bone, traces of blood, tendons, glands. No more than 40% fat.

Photo 2.30 Beef class IV.

Photo 2.31
Beef fat.

Photo 2.32 Beef Class I.

Photo 2.33 Beef Class II.

Photo 2.34 Beef Class III.

Photo 2.35 Beef Class IV.

Beef class I - lean, without connective tissue
Beef class II - lean, with connective tissue
Beef class III - fat meat
Beef class IV - bloody meat cuts
Beef class V - gristle, sinews, connective tissue
Beef class V may be softened up by cooking in water.

Curing

In its simplest form the word 'curing' means 'saving' or 'preserving.' The definition covers preservation processes such as: drying, salting and smoking. When applied to home made meat products, the term 'curing' usually means 'preserved with salt and nitrite.' Meat cured only with salt will have a better flavor but will also develop an objectionable dark color. Adding nitrates/nitrites to meat will:

- Improve flavor – meat cured with nitrates develop a characteristic flavor which is favored by consumers.
- Develop the pink color widely known and associated with smoked meats. Cured meat will develop its true cured color only after cooking to 60-72° C (140-160° F).
- Prevent food poisoning by preventing *C. botulinum* spores from developing into toxins when smoking at low temperatures.
- When combined with salt, sodium nitrite inhibits the growth of meat spoiling bacteria which is very important when making cold smoked products or fermented sausages like salami.

Methods of Curing

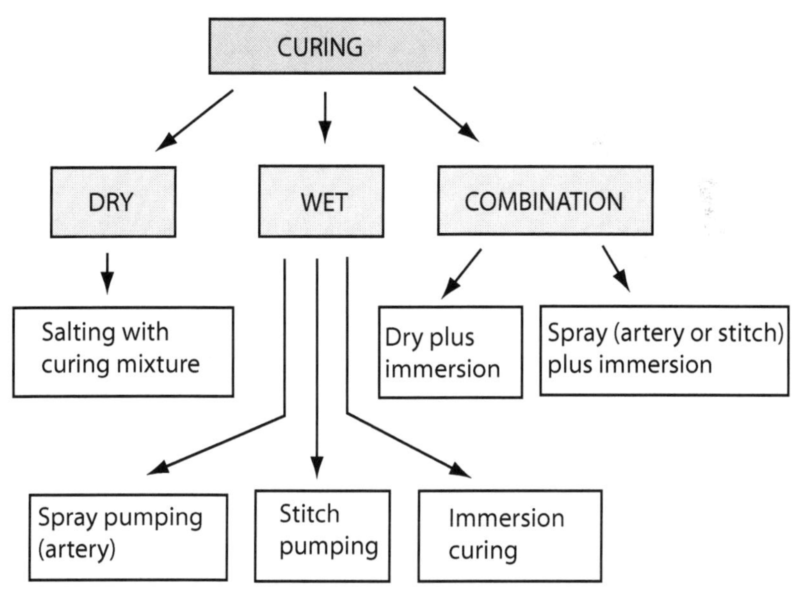

Fig. 2.1 Curing methods.

As this book is about making sausages we are going to limit our discussion to the dry curing method as this is the method used for sausages.

Curing and Meat Color

Meat color is determined largely by the amount of myoglobin a particular animal carries. The more myoglobin the darker the meat, it is that simple. Going from top to bottom, meats that contain the most myoglobin are: beef, lamb, veal, pork, dark poultry and light poultry. The amount of myoglobin present in meat also increases with the age of the animal. Different parts of the same animal, take the turkey for example, will have different colors as well. Parts that are active (legs) need more oxygen to function and they carry more myoglobin making this particular meat darker. A breast works very little and its meat contains less myoglobin making it lighter. This color is pretty much fixed and there is not much we can do about it unless we mix different meats together. Cured meats develop a particular pink-reddish color due to the reaction that takes place between meat myoglobin and nitrate/nitrite. If an insufficient amount of nitrate/nitrite is added to the meat the cured color will suffer. This may be less noticeable in sausages where the meat is ground and stuffed but if we slice a larger cut like a ham, the poorly developed color will be easily noticeable. Some sections may be gray, some may be pink and the meat will not look appetizing. There is a fixed maximum amount of nitrite that the meat can absorb and that depends on the amount of myoglobin. If too much is added the myoglobin will reject the excess of it and the consumer will have to eat it.

Curing Fats

We already know that nitrite will color meat pink. What about pure fat like back fat? It makes no sense to add nitrite to back fat as there is no myoglobin present and there is nothing there for nitrite to do. We will end up eating the chemical. Salting is all we need. If you study the recipes you will see that the more fat in the meat the less potassium nitrate was added. Very fatty meats or back fat are salted only, as the salt alone will cure the fat.

Blood Salting

Blood is a very perishable product and has to be refrigerated. It was preserved by adding 5 kg of salt to 100 kg of blood and mixed well together. Such preserved blood was stored up to 48 hours at 4-6° C (39-42° F). Today an anticoagulation agent is immediately added to freshly collected blood and the blood is either stored at 3° C (37° F) for up to 48 hours or frozen.

Curing With Nitrates/nitrites

Meat cured only with salt, will have a better flavor but will also develop an objectionable dark color. Adding nitrites to meat will improve flavor, prevent food poisoning, tenderize the meat, and develop the pink color widely known and associated with smoked meats. Nitrite also prevents *Cl. botulinum* spores from developing into toxins and slows down rancidity of fat. There is not even one documented incident of food poisoning of a meat cured with salt and nitrates.

The minimum of 50-75 ppm (parts per million) of nitrite is needed to cure meat. Some of it will react with myoglobin and will fix the color, some of it will go into other complex bio-chemical reactions with meat that develop a characteristic *cured meat flavor*. If we stay within Food and Drug Administration guidelines (1 oz. Cure #1 per 25 lbs. of meat – about 1 level teaspoon of Cure #1 for 5 lbs of meat) we are applying 156 ppm of nitrite which is enough and safe at the same time.

Both nitrates and nitrites are permitted to be used in curing meat and poultry with the exception of bacon, where nitrate use is prohibited. *The use of nitrate is going out of fashion because it is difficult to control the curing process.* Sodium Nitrate ($NaNO_3$) *does not cure meat directly* and initially not much happens when it is added to meat. After a while micrococci and lactobacilli bacteria which are present in meat, start to react with nitrate and produce Sodium Nitrite ($NaNO_2$) *that will start the curing process.* If those bacteria are not present in sufficient numbers or the temperature is too low the curing process may be inhibited. Sodium nitrite does not depend on bacteria and by adding sodium nitrite directly to meat we can cure meats faster and at lower temperatures.

Nitrates And The Law

Maximum Ingoing Nitrite and Nitrate Limits in PPM (parts per million) for Meat and Poultry Products as required by the Food Safety and Inspection Service are:

Curing Agent in PPM	Curing Method			
	Immersion Cured	Massaged or Pumped	Comminuted	Dry Cured
Sodium Nitrite	200	200	156	625
Potassium Nitrite	200	200	156	625
Sodium Nitrate	700	700	1718	2187
Potassium Nitrate	700	700	1718	2187

Nitrate Safety Concerns

There has been much concern over the consumption of nitrates by the general public. Studies had shown that when nitrites combine with by products of protein (amines-in the stomach), that leads to the formation of nitrosamines which are carcinogenic (cancer causing) in laboratory animals. Those findings started a lot of unnecessary panic in the 1970's about harmful effects of nitrates in meat on our health. Millions of dollars were spent, a lot of research was done, many researchers had spent long sleepless nights seeking fame and glory but no evidence was found that when nitrates are used within established limits they can pose any danger to our health.

A review of all scientific literature on nitrite by the National Research Council of the National Academy of Sciences indicates that nitrite does not directly harm us in any way. All this talk about the danger of nitrite in our meats pales in comparison with the amounts of nitrates that are found in vegetables we consume every day. The nitrates get to them from the fertilizers which are used in agriculture. Don't blame sausages for the nitrates you consume, blame the farmer. It is more dangerous to one's health to eat vegetables on a regular basis than a sausage.

As our most popular cures are in a pink color it would be very hard to mistake them for common salt. Even if Cure #1, was misplaced in such an unusual way the amount of salt needed to consume as a single dose will even be larger as there are only 156 ppm of sodium nitrite in it. That corresponds to eating 18.26 lbs of meat at one sitting. The only way to consume a fatal dose will be to mistake pure nitrite (it is white) for salt but the general public has no access to it. Note that:

- 1g of nitrite is generally accepted as the life threatening dose.
- 1 PPM (part per million) equals 1 mg/kg.

By the time meats are consumed, they contain less then 50 parts per million of nitrite. It is said that commercially prepared meats in the USA contain about 10 ppm of nitrite when bought in a supermarket. *Nitrite and nitrate are not permitted in baby, junior or toddler foods.*

American Cures

Cure #1 *(also known as Instacure 1, Prague Powder #1 or Pink Cure)* is a mixture of 1oz of Sodium Nitrite (6.25%) to 1 lb of salt. It must be used to cure all meats that will require smoking at low temperatures. It may be used to cure meats for fresh sausages (optional).

Cure #2 *(also known as Instacure 2, Prague Powder #2 or Pink Cure)* is a mixture of 1 oz of Sodium Nitrite (6.25%) along with .64 oz of Sodium Nitrate (4%) to 1 lb of salt. It can be compared to the time-releasing capsules used for treating colds. It must be used with any products that do not require cooking, smoking or refrigeration and is mainly used for products that will be air cured for a long time like: Country Ham, salami, pepperoni, and other dry sausages.

Both Cure #1 and Cure #2 contain a small amount of a FDA approved red coloring agent that gives them a slight pink color thus eliminating any possible confusion with common salt and that is why they are sometimes called pink curing salts. They also go by the name Prague Powder #1 (Instacure #1) and Prague Powder #2 (Instacure #2). Cure #1 is not interchangeable with Cure #2 and vice versa, however, no harm will come to you if they were inadvertently mixed. To add to the confusion Morton® salt manufacturer makes their own curing mixtures that are available in supermarkets. Those cures are premixed with sugar and other ingredients so please read the instructions carefully.

European Cures

There are different cures in European countries and for example: in Poland a commonly used cure goes by the name "Peklosól" and contains 0.6% of Sodium Nitrite to salt. No coloring agent is added so it is white in color.

Country	Cure	% of nitrite in salt
USA	Cure #1	6.25
Poland	Peklosól	0.6
Germany	Pökelsalz	0.6
France	Sel nitrité	0.6
Sweden	Colorazo	0.6
England	Nitrited salt	various
Australia	Kuritkwik	various

In European cures such a low nitrite percentage in salt is self-regulating and it is impossible to apply too much nitrite to meat, as the latter will taste too salty. Following a typical recipe (salt content 2%) you could *replace salt will peklosol* and the nitrite limits will be 120 ppm which is well within the established limits. This is very convenient when dry curing meat as there is nothing to calculate. Just replace salt with *peklosol* (0.6% sodium nitrite) and *the meat is cured and ready for smoking.*

There is a different case with American Cure #1 which contains more nitrite (6.5%) and we have to color it pink to avoid the danger of mistakes and possible poisoning.

Comminuted products: small meat pieces, *meat for sausages,* ground meat, poultry. A proportion of sodium nitrite added to salt in Cure #1 was developed in such a way that if we add 4 ounces of Cure #1 to 100 pounds of meat, the quantity of nitrite added to meat will comfort to the legal limits (156 ppm) permitted by the Meat Division of the United States Department of Agriculture. That corresponds to 1 oz (28.35 g) of Cure #1 for each 25 lbs (11.33 kg) of meat.

Comminuted Meat	Cure #1 in ounces	Cure #1 in grams	Cure #1 in teaspoons
25 lbs	1	28.35	5
5 lbs	0.2	5.66	1
1 lb	0.04	1.1	1/5
1 kg	0.08	2.5	1/2

European regulations permit 150 ppm of nitrite to be added into ground meat. Denmark insisted on lower limits and they can use 100 ppm. The standards specify the *maximum* amount of nitrite that can be introduced to meat. They do not prevent you to use less, but remember that 75 ppm is about the minimum required for any meaningful curing to take place.

Curing Meat for Sausages

All top quality sausages are made from cured meat. The dry curing method is used to cure meat for sausages. Meat should be cut into smaller pieces, about 2 inches (5-6 cm) and not heavier than 0.5 lb (250 g). It should be thoroughly mixed with salt, sodium nitrite (Cure # 1), sugar (if present in a recipe) and packed tightly in a container (to eliminate air pockets), not higher than 8 inches (20 cm). It should be covered with a linen cloth to allow breathing, gas exchange and prevent discoloration of the top layer of the meat.

Meat preparation	Curing temperature	Curing time in hours
Manual, 2" cubes	2-4° C (35-40° F)	48-72
Ground meat	2-4° C (35-40° F)	24-36
The above data are for sodium nitrite (Cure #1, Peklosol)		

At higher temperatures curing times will be even shorter but that will encourage the growth of bacteria and will decrease the shelf life of the product.

Accelerated Curing

Stuffed sausages may contain meat that was not cured in a refrigerator at all or only partially cured. Today, people don't cure meat at all assuming that if the sausage is pink it has been cured. Well, if you mix sodium nitrite with ground meat the sausage will develop a pink color after cooking. Curing is not just coloring meat, curing changes the texture of the meat and develops *curing flavor* what contributes to quality of the product. Meat cured for 2 days in a refrigerator will produce a better quality sausage than meat which was ground, mixed with sodium nitrite (Cure #1) and immediately smoked. All of us are very busy nowadays and we may not want to cure meat in a refrigerator, but we still want a good product. We know that *curing needs time*, so let's find some extra time for the meat to cure, but let's do it inside the casing.

It is a known fact that a smoked sausage will be of higher quality when the meat is seasoned over night which is basically a shorter, simplified version of a curing process that should have been performed earlier. If you want to cure a sausage that way, grind the meat, mix and stuff it, then it can be stored for a day before it goes in the smoker. *Leaving sausages for 12 hours at 2-6° C (35-42° F) or for 2-3 hours at room temperature below 30° C (86° F) will provide this extra time to cure meat. This curing process will continue during smoking and will end when the sausage is cooked.*

Bear in mind that this "simplified" curing method can not be used when curing whole pieces like hams, butts, loins or even chunks of meat that should be *visible* in some sausages. Due to the insufficient curing time they will have an uneven pink and reddish area or even some gray in it that would be easily noticeable when slicing those meats. In those cases a traditional method of curing must be performed.

Commercial processors can cure meat faster and at lower temperatures by using ascorbic acid, erythorbic acid, or their derivatives, sodium ascorbate and/or sodium erythorbate. These additives speed up the chemical conversion of nitrite to nitric oxide which in turn will react with meat myoglobin to create a pink color. They also deplete levels of meat oxygen which prevents fading of the cured meat color in the presence of light and oxygen.

Curing Meats for Head Cheeses, Liver and Blood Sausages

This group of sausages employs an assortment of meats that will be difficult to sell. Many people would restrain from buying a sausage knowing that organ meats or blood are inside and they would refuse to accept the fact that this kind of sausage has a very high nutritional value. In the meantime they prepare sandwiches for work with bologna, hot dogs and other emulsified products which have a very similar meat composition.

Curing jowls, tongues or blood is not something that you can find in a typical sausage making book. We are presenting the actual data and curing tables from the official government manual that was prepared for Polish meat plants in 1959, however, this information holds true today as well. Those products were made and sold in Poland for 50 years and were absolutely wonderful. Most of them are still available although they are made differently today. The *curing* step contributed the most to the high quality of those products. There were three curing procedures:

1. Dry mixture for ground meats (sausages). Dry mixture was prepared by mixing 5 kg of potassium nitrate with 100 kg of salt. Today it is equivalent to adding 2.5 g of Cure #1 to 1 kg of meat or 26 g of Peklosol/1 kg of meat.

2. Salting fats without use of potassium nitrate. As explained earlier it makes little sense to add nitrite to fats as they do not contain myoglobin and nitrite does not react with pure fat. Back fat is pure fat and only salt is needed.

Meat type	**Formula**	**Amount of formula per 100 kg of meat**	**Curing/ salting time**	**Cure #1 per 100 kg of meat**
pork dewlap/ jowls	100 kg salt plus 4 kg *potassium nitrate*	7 kg (455 g *potassium nitrate* and 6.545 kg salt)	12-15 days	0.5 kg cure #1 and 6.1 kg salt
back fat to be smoked	salt	7 kg	14-18 days	7 kg salt, no cure #1
back fat salted	salt	8 kg	14-21 days	8 kg salt, no cure #1
small pieces of fat	salt	2 kg	24-48 hours	2 kg salt, no cure #1

Cure #1 was not used in original recipes, we provide above figures for orientation purposes.

Photo 2.36 *The meat is cured only once*. Different type and grade meats were cured accordingly and the containers were dated and kept in a cooler.

3. Curing solution for bigger meat cuts or organ meats.

Curing solution was prepared by mixing 4 kg of potassium nitrate with 100 kg of salt and the required amount of water.

Salt and water solution		
Meats	**Solution in °Bé**	**Curing time**
Pork skins, beef and lamb tripe, veal casings, cow's udders, pork stomachs	12-14°	48-72 hours at 4-8°C (39-46°F)

Salt, potassium nitrate and water solution				
Meats	**Solution in °Bé**	**Solution in liters per 100 kg of meat**	**Curing time in days**	**Draining time in hours**
Tongues: pork	14	40	5-6	12
veal	14	40	5-6	12
beef	14	40	14-31	12
lamb	14	40	5-6	12
Hearts: pork	14	40	3-4	12
veal	14	40	3-4	12
beef	14	40	4-5	12
lamb	14	40	3-4	12
Heads: pork	16	60	4-6	4-12
veal	14	60	3-4	4-12
beef	14	60	3-4	4-12
lamb	14	60	3-4	4-12
Pork ears	16	40	2	12
Legs	16	60	2-4	12
Veal lips	16	40	4-5	4-12
Beef lips	16	40	4-5	4-12
Pork masks (jowls, snouts)	14	40	3-4	12

The Baumé scale has a range of 0 to 26 degrees. It is a popular method in Europe of measuring the salt density of a solution which is accomplished by immersing a float instrument in a solution. One Baumé degree corresponds to 10 g of salt in one liter of water. In the USA the preferred method is using salt brine tables that have a range from 0 to 100 degrees. Zero degrees is pure water and 100 degrees is water fully saturated with salt (26.395% of salt) at 15° C (60° F). In the tables above only a small range of the Baumé scale is used and the salometer equivalents are given here: 12° Bé = 46° SAL, 13° Bé = 52° SAL, 14° Bé = 54° SAL, 16° Bé = 64° SAL.

The complete brine tables are listed on our web site:
www.meatsandsausages.com/sausage-making/curing/making-brine

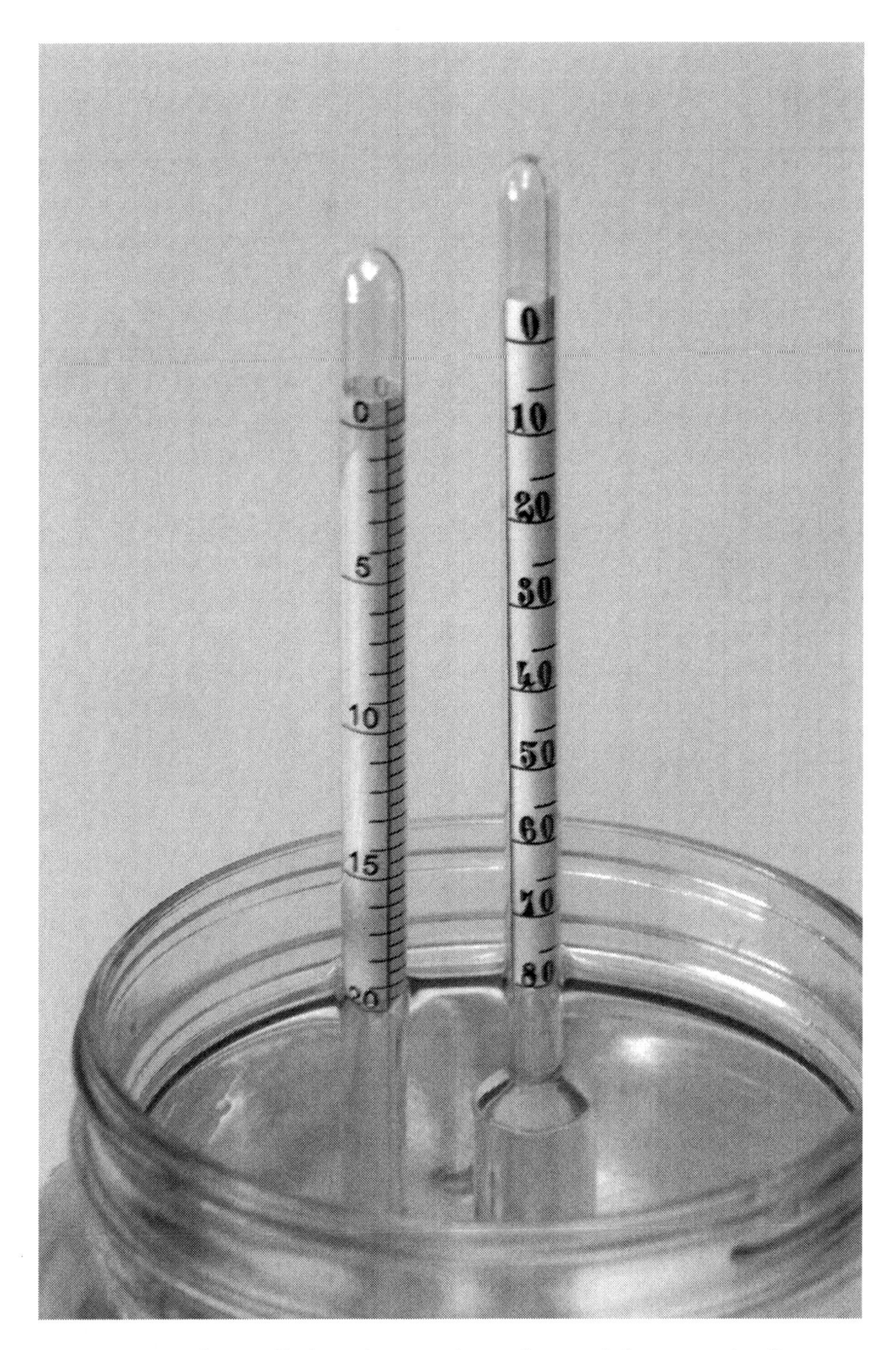

Photo 2.37 A float called a salometer is used to read the strength of a solution. Baumé tester left, SAL tester right.

Cure # 1 is used in the USA and we provide most commonly used solutions in the table below:

Curing Solutions with Cure #1						
Strength SAL degrees	25°	27°	35°	46°	54°	60°
Water, US Gallon (3.8 l)	1	1	1	1	1	1
Salt	5.43 oz (154 g)	6.25 oz (177 g)	9.6 oz (272 g)	14.4 oz (410 g)	1.13 lb (515 g)	1.32 lb (598 g)
Cure # 1	4.2 oz (120 g)	4.2 oz (120 g)	4.2 oz (120 g)	4.2 oz (120 g)	4.2 oz (120 g)	4.2 oz (120 g)
Salt in Cure # 1 accounted for (120 g Cure # 1 contains 112.5 g of salt).						

Except "White Sausage" which is of the fresh variety and special sausages like "Head Cheeses", "Liver Sausages" and "Blood Sausages", others are smoked and `require the use of sodium nitrite as mandated by law in the USA and in European countries. Fresh sausages that will be cooked or grilled at high temperatures don't need to be treated with nitrite though nitrite may be added to develop the pink color. In the USA and most European countries it is 150 ppm (parts per million) which corresponds to 150 mg of sodium nitrite per 1 kg of meat. 75 ppm is considered to be the minimum for curing meat for sausages (adding cure mix directly to meat-dry curing method). Our calculations are based on 120 ppm (using Cure #1 or Peklosol) which is below the max limit. When the recipe calls for 1 flat teaspoon (6 g) of cure 1 and you administer a little less or a little more, it will not really matter much.

Curing Temperatures

The curing temperature should be between 36° and 4-10° C (40° F) which falls within range of a common refrigerator. Lower than 36° F temperature may slow down the curing process or even halt it. In the past we used potassium nitrate exclusively because its derivative, sodium nitrite was not discovered yet. Potassium nitrate was the best and only curing chemical we knew of and it worked wonderfully at 4-8°C (40-46°F) which was fine as refrigeration was not very common yet. If temperatures dropped below 4°C (40°F) the bacteria that was needed to force nitrate into releasing nitrite would become lethargic and the curing would stop.

It was a slow working agent and the meat for sausages had to be cured for 72-96 hours. Sodium nitrite does not depend on bacteria, it works immediately and faster and the curing times are shorter, 48-72 hours at refrigerator temperature 2-4° C (35-40° F). At higher temperatures it will work even faster, however, spoilage bactria will also grow faster which will shorten the shelf life of the product. Nevertheless a stuffed sausage may be conditioned (hanged) for 1-2 hours at room temperature. That means we could perform the curing process out of the refrigerator saving some time and space.

Except fresh and a few special sausages (head cheeses, liver and blood sausages) *all Polish sausages require meat to be cured* and we would like to simplify this procedure for a busy person of today. Curing is an extra process that requires more time, designated containers and valuable space in a refrigerator.

Grinding

The lean meat should be separated from the fat. As a rule, lean meat is ground coarsely, while fatty cuts are ground very finely. Sausage is lean-looking and the fat is hidden inside. It is much easier to grind cold meat taken directly out of the refrigerator. The fat is usually ground through a plate with very small holes and if it is not partially frozen a smeared paste will be produced. The locking ring on the grinder head should be tight and the knife must be sharp, otherwise the meat will smear. To avoid smearing, grinding should be performed at low temperatures 1-3° C (34-38° F). Ideally, meat should always be chilled between 0-2° C (32-35° F) for a clean cut. Since refrigerator temperatures are roughly 3-4° C (38-40° F), we should place the meat in a freezer for about 30 min just before grinding. There are numerous electrical grinders, or processors with grinding head attachments that all work fine. Keep in mind that the meat will have to be stuffed into casings, so the grinder will need to accept tubes of different sizes. The best solution is to use a stand alone sausage stuffer.

Photo 2.38 Grinder is an efficient device, however, it "grinds" meat, it does not produce a clean cut.

Photo 2.39 Bowl cutter pictured below produces a very clean cut. As the bowl slowly rotates a set of knives rotates thousands of times per minute and cuts meat finely. This action generates so much heat that crushed ice or cold water must be added to protect the meat and knives. As a result a fine paste is obtained. *Home food processors can process meat in a similar manner.*

Common Grinder Plate Sizes								
mm	2	3	4	6	10	12	16	19
inch	1/16	1/8	3/16	1/4	3/8	1/2	5/8	3/4

The question may arise, why do we grind different grades of meat through different plates? It will be much easier to use 3/8" plate for everything. There are many reasons for it:

1. You could do just that if you had only high grade meats, let's say pork class I (ham) and pork class II (butt). With such fine meats you would not get any pieces of bone, gristle and sinews that would stick between your teeth. On the other hand we are left with meat scraps of lower classes that we would not be able to eat if they were not finely ground.

2. We want to retain meat juices and water inside the meat and those poor meat grades with a lot of gristle and sinews are loaded with collagen that helps do just that. The better grind we can obtain the stronger binding power meat develops and this is where a bowl cutter starts to shine. A grinder, manual or electrical, cuts meat and pushes meat through plate holes, cutting meat but also mechanically breaking it at the same time. A bowl cutter cuts cleanly without doing mechanical damage to a piece of meat's structure. It develops a lot of heat so ice or cold water are added to cool down the meat and rotating knives. That allows it to emulsify meat into a consistency of fine paste that is able to trap all this ice and water with fat and hold it inside. All scraps of meat with fat, gristle and sinews have become a paste now, the product will be juicier and the manufacturer will make more money.

3. The third reason is that many people do not like to see fat inside of the sausage. By grinding fat through a fine plate the fat will bind with meat and will not be noticeable. There is not any rigid, fixed rule in regard to grinder plates and the selection depends greatly on the type of sausage that we decide to make.

For hundreds of years we chopped meat with knives and stuffed it with fingers through a horn. And the sausages were great. Queen Victoria of England had her own very strict rules about making her sausages:

- The meat had to be chopped, not ground to prevent natural juices from leaking out
- The casings had to be filled by hand, the mixture pressed down through a funnel with the thumbs

Some sausages like "Krakowska Krajana Sausage" are still made from lean meat cut with knives and then stuffed into a large diameter casing.

Mixing

If the meat was previously cured, then the salt, nitrite, and sugar was already added. Now we have to add the remaining ingredients and spices. They can be added during emulsifying in a food processor or they may be mixed with cold water and then poured over the minced meat. The water helps to evenly distribute the ingredients and it also helps soften it during stuffing. We can easily add 1 cup of cold water to 5 lbs of meat because it is going to evaporate during smoking anyway. Water should not be added to products that will be cold smoked, fermented or air dried. The lean meat should be mixed with spices first and to prevent smearing the fat should be added at the last moment. *You have to apply some pressure* when mixing and *kneading* is a good term for it. When the meat feels sticky it is an indication that it was properly mixed. Mixing meat by hand also raises its temperature so it should be done quickly. It takes roughly about 5 minutes to thoroughly mix 10 lbs of meat. The time is important because fat specks start to melt at 35-40° C (95-104° F). We want to prevent this smearing to keep the sausage texture looking great. Taste the sausage before you stuff it, since you still have time to implement any changes.

Stuffing

There is not much we can do to alter the taste of the sausage after it is stuffed. It is strongly recommended to taste the meat when mixing it with spices. People make mistakes when reading recipes, they get confused with ounces and grams and they use different size spoons to measure ingredients. Just make a very tiny quarter size hamburger, throw it on a frying pan and in two minutes you can taste your sausage. After the meat is ground and mixed it has to be stuffed into a casing preferably as soon as possible. Allowing the meat to sit overnight in a container causes it to set up and absorb all this moisture that we have added during mixing and stuffing. The mixture will harden and we'll be struggling filling casings blaming the whole world for it.

Pack the meat tightly inside the grinder, horn, or piston stuffer to prevent air from entering into the casing. The air creates unnecessary resistance during stuffing and creates little air pockets which may fill with water and produce spoilage. Besides, when water evaporates the finished product may have little holes visible after slicing. The majority of piston stuffers come equipped with an air valve that allows accumulating air to escape outside. After the sausage is stuffed, any air pockets are simply pricked with a needle. There is no need to worry about tiny holes that will be gone as fast as they were made. The exception to the above hard stuffing rule is when a long rope sausage is made as it will be divided to equal links by twisting them. That would be impossible to achieve if the casing was stuffed hard. Liver and blood sausages are stuffed loosely as they often contain filler material such as buckwheat and barley groats, rice, rusk bread crumbs, semolina flour or soaked rolls. Those materials can expand during the cooking process. The casing should have a little water inside as it acts as a lubricant for the entering meat. By the same token pouring water over the stuffing tube is recommended to increase lubrication. Some people grease the tube lightly. When placing a casing on a stuffing tube, it should go on loosely otherwise it might break.

The natural casings are ideal casings for a home sausage maker though they require some practice. After the first sausage session they become easy to work with and are always ready to be used at a moment's notice. After stuffing, any remaining casings should be packed with canning salt and stored at refrigerator temperature 3-4° C (38 - 40° F) where they will last almost indefinitely.

Conditioning

At the first look this step seems to be insignificant but in reality it is very important. It is a kind of drying-setting up-seasoning combination step that influences the color of the sausage, both inside and outside. Conditioning provides extra curing time and allows the surface of the casing to become dry as it should be if we want to obtain a nicely colored smoked sausage.

The sausages can be placed in the area with some moving air and the moderate use of a fan will definitely be of help. Air-fan drying should not be used for an extended period of time as it may harden the surface of the smaller meat pieces/sausages. Conditioning is a short, hardly noticeable process and when making a lot of sausages, before the last casings are stuffed, the first ones are ready for smoking.

Stuffed sausages that are subject to smoking may follow a drying procedure inside the smoker which lasts about 1 hr (no smoke applied) at 40-60° C (104-140° F) until *the casings feel dry or at least tacky to the touch.* Leave draft controls or the top of your smoker fully open. If a natural wood is used for fuel, enough wood must be burned to produce hot embers that would be releasing heat without creating smoke to dry out the casings. This is a welcome scenario as preheating a smoker to eliminate humidity inside is a must step for any kind of a smoker.

Smoking

There are two distinctive methods of smoking:

1. Cold smoking, usually at 22° C (71° F) or less.

2. Hot smoking. This method covers a large range of temperatures and at lower range is often called *warm smoking* and as the temperature raises it becomes *hot smoking*.

The dividing line is when meat or fish proteins start to cook. Throw an egg on a cold frying pan and start raising the heat. At a certain point the white of the egg which actually looks like a clear jelly starts changing color and becomes cooked egg whites. The technical term is *coagulation of protein*, this is when the product starts to cook. In meat this usually happens at around 29° C (85° F), there is a rapid loss of moisture and the texture of the meat becomes hard. The fish starts to cook at 29° C (85° F) and if you want to make cold smoked salmon that can be sliced paper thin you cannot exceed 29° C (85° F). In simple terms *cold smoking should be performed below 29° C (85° F).* Dry wood should be selected for cold smoking.

Cold Smoking

You will find that different sources provide different temperatures for cold smoking. All Polish, German, Russian or Lithuanian technology books agree that cold smoke should be applied around 22° C (72° F). Occasionally a book calls for 25° C (77° F). Old German books specify temperature of cold smoke as 18° C (64° F) or lower. Any recipe that calls for cold smoke *higher* than 29° C (85° F) makes little sense, as at this temperature proteins coagulate and the texture of the meat changes. The meat gets cooked. The surface area will harden preventing moisture removal and the product may rot inside. This hardened ring will also slow down smoke penetration. In the past sausages were smoked for different reasons. Our ancestors did not care much about the flavor of the meat or the sausage. What they needed was a method that would preserve food for later use. They tried different ways to preserve meat and this eventually lead to methods like salt curing, drying, smoking and fermenting. It was discovered that salted meats could be air dried and would keep for a long time.

Photo 2.40 and **2.41** Using the weather to his advantage, Waldemar Kozik has no problems with cold smoking in Catskill Mountains of NY.

Two different methods of drying developed in Europe. In Northern European countries, winters were cold and the only way meat could be dried at low temperatures was placing them close to the fire. Originally that took place in caves where fire was the center of all social activities, then separate enclosures (smokehouses) were built for drying and storing meats. As the temperature had to be higher than freezing temperatures outside, the fire was slowly burning on the ground providing suitable temperatures for drying. It is common knowledge that fire produces smoke so the meats and sausages were dried and smoked at the same time. They were just flavored with cold smoke which not only further preserved the product but gave it a wonderful aroma. In addition it prevented molds from growing on the surface. Those advantages of applying smoke were not ignored by our ancestors and smoking became an art in itself. The meat, however, was preserved by drying and the benefits of smoke flavor was just an added bonus.

The majority of hobbyists think of cold smoking as some mysterious preservation technique that will produce a unique and superb quality product. What makes matters worse is that they start to experiment with different smoke temperatures and establish their own rules which then spread around and are repeated by newcomers into the field of smoking meats. Let's put some facts straight:

- cold smoking is not a preservation method, it will not preserve meat unless the meat will be dried.
- the higher amount of salt is added to meat to inhibit the growth of spoilage bacteria.
- cold smoking is an additional safety hurdle that helps to achieve microbiological safety of meat.

Cold smoking is an old technique that was practiced not because it produced great flavor, but because it helped to preserve meats. Cold smoking was nothing else, but a drying method. Its purpose was *to eliminate moisture so that bacteria would not grow*. This technique developed in North Eastern European countries where the climate was harsh and winters severe. When meats were cold smoked for 2-3 weeks, yes, the meat became preserved due to the loss of moisture, but it was drying that made the meat safe. If the same meat was dried at 12° C (54° F) without any smoke present, it would be preserved all the same.

Cold smoking is drying meat with smoke.

The pigs were traditionally slaughtered for Christmas and the meat had to last until the summer. Noble cuts were cooked or salted, but trimmings were made into sausages that were dried which was not easy with freezing temperatures outside. The only way to heat up storage facilities was to burn wood and that produced smoke. Too much heat was not needed as it consumed too much wood and it would cook the product instead of preserving. They were two choices:

- hang meats 5 feet above a small smoldering fire OR
- burn wood in a firebox that was located outside. Thc firebox was connected with the smokehouse by an underground channel that would supply heat and smoke at the same time.

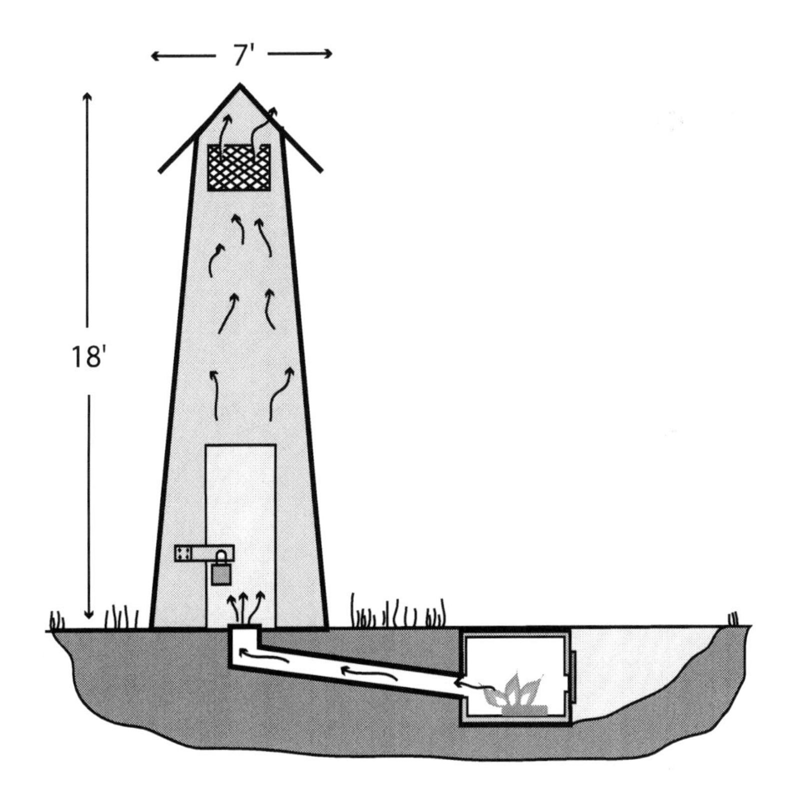

Fig. 2.2 An old Polish smokehouse.

A large smokehouse was also a storage facility where smoked meats hung in a different area where they continued to receive some smoke, although on a much smaller scale. This prevented any mold from growing on the surfaces of hams or sausages, as molds need oxygen to grow.

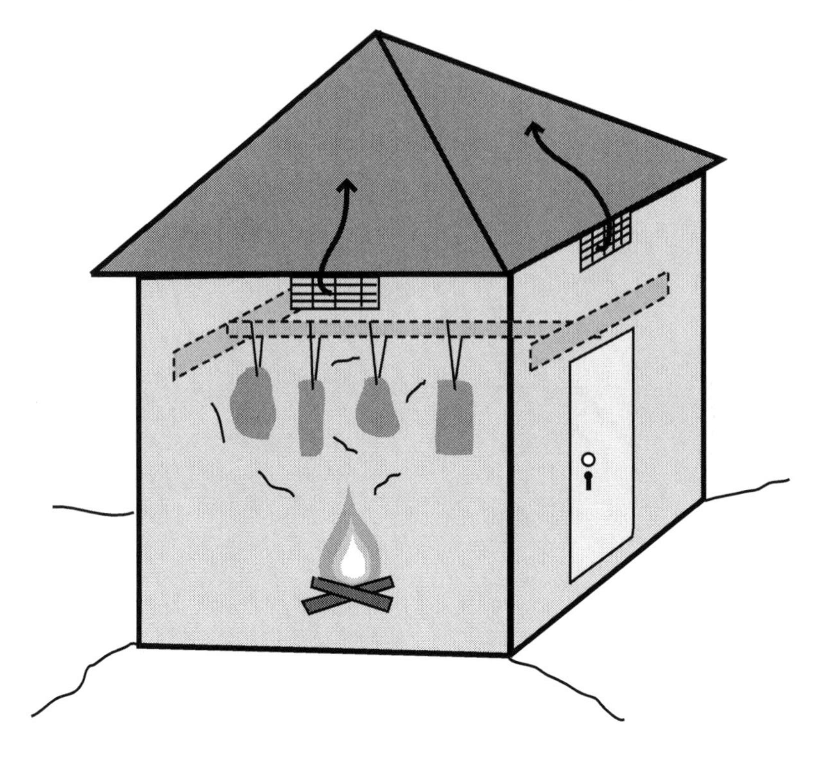

Fig. 2.3 An old smokehouse.

It had been established that meats dried best when the temperatures were somewhere between 10-15° C (50–60° F) and although the temperature of the smoke leaving the firebox was higher, it would be just right by the time it made contact with meat. Whole logs of wood were burnt. The fire was allowed to die out as people went to sleep. The meats hung until the morning and the fire would be re-started again. So, when you see an old recipe saying that ham or sausage was smoked for 2 weeks, well, it really was not, as it probably received smoke for about 1/3 of the time. Those meats were not cooked, they were dried and could be considered fermented products. There is little difference about Italian salami, Hungarian salami or Polish Cold Smoked Sausage. Italian salami is dried without smoke and Hungarian salami or Polish sausage were dried with cold smoke.

Italians and Spaniards were blessed with a climate that provided cool prevailing winds at right temperatures. There was no need to burn wood to warm up the drying chambers. As a result products did not carry a smoky flavor. For this reason people in the Mediterranean basin are not particularly fond of smoked products, and people in Germany, Poland, Russia, Lithuania love them, but don't generally like uncooked air dried products. The majority of all processed meat products in Northern Europe are of smoked variety.

The purpose of cold smoking was to dry meats. The product was drying out and the smoke happened to be there. Preservation was on people's mind rather than creating cold smoked flavor. Very few products are cold smoked today, notably cold smoked salmon known as "lox." The texture of cold smoked products is firmer and they can be sliced paper thin. The taste is a different story, you must acquire a liking for cold smoked products. In the past people already knew what we know today, that hot smoked products taste better. Cold smoking was our answer to the lack of refrigeration in the past. Do you think we would have bothered to smoke meats for weeks if refrigeration had been present? No, we would hot smoke them for a few hours and then they would go into the refrigerator.

Cold smoking – 12-22°C (52-71°F), from 1 - 14 days, applying *thin* smoke with occasional breaks in between. Cold smoking is not a continuous process, it is stopped a few times to allow fresh air into the smoker. Cold smoking slows down the spoilage of fats, which increases the shelf life of meat. The product is drier and saltier with a more pronounced smoky flavor. The color varies from yellow to dark brown on the surface and dark red inside. *Cold smoked products are not submitted to the cooking process.* Cold smoking assures us of total smoke penetration inside of the meat. The loss of moisture is uniform in all areas and the total weight loss falls within 5-20% depending largely on the smoking time.

It is obvious that you cannot produce cold smoke if the outside temperature is 32° C (90° F), unless you can cool it down, which is what some industrial smokers do. With careful planning you can even cold smoke in tropical areas like Florida, however, you are limited to the winter months only and the smoking must be done at night when temperatures drop to 4-16° C (40 - 60° F) or even lower.

The question arises to how to continue cold smoking when temperature increases to 27° C (80° F) at day time? Well, do not smoke, move meat to the area of 10° C (50° F) or refrigerate. Then when the temperature drops in the evening, start smoking again.

Warm Smoking - 23-40° C (73-104° F), continuous smoking from 4-48 hours depending on the diameter of the meat, humidity 80%, and *medium* smoke. The weight loss varies between 2-10%, with the difference being largely dependent on time spent smoking. The surface of the product becomes quite dry but the inside remains raw. Because of the warm smoke, the product receives more smoke in its outside layers. This dry second skin helps increase shelf life, as well as prevent the loss of its natural juices. The color ranges from yellow to brown and has a little shine due to some fat moving outwards.

Hot Smoking - continuous smoking at 41-60° C (105-140° F), 0.5-2 hours, 5-12% weight loss, *heavy* smoke. This is not recommended for large pieces of meat. Although it is the fastest method, there is not enough time for adequate smoke penetration. This results in a higher moisture content thus reducing the product's shelf life. This type of smoking can be divided into three separate phases:

1. Drying out the surface of the meat for 10-40 min at 45-55° C (112-130° F), some very light smoke is acceptable, although not necessary. Besides drying out the surface of the meat, the temperature speeds up nitrite curing. Keep in mind that draft controls must be fully opened to eliminate any moisture residing inside of the smoker. Initially smoking at temperatures higher than 54 -60° C (130-140° F) will prematurely dry out the casings on the surface of the meat and will create a barrier to smoke penetration.

2. This is the proper smoking stage at 45-60° C (112-140° F) for 30-90 min, using medium to heavy smoke. The color becomes a light yellow to dark brown with a shade of red. In this state, the natural casings become strong and fit snugly on the sausages.

3. About 10-20 min baking on the sausage surface at 60-80° C (140-176° F). Temperatures as high as 194° F (90° C) are permitted for a short period of time. Proteins are denatured in the outside layers of the product, but the inside remains raw with temperatures reaching only 40° C (104° F).

If a smoker is used to cook the meat, for example Kabanosy or Hunter's Sausage *(Myśliwska)* the temperature in the last stages of hot smoking is increased to 75-90° C (167-194° F) until the inside of the meat reaches 67° C (152° F). The majority of smoked sausages are cooked in water at 80° C (176° F). This type of cooking (poaching) is more economical to baking (less weight loss). Hot smoked casings fit very snugly, become shiny, and develop a few wrinkles. This is a welcomed scenario; lots of smoked products are subsequently poached. Acting like a barrier, the drier and stronger casings prevent the loss of juices. Because of a relatively short smoking time, hot smoked products should be kept in a refrigerator and consumed relatively quickly. Hot smoking is the fastest and most common method of smoking.

Wet Smoking - hot smoking that employs a water dish placed inside of the smoker to increase humidity levels. Dampening wood chips into water one hour before smoking will produce a similar effect. One reason small smokers need a water dish is that their fuel (charcoal briquettes, heating element) does not contain moisture. On the other hand wood logs always contain some moisture, even when perfectly dried. During the first stage of combustion wood dries out and any remaining moisture evaporates with the smoke into the chamber. Once the wood has burned out, the remaining charcoal has no water left and in dry climates the product may be too dry. Ready made charcoal briquettes or an electric heating wire have no internal moisture, so we have to supply the water in a pan.

Another reason for the water pan is that most little factory made smokers are enclosed units that don't receive a steady supply of air. Fresh air contains moisture which cools sausage casings or the surface of the meat. When smoking with an open fire, lots of fresh air enters the smoker and keeps the meat from drying out. As the water boils at the constant temperature of 100° C (212° F), placing a water filled pan inside of a small smoker will also help to control and maintain temperature at that level. Bear in mind that this temperature is too high for smoking quality meats and sausages.

Wood for Smoking

All hard woods are suitable: oak, alder, beech, hickory, nut, fruit and citrus trees. Stay away from evergreen trees such as pine, spruce, fir and others. These are soft trees that are rich in resin. They impart a turpentine like flavor to meat and they produce a lot of soot which will induce a dark color to smoked meats.

Smoking Temperature

There is no steadfast rule that dictates exact temperature ranges for hot smoking. A few degrees one way or the other should not create any problems as long as the hot smoking upper temperature limit is not crossed. Smoking temperature is one of the most important factors in deciding quality. When smoking, the inside temperature of the smoker cannot exceed 78° C (170° F) for any extended time. At this temperature, fat starts to melt quickly affecting the texture of the sausage. Once it melts the sausage will be greasy outside with a mass of bread crumbs inside, it will lose its shine and will have an inferior taste. If your sausage:

- Is greasy on the outside.
- Drips grease onto the ground.
- Is too shriveled and wrinkled.
- Has lost its shine and looks opaque.
- Is crumbly inside with little empty pockets.

it means that the internal temperature of the sausage was too high during smoking or cooking. Determining temperature is as easy as inserting a stem thermometer through the wall or the door of the smoker. To sum it all up:

- Meat smoked with dry wood has a more pronounced smoky flavor.
- Dry wood may be soaked in water and used for hot smoking.
- Dry wood must be selected when cold smoking.

Humidity

Ideally the meat should be cold smoked at 80% relative humidity. If the humidity were increased, the intense smoke penetration would bring extra moisture inside. Extra moisture in the meat causes bacterial growth, which is exactly what we are trying to avoid. Extremely low humidity, such as in Arizona and New Mexico will cause excessive drying of the sausage casing or the surface of the ham. This will prevent internal moisture from escaping the meat. Humidity control plays an important role when making products that cure very slowly in open air. Not having enough humidity will produce meat that is still moist and raw on the inside and dry outside. Once the meat is cut there will be two different noticeable shades.

Choosing the time of the day is an effective method of humidity control. The humidity is always higher at night when the temperatures are lower. As the temperature drops down the air loses its ability to hold moisture and more moisture is present. In warm climates night is the best time for cold smoking.

Using *dry wood* is of utmost importance when cold smoking. By following these rules we achieve 75-85% humidity, creating the best conditions for moisture removal. This in turn prevents the growth of bacteria. Once the moisture content drops low enough the salt present in meat will further inhibit the development of bacteria and the products can hang in the air for months losing more moisture.

Cooking Sausages

Sausages, hams and other pieces of meat are considered a raw product unless heated to an internal temperature of 68-72° C (154-160° F). It is of no importance whether it is done by boiling, steaming, grilling, or baking. A sausage smoked for 6 hours at 38° C (100° F) will have a great smoky taste, flavor and color, but it will still be a raw sausage like a fresh sausage that was only ground, mixed with spices, and stuffed into casings. Both of them must be cooked to safe temperatures before consumption.

Methods of Cooking

You could smoke your meat in the most primitive conditions outdoors, then bring it home, cook in water and it will be a great product. We can use the following cooking methods:

- Baking in a smoker.
- Baking in the oven.
- Cooking in water.

All we have to do is remember that fat melts down at low temperatures and although it solidifies again, its looks are already gone. Fry a piece of solid fat on a frying pan and see what happens when it solidifies, it doesn't look the same. We can't avoid it altogether (unless we make cold smoked and air dried products), but there is no reason to intensify the problem by creating unnecessarily high temperatures.

Cooking in a Smoker

It makes a lot of sense to cook meat in the smoker as it is already there. Besides, it will have a slightly better taste than sausage cooked in water and it will shine more. On a downside, it will lose more weight than other methods. It is also the *slowest* and the most difficult method that largely depends on the technical possibilities of the smoker. A slow but regularly increasing temperature inside the smoker will produce the best effects. Two thermometers are needed – one to monitor the temperature of a smoker and the other to monitor the inside temperature of the meat or sausage in its thickest part. It helps to have a thermometer with an alarm sounder in it, this way we get an audible warning when meat has achieved its pre-set temperature. Cooking meats in a smoker is a slow process. While it takes 2 –3 hours to smoke a sausage, it may take an additional 5 hours to bake it. It will largely depend on the inside temperature of the meat when smoking was stopped. If it was 38° C (100° F) we have a long way to go, if it was

66° C (150° F) we are almost there. A lot will depend on outside conditions and how well the smoker is insulated. Of course we take for granted that our smoker is fully capable of providing heat on demand. The other easier method will be to increase the temperature of the smoker to about 80° C (176° F) and wait until the meat's inside temperature reaches 68-72° C (154-160° F).

Cooking in Water

This is a common, acceptable and professional method of cooking meats and sausages. It is also easier and faster to apply than cooking in the smoker and the meat weight loss is also smaller. Water is brought to the temperature of 70-90° C (158-194° F) and the meats or sausages are immersed in it. For instance, home made hams are poached at 80° C (176° F) and this temperature is maintained until the meat internal temperature reaches 68-72° C (154-160° F).

Note: according to United Stated Department of Agriculture meats that *were not cured and smoked* should be cooked to the following temperatures:

- Fish should reach 63° C (145° F).
- All cuts of pork to 72° C (160° F).
- Ground beef, veal and lamb to 72° C (160° F).
- All poultry should reach a safe minimum internal temperature of 74° C (165° F).
- Leftovers to 74° C (165° F).

Baking in Oven

Baking in an oven is also an option as long as the temperature can be kept at 93° C (200° F) or less.

Smokehouse

The simplest smokehouse will be the one that is dedicated to smoking only. The outside temperature will determine whether such a smoker can be used for cold smoking. Any smoking done over an open fire or inside of any simple box or barrel will fall into this category. The design of a smoker remains relatively easy unless we want to use it for baking sausages. In cold climates such an outside smoker will use plenty of fuel unless it is well insulted.

But why cook a sausage in a smoker? The majority of processed meats are cooked in water or in steam. The design of the smoker becomes very simple if cooking is accomplished in a different appliance. There are many commercially produced small electric smokers that are suitable for smoking and baking small amounts of sausages.

In some Polish homes a chimney was a part of the smokehouse.

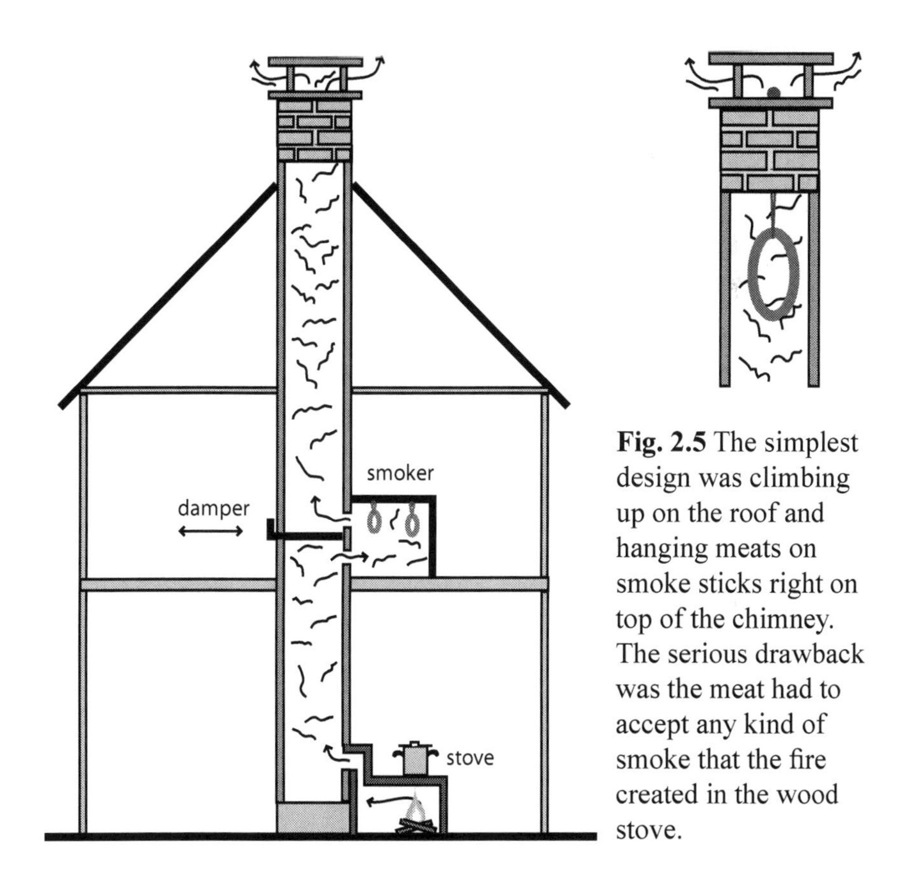

Fig. 2.5 The simplest design was climbing up on the roof and hanging meats on smoke sticks right on top of the chimney. The serious drawback was the meat had to accept any kind of smoke that the fire created in the wood stove.

Fig. 2.4 Home chimney smoker.

A much better design was placing a proper smokehouse on the second floor. Two holes were made in the chimney: one for the smoke to enter the chamber and another to allow it to escape.

Most unusual but effective smoker made from the stump of an old oak tree. Smoker located on Poliwoda Fishing Grounds, Opole, Poland. Smoked trout ends up on a dinner plate in a popular tourist restaurant which is located on the same grounds.

Photo 2.42 above. Brined fish being inserted on smoke sticks.

Photo 2.43 A separate fire pit burning wood logs can be seen in front. It is connected with a smoker by an underground pipe. Black item lying on the ground to the right of the smoker is an old potato burlap bag that is used as a smoker's cover.

Chapter 3

Food Safety

Restricting bacteria growth is the first step towards successful production of quality meats. Under correct conditions, bacteria reproduce rapidly and the populations can grow very large. Temperature and time are factors that affect bacterial growth most. Below 7° C (45° F) bacteria grow slowly and at temperatures above 60° C (140° F) they start to die. In the so called "danger zone" between 6 - 60° C (40-140° F) bacteria grow quite well. Most bacteria will grow exponentially at temperatures between 21° C (70° F) and 49° C (120° F). Bacteria don't grow in size but reproduce by dividing. It is assumed that under ideal conditions bacteria divide every 20 minutes.

What is Botulism?

Botulism, once known as a sausage disease, is a rare but serious food-borne disease that can be fatal. Food borne botulism can be especially dangerous because many people can be poisoned at once. *Clostridium botulinum* is found in soil and aquatic sediments all over the world. The bacteria can form a spore that is very resistant to heat and chemicals. Like plant seeds, it can lie dormant for years. The optimal temperature range for the growth of botulinum bacteria is 26-35° C (78-95° F) and it significantly slows down at 48° C (118° F). At 60° C (140° F), botulinum spores do not develop into toxins, although they are heat resistant. They will survive in boiling water 100° C (212° F) for up to 5 hours.

How To Prevent Botulism

The answer lies in the use of nitrates/nitrites. When present, they prevent the transformation of *C. botulinum* spores to toxins. It is almost like applying a vaccine to eliminate a disease. Nitrates are cheap, commonly available, and completely safe in amounts recommended by the Food and Drug Administration. So why not use them? All commercial plants do. Nitrates are needed only when smoking meats. You don't need nitrates when barbecuing or grilling, as the temperatures are high enough to inhibit or kill botulinum spores. Botulinum spores will die in a matter of minutes at 121° C (250° F).

Trichinae

Trichinae is an illness caused by the consumption of raw or under cooked meat infected with *"trichinella spiralis."* It is a round worm that can migrate from the digestive tract and settle in the form of cysts in various muscles of the body. The disease is almost non-existent in American pigs due to their strictly controlled feed, but it can still be found in wild boar and wild game. Venison meat is safe as deers are herbivores; they eat leaves, bushes and shrubs and they don't contract the disease. Trichinae in pork is killed by raising the internal temperature of meat to 58° C (137°F). The U.S. Code of Federal Regulations requires pork to be cooked for 1 minute at 60° C (140° F). We can not apply these procedures to a product that is not supposed to be cooked. Fortunately, *storing pork at low temperatures also kills trichinae.* The U.S. Department of Agriculture's Code of Federal Regulations, Title 9, Volume 2, Citr: 9 CFR318.10 requires that pork intended for use in processed products be frozen at:

Group 1 - comprises product in separate pieces not exceeding 6 " (15 cm) in thickness, or arranged on separate racks with layers not exceeding 6" (15 cm) in depth, or stored in crates or boxes not exceeding 6" (15 cm) in depth, or stored as solidly frozen blocks not exceeding 6" (15 cm) in thickness.

Group 2 - comprises product in pieces, layers, or within containers, the thickness of which exceeds 6" (15 cm) but not 27" (68 cm) and product in containers including tierces, barrels, kegs, and cartons having a thickness not exceeding 27" (68 cm).

Table 1. Required Period of Freezing Indicated			
Temperature		Days	
° F	° C	Group 1	Group 2
5	-15	20	30
- 10	-23.3	10	20
- 20	-28.9	6	12

The product undergoing such refrigeration or the containers thereof shall be so spaced while in the freezer as will insure a free circulation of air between the pieces of meat, layers, blocks, boxes, barrels, and tierces in order that the temperature of the meat throughout will be promptly reduced to not higher than -15° C (5° F), -23.3° C (-10° F), or -28.9° C (-20° F). Microwaving, curing, drying or smoking is not effective in preventing Trichinae. It should be noted that *freezing will not kill larval cysts in bears and other wild game that live in Northwestern U.S. and Alaska.* That meat has to be cooked to 72° C (160° F) internal temperature.

Good Manufacturing Practices that Can be Applied in the Everyday Kitchen

Meat of a healthy animal is clean and contains very few bacteria. Any invading bacteria will be destroyed by the animal's immune system. Most bacteria are present on the skin and in the intestines. The slaughtering process starts introducing bacteria into the exposed surfaces. In a large piece of meat the outside surface serves as a natural barrier preventing access to bacteria. Every time we create a new surface cut with a knife we create an opening for bacteria to enter the meat from the outside and start spoiling it.

The more cuts, the more spoils of meat and that is the reason why ground meat has the shortest shelf life. In a stressed animal bacteria are able to travel from the animal's gut right through the casing into the meat. Duties like cutting meat, grinding, mixing or stuffing all increase meat temperature and should be performed in the kitchen at the lowest possible temperatures and as fast as possible. Otherwise we create conditions for the growth of bacteria and that will decrease the shelf life of the product.

To sum it up make sure that:

- ***Meat is very fresh and always kept cold.***
- ***Facilities and tools are very clean.***
- ***Working temperatures are as low as possible.***
- ***Take only what you need rule always applies.***

Temperature Control

If you live in a tropical climate without air conditioning, try to process meat in the evening or early morning hours and work with a small portion of meat at one time. Other factors which influence your product quality and can eliminate the danger of any food poisoning are the 4 C's of Food Hygiene:

- Cleanliness-wash hands, prevent insects, use clean equipment.
- Cooking-cook meat, poultry and fish to proper internal temperature.
- Cooling and storage-keep food at refrigerator temperature.
- Cross-contamination-don't mix raw and cooked meats, use clean knives, keep separate chopping boards for cooked and raw meat.

Storing Meat

Treat fresh or smoked meats and sausages as fresh meat. We can keep at hand an amount that will be consumed within a few days but the rest should be frozen. A ready to eat product should not be stored for more than 7 days if held at 5° C (41° F), or 4 days at 7° C (45° F). Meats should be stored at 0-4° C (32-40° F). We should bear in mind that there are differences between home and commercial refrigerators and freezers:

Home refrigerator	Butcher's cooler
2° - 4° C (36° - 40° F)	0° C (32° F)
Home freezer	Butcher's freezer
-18° C (0° F)	- 32° C (-25° F)

Freezing Meat

Freezing prevents the spoilage of sausage, however, keeping it in a freezer for longer than 6 weeks will lower its quality due to internal changes of fats known as "rancidity." The sausage, however, will still be nutricious and perfectly safe to eat.

Thawing Meat

Thawing must be done slowly, preferably at refrigerator temperature, which will allow for the ice crystals to dissipate slowly without creating significant damage to the texture of the meat. Preferred methods of thawing are:

- In the refrigerator 2-4° C (36-40° F).
- In cold water.
- In the microwave.

Chapter 4

Polish Sausages

Official Classification

Polish sausage classification sounds very technical and is somewhat confusing. It divides sausages by the size of the minced meat. You may say that the the size of the grinder plate establishes sausage type:

- Homogenized.
- Finely minced - meat particles below 5 mm (3/16").
- Finely minced uncooked.
- Finely minced "wysokowydajne" - gain of the finished sausage is more than 135% in relation to the original meat weight.
- Medium minced - meat particles between 5-20 mm (3/16 - 3/4").
- Medium minced uncooked.
- Medium minced, high yield ("wysokowydajne") - gain of the finished sausage is more than 120% in relation to the original meat weight.
- Medium minced semi-dry.
- Coarse minced - meat particles over 20 mm (over 3/4").
- Coarse minced uncooked.
- Coarse minced.
- Coarse minced, high yield - gain of the finished sausage is ***more*** than 115 % in relation to the original meat weight.
- Coarse minced dry.

A finished high yield sausage *("wysokowydajna")* weighs more than the original weight of the meat. This is due to the addition of water and chemicals that will hold this water inside. Note that there is no upper limit. Almost all sausages are called by the general word Kielbasa ("sausage") which is followed by its proper name, for example: Kielbasa Szynkowa, Kielbasa Wiejska, Kielbasa Serdelowa, Kielbasa Krakowska, Kielbasa Mysliwska etc. As explained earlier the word "kielbasa" (a sausage) has little meaning if you do not follow it with the proper name.

Then there is a more practical classification:

- Dry and semi-dry sausages - cold smoked, not cooked.
- Dry and semi-dry sausages-smoked and cooked (baked or poached).
- Regular smoked sausages-smoked and poached in water.
- Emulsified sausages - like American hot dogs or bologna.
- Fresh sausages-not smoked, need to be cooked before consumption.

plus a special group of sausages:

- Head cheeses.
- Liver sausages.
- Blood sausages.

Sausages in the special group are made with offal meat: liver, heart, lungs, brain, spleen, tripe, casings, jowls, dewlap, skins, snouts and blood. When you see the word "kiszka" in the name it signifies the fact that organ meats and often the blood were used as materials. The special group of sausages are cooked in water and usually are not smoked so the entire process can be accomplished in the kitchen. However, at your discretion after cooking and cooling they may be briefly *cold* smoked to extend their keeping qualities.

There are very few books that explain how to make those unique products so we provide detailed information in the corresponding chapters. Once a reader understands the process he will not be intimidated by the recipes and he might give them a try. This is a much simpler process than it looks. In addition these sausages are usually not smoked. A peculiar characteristic of the special group sausages is that the cooking process is employed twice:

1. To cook meats and materials in water before grinding and emulsifying.

2. To poach sausages in water to the safe internal meat temperature.

The casings are filled loosely as the semi-cooked groats or rice often expand further and the sausage casings may burst.

Names of Sausages

An average person is not really aware and could not care less about this technical classification as all sausages have their own names and people know them. Most Polish sausages derive their name from:

- The part of Poland where they were once originally made: Bydgoska Sausage, Lithuanian Sausage, Krakowska Sausage.

- The name of the meat part or spice that plays a dominant role in the recipe: Bacon Sausage, Garlic Sausage, Juniper Sausage.

It is possible to make different types of a particular sausage not changing its original recipe but employing different manufacturing techniques. And the same sausage will have a different texture, will have a different degree of saltiness and will have different preservation qualities. White Sausage and Polish Smoked Sausage (cold or hot smoked) are made up of the same ingredients but are different products.

A very interesting group of sausages were cold smoked products made in Poland and Russia. When thinking about Russia, a picture of a poor farmer laboring his land often comes to mind. Well, there were also aristocrats, Tzar families and royalty who liked good food, sausages not being an exception. The same happened in Poland and continued during the communist regime when the privileged class (party members) had access to the special state run stores where the best domestic and imported foods were available.

Processed meat products had to exhibit superior quality and last a long time as there was no refrigeration. Such requirements forced the development of a manufacturing process which guaranteed that the end product was microbiologically stable, and had an almost indefinite shelf life. Many of these sausages were naturally fermented cold smoked products which could have been called salami.

Starter cultures were not around yet and the final product exhibited none of the sourly flavor so common today. The procedure was as follows:

- Top quality meats were selected and cured for 3-4 days with salt and nitrate at low temperatures.
- Sausages were cold smoked for weeks at the time. This allowed natural fermentation and drying to take place inside of the smokehouse. Due to the action of the smoke, there was no mold on sausages and if it developed, it would be wiped off.
- Sausages were left hanging in a smokehouse or in a different chamber and were consummed on a need basic. The sausages kept on drying out and during this "ripening" process were developing salami like flavor.

We could classify these sausages as:

- Cold smoked sausages - as salami,
- Metka sausages - spreadable fermented sausages.

Authentic Polish Sausage Recipes and What You Need To Know to Understand Them

The "*Internal Regulations # 16 for Making Meat Products and Sausages*" printed in 1959 in Warsaw, was the first official government guide for making processed meats. This 300 page internal guide was reserved for personnel employed in the production of meats and sausages. It covered meat curing and salting, brine preparation, meat selection and official recipes with detailed instructions for making and smoking products like hams, butts, loins, ribs and sausages. A lot of research was based on Russian Meat Technology which was very advanced even in the years before the war. For instance one of the best early books on meat technology that we have seen anywhere is the *"Meat Technology and Making Meat Products"* by A.A. Manergerger and E.J. Mirkin, printed in Russian, 1949 Moscow edition.

In 1964 the Polish Government issued "Internal Regulations # 21 for Making Meat Products and Sausages" (760 pages long) which was the expanded version of the 1959 guide. In the following years more guides followed, however, in the later editions starting in 1982 additives which were never used before started to appear. The situation deteriorated further when Poland joined the European Common Market in 2004 and had to submit to new common regulations. The meat industry had to accept new additives and chemicals and Polish sausages were never the same.

The recipes presented in this book come from 1959-1964 archives so they do not contain any chemicals, save sodium nitrite which is required in smoked products in every country. They are a treasure chest of sausage history and sausage making secrets. One can learn a new trade by just studying their composition and detailed instructions of their making.

The recipes were prepared for meat plants and the original formulas were for 100 kg (220 lbs) and 1000 kg (2,200 lb) of sausage. As this is too large of an amount for even the hungriest families we have scaled them down to 1 kg (2.2 lbs) of meat. Original instructions were left intact and even though the purchase of some parts such as hearts, tongues or head meat are beyond the reach of an average hobbyist, the recipes were left in the original form and will provide an excellent reading on the art of sausage making. You will notice that some sausages were smoked on three separate times and about 3 weeks of time was needed to produce them. This resulted in a product with a long shelf life. It is unlikely that a modern meat plant could afford itself the luxury of so much time to make a sausage. Most of those sausages are still made today using modified and faster methods of production. Once the sausage is fully cooked it is done and may be placed in a refrigerator. Because refrigerators were not common when the war ended, additional drying steps followed to make products stable at room temperature. Many people still make those original products at least from time to time. And of course in Poland those times will be Christmas and Easter when only the best of the best qualifies to be displayed on the dinner table.

Herbal Pepper *(Pieprz ziołowy)*

Spices like pepper, nutmeg, or allspice do not grow in cold Polish climate and had to be imported. Poland had salt mines but shortages of pepper were quite common. Human ingenuity came to the rescue and the herbal pepper was invented. Although it was not as potent as the original pepper, it had an advantage: it was mainly made from locally grown herbs.

As a rule of thumb a double amount of herbal pepper is needed to replace regular pepper. It has also been said that in meat products the full effect of herbal pepper use is noticeable after about 48 hours. Herbal peppers are used in many countries, for example French Quatre-èpices: (pepper, nutmeg, cloves) or Italian seasonings (marjoram, thyme, rosemary, savory, sage, oregano, and basil).

Different combinations were created and the herbal pepper became such a hit that it is still being sold in every store in Poland. The table lists the herbal pepper formula that was approved for use in meat products.

Spice Name	% used
coriander	26.6
dry horseradish	17.6
caraway	8.8
cayenne pepper	4.3
white mustard seed	17.6
marjoram	0.9
black mustard seed	17.6
gentian	0.004
fennel	6.6

Another herbal pepper typical formula: white mustard seed, caraway, marjoram, chili, hot and sweet paprika, bay leaf.

Buckwheat and Barley Groats *(Kasza gryczana and jęczmienna)*

Those groats are used in many blood sausages. They are very popular in Germany, Poland, Russia, Spain and England. Barley is big in Scotland too but for a different reason: Scotch Whiskey is made from it.

Bread Crumbs and Dry Rolls *(Bułka tarta i czerstwa)*

Bread crumbs need very little introduction as they are used for general cooking. Only rolls baked from pure wheat flour were used in the meat industry. Except for wheat, no other ingredients like rye or sugar were permitted in the manufacturing. Dry rolls were soaked in leftover meat stock or just in plain water. Bread crumbs were made by slicing dry wheat rolls through a grater. Bread crumbs that are sold in supermarkets today are a poor choice for making sausages as they contain too many foreign ingredients that may go sour. You are better off buying a few Portuguese wheat rolls and leaving them on a shelf to dry out. The practice of adding rolls to meat was widely used after the war and it was the question of economics. There was no meat and sometimes there were leftover rolls and bread that nobody would throw away.

It was a cardinal sin to throw away any kind of food, especially bread. When a piece of bread was dropped people would pick it up and kiss it as the way of saying I am sorry. We are talking about times when the diet consisted of stinging nettle soup, wild mushrooms or dandelion wine. If you add soaked rolls or bread crumbs to your hamburger meat, add raw egg to bind it together, fry some finely diced onions until glassy, and mix it together you have created a whole new dish. Ever heard of Wiener Schnitzel? It is basically a veal fillet, soaked on both sides in beaten egg, then dipped on both sides in bread crumbs and fried on a frying pan. You can do the same with a pork chop or a boneless and skinless chicken breast.

Semolina *(kasza manna)* is made during the grinding of wheat to make flour. The particles are round, 0.60-0.65 mm (1/32") in diameter and white with a yellow tint. Healthy, high caloric food (325 cal per 100 g) semolina was often given with milk and sugar to children for breakfast. When making sausages it is used to bind meats together in products like Liver Sausage, Jowl Sausage and Blood Head Cheese.

Skwarki

Skwarki are basically ¼ cubes of pork fatback fried on a pan, until becoming light brown in color. Kind of bacon bits. Skwarki is the by product of making lard (*smalec* in Polish) by fat rendering. They are remaining bits of pure fat or very fatty meat, about ¼" in size, which are obtained by melting down back fat. The melting process must be stopped when they become gold or light brown otherwise they will burn and taste bitter. They are often added to blood sausages. Skwarki are usually present in home made lard. In the early 20th century lard's popularity was equal to butter and it was commonly used as a cooking fat or as a spread. Today its use has diminished by its negative image among health conscious consumers. But if one can put this perception aside for a minute and look at lard's chemical composition, it will become clear that lard has less saturated fat and less cholesterol than an equal amount of butter. At the last moment, when skwarki are almost done, a finely chopped onion may be added into the melted lard and when the onions acquire a golden color the heat must be turned off. A small amount of salt may be added. The lard with skwarki is poured into containers where it will last a long time even at room temperature. Such lard when spread on a slice of bread became a high calorie food. You can made lard and skwarki from back fat or belly slabs.

Photo 4.1 Lard rendering.

Photo 4.2 Lard cracklings *(skwarki).*

Spices

You will easily notice that by today's standards these recipes call for a small dosage of spices. With high quality meat available and no chemicals or binders used it was sufficient to produce a great sausage. Today, extra water and the whole array of extra ingredients are added which dilutes the flavor. To make up for that we need to add flavor enhancers and more spices.

Sugar

Less crucial, normally used to offset the harshness of salt. Amount used is about 10% of the salt used in the recipe. Sugar is normally used with salt when curing meat. As a flavoring ingredient, sugar plays a little role in making sausages. No more than 3 g of sugar is added to 1 kg of meat otherwise it can be noticeable.

Fat

The meat needs about 25 - 30% fat in it. This will make the sausage tender and juicy, without fat it will feel dry.

Salt

Sausage needs salt. The proper amount of salt in meat (tastes pleasant) is 2 – 3%, though 1.5 – 2% is usually an average. Poland lies on a similar latitude to Quebec in Canada which provides good conditions for storing food at room temperatures for the most of the year. Those conditions plus the right amount of salt, nitrate and proper manufacturing procedures (curing, cold smoking) allowed the creation of stable meat products with a very long shelf life. The original recipes called for about 2.3% of salt which was needed when the main objective was meat preservation and refrigerators were unheard of. We all have access to refrigerators and most typical sausages contain about 2% or less of salt.

Salt perception can be an acquired taste. If you decide to go on a low sodium diet and start decreasing the amount of salt you consume, in about three weeks time you may reach a point when your food tastes enjoyable, though you use less salt than before. This is fine as long as you prepare those meals for yourself. When smoking meats, sausage or fish for your friends try to adhere to the amount of salt the original recipe calls for as other people will probably like more salt than you.

When smoking large amounts of meat that will be kept for a week or longer in the kitchen or refrigerator, remember that *it will keep on drying out* (losing moisture). *Salt will, however, remain inside and your sausage will now taste saltier and will be of a smaller diameter.* The meat flavor will also be stronger now. In such a case you may use less salt than originally planned for, let's say 1.5 mg/kg. That will not apply when making a fresh sausage which will be consumed in a matter of days and 1.8 - 2.0 mg salt per one kilogram of meat will be fine.

Pepper

The most popular spice "pepper" comes in two forms:

- black pepper - unripe seeds of the plant with the skin left on
- white pepper - ripe seeds with the skin removed

Pepper is available as whole seeds but you have to grind it. Like in the case of coffee beans, the advantage is that you get a fresher aroma when grinding seeds just before use. It is available as coarse grind, sometimes called butcher's grind or fine grind. A recipe will call for a particular grind but the final choice will be up to you. *The dividing line is whether you want to see the pepper in your product or not.* Otherwise it makes no difference and you can replace black pepper with the same amount of white pepper, although the black pepper is a bit hotter.

General Notes

By studying the recipes one will notice that most are made of pork and different proportions of beef, sometimes veal. In Israel or in Muslim countries pork will be omitted on religious grounds as in those times it was thought to be an inferior meat. The reason was not the meat itself but the insufficient knowledge we had on the subject as the meat was often infected with *trichinae worms* due to eating raw garbage and dead rodents. The climate in those countries was much warmer than in Northern Europe and pork meat did not last long either. If you follow cases of food recalls in the USA, you will see that they were mainly created by beef that was infected by *E.coli*.

Geographical location plays a significant role when making up new recipes. Mountain people or highlanders raise animals such as sheep or goats and in their recipes those meats will play a dominant role. They would probably love to eat more pork but the rocky terrain was ill suited for pigs to prosper.

Choosing only lean meat will not produce a high quality sausage. It will be a poor quality sausage as it will not have enough fat in it. We may think of all those little scraps of meats with gristle and sinews as inferior meats, but they are rich in collagen and will produce gelatin which will bind all ingredients together. Those scraps are processed in a bowl cutter until a fine paste is obtained. Rotating knives generate so much heat that flaked ice is added to keep the temperature under control and all those scraps of meat, skins included, can swallow large amounts of ice and water and hold it thus making the product feel juicy. Fat carries the flavor, in addition it provides a pleasant mouth feel. Fat foods such as ice cream, cream cheese, mayonnaise, butter, sauces, fat hamburger; they all feel pleasant to our palate. Remove the fat and the sausage feels like bread crumbs. There are low fat equivalents of ice cream, yogurt, cream cheese and other foods that to a certain point they can imitate the original flavor of the product, but they are made with special ingredients known as hydrocolloids, for example microcellulose or a variety of gums.

People like to apply double standards to whatever they consider to be good food. Mention smoked eel to a friend and he is already shaking seeing in his mind a nasty rattler going after him. He does not even want to hear that quality smoked eel can be spread with a knife on a roll like butter. Until the 1970's one could not find a single eel in a fish store in New York City. Then an influx of immigrants from the Far East had brought new customs and cuisines. The eels started to swim in fish tanks everywhere.

Take "carp" for example, the fish originally came from Japan to China, then to Europe and finally to the USA. Served in aspic or cooked Jewish style, in Poland carp has been the traditional Christmas Eve dish for centuries. In 1985 when I was trained in New York as a scuba diver, my manual stated that the fish was non-edible. The probable cause was that the fish being a bottom dweller, could develop a slight muddy flavor especially as it grew larger. It also contains more bones than other species and ourselves being a busy species today, we expect to order our meal, swallow it and rush out to watch a baseball game. In Poland there were no stores nor proper distribution systems when the war ended and live carp was sold on street corners before Christmas. People would buy a few fish a week earlier and keep them swimming in a bathtub full of water until they were ready to process and cook them.

How many of us ate Steak Tartare which is a raw ground beef (originally horse meat). It is is served with an egg, chopped onions, and a pickle, not forgetting a glass of cold beer. Most of us will eat a bloody rare steak, but will not touch a fully cooked blood sausage. Mention to someone that skins and tongues are used to make a head cheese and he'll never touch it. In the meantime, all his life he eats hot dogs not realizing that they are made from tongues, skins, organs, head meat and bone scraped meat. Special machines are designed to scrape off the tendons and remaining pieces of meat from the bones until they are bare.

In European countries the consumer accepts head cheese or blood sausage as a fine product. You can buy sausages made from horse meat in Europe and nobody is surprised. Here in the USA there is a lot of prejudice, but we are very practical people. In order not to confuse folks with names like head cheeses or blood sausages, we dump all parts of animal into bologna, hot dogs and frankfurters.

Sausage Names

Where practical the English name was substituted: Kielbasa Litewska (Lithuanian Sausage), Kielbasa Ukraińska (Ukrainian Sausage) or Juniper Sausage (Kiełbasa Jałowcowa). In other instances due to the established popularity of the sausage the Polish name was left intact, even though it sounded difficult to pronounce: Krakowska Sausage, Mysliwska Sausage or Rzeszowska Sausage (Kiełbasa Rzeszowska). We have tried to avoid creating names that are neither English nor Polish. Where possible we are providing a particular sausage history and you will be able to understand that Zywiecka Sausage (Kiełbasa Żywiecka) means a sausage that comes from the region of Żywiec, the same region where the popular Polish beer "Żywiec" is made. Many sausage names contain words or letters that are common to different languages, notably German. For hundreds of years certain areas in Poland were populated by different ethnic groups living either together or next to each other. This has recently changed as fresh meats and sausages are kept in refrigerators. Barbecue and grill units are everywhere and fresh sausages are cooked outside and immediately eaten. This has made the manufacturing process easier compared to traditional methods of food preservation.

Photo 4.3 A section of a typical Polish meat store.

Recipe Guidelines

As all of original Polish sausage recipes ask for pork, beef or veal meat class I, II, III or IV we have faced a little dilemma. We could have substituted pork, beef or veal meat grades with names like ham, butt, loin and other cuts but this would not be a true representation of the original. In addition most sausages require some connective tissue and one cannot just walk into the store and ask for one pound of connective tissue meat. You have to trim it out yourself. A recipe might call for pork class II B but it really *does not matter whether this meat comes from ham, butt, picnic or from meat trimmings* as long as it fulfills the requirements of the recipe.

In order to select right meat cuts it is absolutely essential that one studies Chapter 2, especially *meat classes*. Lean ham or butt can be used for pork class I. Pork butt will do fine for class II. Keep in mind that ham and butt will provide meats of all classes. To make a quality sausage you need to understand Chapter 2, that simple.

Many recipes call for the addition of *dewlap* which is seldom mentioned in American sausage recipes. Instead the word *jowl* (cheek) is predominantly used and it covers dewlap and jowls at the same time. When one ends and the other begins depends how the head is separated from the body but the meat itself remains pretty much the same in both cases.

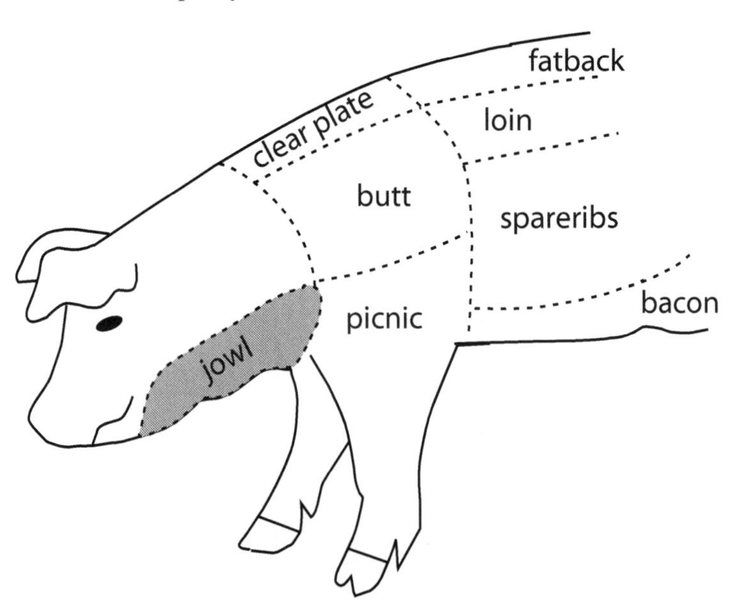

Fig. 4.1 Jowl/dewlap.

- In the Polish meat industry a clear distinction is made between the two. The front part (cheek) is called jowl and the back (lower) part is called dewlap. The jowls look very much like bacon and sometimes you will meet a definition of "jowl bacon." The difference is that bacon is a soft belly fat and jowls fat is a hard one.
- Many recipes call for garlic. Too much garlic may be sensed in a fresh sausage which is eaten within a day or two, but its potent flavor dissipates rapidly in time. Because of that more garlic can be added to smoked sausages. Fresh garlic is applied in a minced or crushed form.
- Many sausages are smoked-*cooked*-smoked-dried. The sausage is finished when cooked to safe temperature. Those additional steps were performed to make a drier sausage that would last for a longer time at room temperature. They may be omitted when a sausage is kept refrigerated.
- You should use a thermometer, however, you can estimate cooking time in *water* at 176° F (80° C): allow 10 minutes for 10 mm (1 cm) casing diameter, 36 mm casing requires 36 minutes of cooking time.
- You can be flexible with casings. Stuff into any casings - the main criteria is whether they are permeable to smoke. Casings for head cheeses, liver and blood sausages may be waterproof and not permeable to smoke. You can be flexible with the diameter of the casing, however, if you change casing diameter you may need to readjust smoking and cooking time.
- You could probably use pork butt for most of the sausages. You should, however, trim it into separate classes and finely grind/emulsify trimmings rich in connective tissue.
- When smoking times are long you should periodically re-arrange smokesticks to allow uniform smoke distribution.
- Occasionally you may find salted meats only, soak them in cold running water for 3 hours or change water 2-3 times. Fresh back fat is very hard to find, but supermarkets usually carry it in the form of salt pork. It is very salty, however, you could desalt it in water in a refrigerator. You will need at least 24 hours. Taste it to see how salty it is.
- Get into the habit of tasting every sausage mixture before it is stuffed into a casing.

If you follow safety rules and the proper manufacturing methods it does not really matter how close to the original recipe the amount of spices in your sausage is. It is like roasting chicken in a rotisserie, as long as you add salt and pepper to it, the chicken will come out beautifully. You may add paprika to it, lemon juice, garlic or any other spices you like but it will still remain a fine meal. But if you roast it too long, now it is a different story. The same applies to a sausage, as long as you stay within certain temperatures and times, the sausage will turn out great. Let us quote Madame Benoit, the famous Canadian cookery expert and author who once said:

> ***"I feel a recipe is only a theme, which an intelligent cook can play each time with a variation."***

Most likely you will be making sausages for yourself so use spices that you and your kids like, after all you will end up eating it. We have seen recipe books with names like these: Sausage #1, Sausage #2, Sausage #3. You can do the same but be original and name it after your kids, friends or even your dog or a cat. Just put more oregano to one recipe because John likes more oregano on his pizza and put caraway into the second recipe because Elizabeth likes bread with caraway seeds. Now you have John and Elizabeth Sausages with family history.

I will never forget when I made my first Polish smoked sausage that turned out very well and I proudly gave it to my friend - professional sausage maker Waldemar to try. I included salt, pepper, garlic, and added optional marjoram. I also added nutmeg and other spices that I liked. Well my friend's judgement was as follows:

> ***"Great sausage but why all those perfumes?"***

For him it was supposed to be the classical Polish Smoked Sausage and all it needed was salt, pepper and garlic.

Combining meat with salt and pepper already makes a great product providing that you will follow the basic rules of sausage making. It's that simple. If you don't cure your meats properly or screw up your smoking and cooking temperatures, all the spices in the world will not save your sausage.

Recipe Index

Sausage Recipes by Type

List of Polish Sausages from the Polish Government Archives (1945-1989)

Long Lasting Hot Smoked Dry and Semi-Dry Sausages *From the Polish Government Archives (1945-1989)*		
Name	**Original Polish Name**	**Page**
1. Baltycka Sausage	*Kiełbasa bałtycka*	108
2. Beef Sausage	*Kiełbasa wołowa krajana*	110
3. Beer Sausage	*Kiełbasa piwna*	111
4. Beer Sausage with Goose	*Kiełbasa piwna z gęsiną*	113
5. Belzka	*Kiełbasa bełzka*	114
6. Bialostocka	*Kiełbasa białostocka*	115
7. Bialostocka with Goose Fat	*Kiełbasa białostocka z gęsim tł.*	116
8. Bielska	*Kiełbasa bielska*	117
9. Camp Sausage	*Kiełbasa wczasowa*	118
10. Debowiecka	*Kiełbasa dębowiecka*	119
11. Farmer Sausage	*Kiełbasa wiejska*	120
12. Hunter's Sausage	*Kiełbasa myśliwska*	121
13. Husarska	*Kiełbasa husarska*	123
14. Hutnicka	*Kiełbasa hutnicka*	124
15. Juniper Sausage	*Kiełbasa jałowcowa*	125
16. Kabanosy	*Kabanosy*	127
17. Knyszynska	*Kiełbasa knyszyńska*	129
18. Krakowska Cut Sausage	*Kiełbasa krakowska krajana*	130
19. Krakowska Dry Sausage	*Kiełbasa krakowska trwała*	132
20. Kujawska	*Kiełbasa kujawska*	134
21. Limanowska Sausage	*Kiełbasa limanowska*	135
22. Lithuanian Sausage	*Kiełbasa litewska*	136
23. Loin Sausage	*Kiełbasa polędwicowa*	137
24. Lowiecka	*Kiełbasa łowiecka*	138
25. Olawska	*Kiełbasa oławska*	139
26. Podhalanska Sausage	*Kiełbasa podhalańska*	140
27. Podkarpacka	*Kiełbasa podkarpacka półtrwała*	140
28. Rzeszowska Sausage	*Kiełbasa rzeszowska*	143
29. Salami Krakowskie	*Salami krakowskie*	144
30. Serbian Sausage	*Kiełbasa serbska*	145
31. Servolatka	*Serwolatka*	146
32. Tarnogorska	*Kiełbasa tarnogórska podsuszana*	147
33. Tarnowska	*Kiełbasa cielęca tarnowska*	148

Hot Smoked Sausages, Finely Ground (Emulsified), With Limited Shelf Life *From the Polish Government Archives (1945-1989)*		
Name	**Original Polish Name**	**Page**
1. Bacon Sausage	*Kiełbasa boczkowa*	187
2. Bytomska	*Kiełbasa bytomska*	188
3. Mortadella	*Mortadela*	189
4. Sausage Links	*Kiełbaski porcjowe*	191
5. Serdelki	*Serdelki*	193
6. Serdelowa Sausage	*Kiełbasa serdelowa*	194
7. Serdelowa Veal Sausage	*Kiełbasa serdelowa cielęca*	195
8. Steamed Sausage	*Kiełbasa parówkowa*	196
9. Steamed Sausage Links	*Parówki*	197
10. Veal Mortadella	*Mortadela cielęca*	198

Fresh Sausages *(Not Cooked and Not Ready to Eat, Raw Meat)* *From the Polish Government Archives (1945-1989)*		
Name	**Original Polish Name**	**Page**
1. White Sausage	*Kiełbasa biała surowa*	*202*

Head Cheeses *From the Polish Government Archives (1945-1989)*		
Name	**Original Polish Name**	**Page**
1. All Trimmings Head Cheese	*Salceson podrobowy*	209
2. Black Head Cheese	*Salceson czarny*	210
3. Brunszwicki Head Cheese	*Salceson brunszwicki*	212
4. Farmer Head Cheese	*Salceson wiejski*	213
5. Italian Head Cheese	*Salceson włoski*	214
6. Mazowiecki Head Cheese	*Salceson mazowiecki*	215
7. Pomorski Black Head Cheese	*Salceson czarny pomorski*	216
8. Silesian Head Cheese	*Salceson śląski*	217
9. Tongue Head Cheese	*Salceson ozorkowy*	218
10. White Head Cheese Supreme	*Salceson biały wyborowy*	220
11. Wolsztynski Head Cheese	*Salceson wolsztyński*	221

Kiszki *(Liver and Blood sausages)*

Liver Sausages *(Kiszki Pasztetowe i Wątrobianki)* *From the Polish Government Archives (1945-1989)*		
Name	**Original Polish Name**	**Page**
1. Liver Sausage	*Kiszka wątrobiana*	227
2. Liver Påtė Sausage	*Kiszka pasztetowa*	228
3. Liver Påtė Sausage with Semolina	*Kiszka pasztetowa z manną*	230
4. Obornicka Liver Sausage	*Kiszka wątrobiana obornicka*	232

Blood Sausages *(Kiszki krwiste)* *From the Polish Government Archives (1945-1989)*		
Name	**Original Polish Name**	**Page**
1. Blood Sausage	*Kiszka krwista*	236
2. Blood Sausage with Bread Crumbs	*Kiszka bułczana krwista*	237
3. Blood Sausage with Rice	*Kiszka krwista z ryżem*	238
4. Lodzka Blood Sausage	*Kiszka łódzka*	239
5. Popular Blood Sausage	*Kiszka kaszana popularna*	240
6. Silesian Krupniok	*Krupnioki śląskie*	242
7. Simple Blood Sausage	*Kiszka krwista zwyczajna*	244
8. Supreme Blood Sausage	*Kiszka kaszana wyborowa*	245

Other Kiszki *(Inne kiszki)* *From the Polish Government Archives (1945-1989)*		
Name	**Original Polish Name**	**Page**
1. Brain Sausage	*Kiszka mózgowa*	248
2. Jowl Sausage	*Kiszka podgardlana*	249

Old Sausages		
Name	**Polish Name**	**Page**
1. Finger Sausage	*Palcówka*	253
2. Kindziuk	*Kindziuk*	254
3. Nobility Sausage	*Kiełbasa szlachecka*	255
4. Staropolska Sausage	*Kiełbasa staropolska*	257

Sausages of Merit		
Name	**Polish Name**	**Page**
1. Grandpa's Pork and Turkey Sausage	*Kiełbasa dziadka wieprzowo indycza*	259
2. Grill Sausage with Cheese	*Kiełbasa grillowa z żółtym serem*	261
3. Pork And Beef Sausage	*Kiełbasa wieprzowo-wołowa*	262

Chapter 5

Cold Smoked Dry, Semi-Dry & Spreadable Sausages

(Not Cooked, Ready to Eat)

Salami and Hungarian Salami were made in a real traditional way without the cooking process and without starter cultures which were not around yet. Today all fermented sausages are made with starter cultures as these allow to produce a product of constant quality regardless of the climate zone or meat plant location. Salami Krakowskie fits into modern methods of manufacture, after smoking it undergoes the cooking process and then continues drying. Cold smoked sausages can fit into the definition of fermented products as well:

- Polish Cold Smoked sausage is cold smoked and air dried. In time it will become nothing else than a traditionally made salami.
- Metka sausages can be classified as raw fermented spreadable sausages like German Mettwurst or Teewurst types.
- Hungarian Smoked Sausage can be considered a raw spreadable sausage and it should be stored in a refrigerator.

Do not decrease the amount of salt and Cure #1 (sodium nitrite) as they are the only means of protection against bacteria in the initial processing stage.

The amount of sugar added to Salami and Hungarian Salami is insufficient to increase meat acidity (pH drop) to a level that will guarantee safety. This is why the sausage will not develop the sourly flavor typical of fast fermented sausages. The safety of the product depends on drying (moisture removal) and that can only be accomplished in time. The curing step is needed as it allows for the growth of beneficial bacteria (lactic acid and color and flavor forming).

Bydgoska Sausage

(Kiełbasa bydgoska surowa)

Pork class II (pork butt), 1000 g (2.2 lb)

Ingredients per 1 kg (2.2 lb.) of meat

Salt, 21 g (3-1/2 tsp)
Cure # 1, 2.5 g (1/2 tsp)
Pepper, 1.5 g (1 tsp)
Marjoram, 1.0 g (1/2 tsp)
Sugar, 2.0 g (1/2 tsp)

Curing	Cure meat, see page 44.
Grinding	Grind meat through 13 mm (3/8") plate.
Mixing	Mix ground meat with spices until sticky.
Stuffing	Stuff into 32-36 mm hog casings forming 15 cm (6") long links. Leave links in long coils.
Conditioning	Hang for 1-2 days at 2-6° C (35-42° F) and 85-90% humidity.
Smoking	With a thin cold smoke for 1-1.5 days until the casings develop yellow-light brown color. Re-arrange smoke sticks or smoke carts during smoking.
Drying	At 10-12° C (50-53° F) and 75-80% humidity until the yield is 87% in relation to the original weight of the meat. This should take about 2 weeks. Divide sausage coils into pairs.
Storing	Store at 12° C (53° F) or lower.
Note	87% yield means that the finished sausage has retained 87% of its original unprocessed weight. In other words it has lost 13% of the moisture.

Delicatessen Sausage

(Kiełbasa delikatesowa)

Pork class I, 400 g (0.88 lb)
Beef class II, 400 g (0.88 lb)
Back fat, 200 g (0.44) lb

Ingredients per 1 kg (2.2 lb) of meat

Salt, 28 g (5 tsp)
Cure #1, 5.0 g (1 tsp)
Sugar, 4.0 g (3/4 tsp)
Pepper, 2.0 g (1 tsp)
Sweet paprika, 1.0 g (1/2 tsp)
Ginger, 1.0 g (1/2 tsp)
Nutmeg, 1.5 g (3/4 tsp)
Garlic, 1.5 g (1/2 clove)

Curing	Cure meat, see page 44.
Grinding	Grind all meats and fat through 5 mm plate.
Mixing	Mix ground meats with spice until mixture feels sticky.
Conditioning	Place the mixture in a container for 24 hours at 2-4° C (35-40° F) which is refrigerator temperature.
Stuffing	Stuff into 60 mm synthetic fibrous casings.
Aging	Place sausages in a container one on top of another and hold for 4-5 days at 2-4° C (35-40° F), 85-90% humidity. Remove and hang for 2-3 days at 8-10° C (46-50° F), 80-85% humidity.
Smoking	Apply cold smoke for 2-3 days until brown in color.
Drying	Cool in air to 10-12° C (50-53° F) or lower. Hold at this temperature, 75-85% humidity for 7-10 days.

Hungarian Salami

(Salami węgierskie)

Although this salami carries a Hungarian name, it has been always made in Poland and might as well be considered a local product.

Pork class I, 800 g (1.76 lb)
Pork back fat, 200 g (0.44 lb)

I*ngredients per 1 kg (2.2 lb.) of meat*

Salt, 28 g (5 tsp)
Cure # 2, 5 g (1 tsp)
Pepper, 4.0 g (2 tsp)
Paprika, 2.0 g (1 tsp)
Sugar, 2.0 g (1/2 tsp)
Garlic, 3.5 g (1 clove)

Moisture Removal	Cut meat into 10 cm (3-4") pieces and place in a slightly raised container with holes in the bottom to allow for draining of liquid. Leave for 24 hours at 1-2° C (33-35° F), then grind with ¾" plate and leave for additional 2-3 days. During that period turn meat around 1-2 times. Leave sheets of unsalted back fat for 2-3 days at -2° C (28° F) to - 4° C (24° F) and then cut into 3 mm (⅛") cubes.
Grinding	Mix meat, back fat, salt, nitrite and spices together. Grind through 3 mm (⅛") plate.
Curing	Leave the sausage mass for 36-48 hours at 2-4° C (35-40° F).
Stuffing	Stuff firmly into 55-60 mm beef middles. Make links 16-18" long. Lace up with twine: once lengthwise and every 4-5 cm (1.5-2") across. The ends tied up with a twine, 10-12 cm (4-5") hanging loop on one end.
Conditioning	Hang for 2-4 days at 2-4° C (35-40° F), 85-90% humidity.
Smoking	With thin cold smoke 16-18° C (60-64° F) for 5-7 days, until dark red color is obtained.
Aging	In a dark, lightly drafty area at 10-12° C (50-53° F), humidity 90%, for 2 weeks until salami develops white, dry mold on outside. If green mold appears it has to be wiped off and the sausages moved for 4-5 hours to a drier place. Then they may go back to the original room for drying.
Drying	Place covered with white mold sausages for 2-3 months in a dark and lightly drafty area at 12-16° C (54-60° F), 75-85% humidity, until about 63% yield is obtained.

Hungarian Sausage

(Kiełbasa węgierska wędzona)

Beef class I or II, 300 g (0.66 lb)
Back fat, 700 g (1.54 lb)

Ingredients per 1 kg (2.2 lb) of meat

Salt, 21 g (3-1/2 tsp)
Cure # 1, 2.5 g (1/2 tsp)
Pepper, 1.5 g (3/4 tsp)
Sweet paprika, 1.5 g (3/4 tsp)

Curing	Cut meat into 5 cm (2") pieces and mix with 1/3 (8 g) salt and Cure #1. Pack tightly in container, cover and keep in refrigerator for 3 days. Cut back fat into strips, rub in 2/3 (16 g) salt into fat strips and hold for 10 days in refrigerator. Back fat does not need Cure #1.
Grinding	Grind beef through 2-3 mm plate. Dice back fat into 15 mm (5/8") cubes.
Mixing	Mix ground beef with pepper until sticky. Mix back fat with paprika and then mix all together.
Stuffing	Stuff firmly into 40 mm beef rounds or hog casings and form rings. Tie both ends with twine.
Conditioning	Hang for 1-2 days at 2-4° C (35-40° F), 85-90-% humidity.
Smoking	Apply cold smoke for 2-3 days until yellow in color.
Cooling	Cool in air to 10-12° C (50-53° F) or lower. Keep refrigerated.

Metka

(Metka)

Metka is a cold smoked sausage that has its origin in German Mettwurst. Metka sausages are not cooked and this why they were less popular in summer months. With the advent of refrigeration the storing problem has been eliminated.

Pork class II, 600 g (1.32 lb)
Beef class IV, 400 g (0.88 lb)

Ingredients per 1 kg (2.2 lb.) of meat

Salt, 21 g (3-1/2 tsp)
Cure 1, 2.5 g (1/2 tsp)
Pepper, 1.0 g (1/2 tsp)
Paprika, 1.0 g (1/2 tsp)
Sugar, 2.0 g (1/2 tsp)

Curing	Cure meat, see page 44.
Grinding	Pork class II and beef class IV ground through 3 mm plate.
Mixing	Mix pork class II with beef class IV until sticky. During mixing add remaining ingredients.
Stuffing	Stuff into 36-40 mm beef rounds or synthetic cellulose or fibrous casings.
Conditioning	Hang for 1-2 days at 2-6° C (35-43° F) and 85-90% humidity.
Smoking	With a thin cold smoke for 1-2 days until casings develop brown color with pink-reddish tint. Re-arrange smoke sticks or smoke carts during smoking.
Cooling	Cool in air to 12° C (53° F) or lower.
Storing	In refrigerator.

Metka Brunszwicka
(Metka Brunszwicka)

Origin of this Metka Sausage is to be found in the German town of Brunszwik.

Pork class II, 400 g (0.88 lb)
Beef class IV, 400 g (0.88 lb)
Jowls, skinless, 200 g (0.44 lb)

Ingredients per 1 kg (2.2 lb.) of meat
Salt, 21 g, (3-1/2 tsp)
Cure # 1, 2.5 g (1/2 tsp)
Pepper, 2.0 g (1 tsp) g
Paprika, 1.0 g (1/2 tsp)
Nutmeg, 0.5 g (1/4 tsp)

Curing and Grinding Cure meat (page 44). All meats ground through 2 mm plate, then emulsified in a food processor without adding water.

Mixing Add spices when emulsifying.

Stuffing Stuff into 40 mm cellulose casings and form 20-25 cm (8-10") straight links.

Conditioning Hang for 1-2 days at 2-6° C (35-43° F) and 85-90% humidity.

Smoking With a thin cold smoke for 1-2 days until casings develop brown color with pink-reddish tint.

Cooling Cool in air to 12° C (53° F) or lower. Store in refrigerator.

Photo 5.1 Metka sausage.

Metka Salmon Style

(Metka łososiowa)

There is no salmon inside though the name may imply it. Certain Polish meat products that call for bacon or pork loin in a recipe have the "salmon" nickname added. For instance, Smoked Pork Loin-Salmon Style. The reason is that the loin resembles the shape of a salmon. Both pork loin and salmon are very popular in Poland and are considered delicacies.

Beef class II or III, 1 kg (2.20 lb)
Pork belly, skinless, 4 kg (8.80 lb)

Ingredients per 1 kg (2.2 lb.) of meat

Salt, 21 g (3-1/2 tsp)
Cure # 1, 2.5 g (1/2 tsp)
Pepper, 2.0 g (1 tsp)
Nutmeg, 0.5 g (1/4 tsp)
Paprika, 1.0 g (1/2 tsp)

Curing Cure meat, see page 44.

Grinding Pork belly and beef ground through 2 mm plate then emulsified for short time in a meat chopper without adding water.

Mixing Mix spices when emulsifying.

Stuffing Stuff into 40 mm synthetic cellulose or fibrous casings and form 20-25 cm (8-10") links.

Conditioning Hang for 12 hours at 10° C (50° F) and 85-90% humidity.

Smoking With a thin cold smoke for 10-12 hours until casings develop gold brown color. Re-arrange smoke sticks or smoke carts during smoking.

Cooling Cool in air to 12° C (53° F) or lower.

Storing In refrigerator.

Note Nutmeg may be substituted with double amount of white mustard seed.

Polish Cold Smoked Sausage

(Polska kiełbasa wędzona)

This is the predecessor of the Polish Smoked Sausage as it came to be known all over the world. When it was originally made food preservation was of the primary concern and that is why it was cold smoked. Today its hot smoked version is more popular as it requires less time to make.

Pork class I, 400 g (0.88 lb)
Pork class II, 600 g (1.32 lb)

Ingredients per 1 kg (2.2 lb.) of meat

Salt, 21 g (3-1/2 tsp)
Cure # 1, 2.5 g (1/2 tsp)
Pepper, 1.5 g (1 tsp)
Marjoram, 1.0 g (1/2 tsp)
Sugar, 2.0 g (1/2 tsp)
Garlic, 2.5 g (small clove)

Curing Cure meat, see page 44.

Grinding Pork class I and pork class II ground through 13 mm plate.

Mixing Mix pork class I and pork class II together until mixture becomes sticky. Add spices during mixing.

Stuffing Stuff into 32-36 mm hog casings forming 30-35 cm (one foot) long links. Leave links in long coils.

Conditioning Hang for 1-2 days at 2-6° C (35-42° F) and 85-90% humidity.

Smoking With a thin cold smoke for 1-1.5 days until the casings develop yellow-light brown color. Re-arrange smoke sticks or smoke carts during smoking.

Drying At 10-12° C (50-53° F) and 75-80% humidity until the yield is 87% in relation to the original weight of the meat. At that point the temperature of the sausage should be below 12° C (53° F). Divide sausage coils into pairs.

Storing Store at 53° F (12° C) or lower.

Note Marjoram may be removed from the recipe and the amount of garlic may be increased.

Pomerania Metka

(Metka pomorska)

Metka Sausage has its origin in the Northern areas of Poland known as Pomerania (Pomorze).

Beef, class II or class III, 200 g (0.44 lb)
Beef, class V (no blood), 100 g (0.22 lb)
Back fat or fat trimmings, 650 g (1.43 lb)
Beef kidney fat, 50 g (0.11 lb)

Ingredients per 1 kg (2.2 lb.) of meat

Salt, 21 g (3-1/2 tsp)
Cure # 1, 1.5 g (1/3 tsp)
Pepper, 2.0 g (1 tsp)
Paprika, 1.0 g (1/2 tsp)
Sugar, 2.0 g (1/2 tsp)

Curing Cure meat, see page 44.

Grinding All meats ground through 2 mm plate. Then (optional step), they may be briefly chopped (emulsified) in bowl cutter (food processor) *without* adding water. During emulsifying the temperature of the meat should not exceed 15° C (59° F).

Mixing Mix meat, fat and spices together *without* adding water.

Stuffing Stuff into 50 mm synthetic cellulose or fibrous casings. Form straight 20-25 cm (8-10") long links.

Conditioning Hang for 1-2 days at 10° C (50° F) and 85-90% humidity.

Smoking With a thin cold smoke for 1-2 days until casings develop light brown color. Re-arrange smoke sticks or smoke carts during smoking.

Cooling Cool in air to 12° C (53° F) or lower.

Note If using bowl cutter (food processor), you can add spices to ground meat and let the food processor do the mixing. Don't add water as the purpose of cold smoking is to eliminate moisture and not to bring it in.

Salami
(Salami)

Although salami is of Italian origin, almost every country has its own version and Poland is no exception.

Pork, class I, 400 g (0.88 lb)
Beef, class I, 300 g (0.66 lb)
Pork back fat, 300 g (0.66 lb)

Ingredients per 1 kg (2.2 lb.) of meat

Salt, 28 g (5 tsp)
Cure # 2, 5.0 g (1 tsp)
Pepper, 2.0 g (1 tsp)
Cardamom, 0.5 g (1/4 tsp)
Sugar, 2.0 g (1/2 tsp)

Curing Cut meat into 5-6 cm (2") pieces, mix with 2/3 salt, sugar and Cure #1. Place in a slightly raised container with holes in the bottom to allow for draining of curing liquid. Leave for 5 days at 2-4° C (35-40° F). Cut back fat into strips and rub in 1/3 of the salt. Back fat does not require nitrite (Cure #1) and can be kept separately at 2-4° C (35-40° F).

Grinding Grind pork with 5 mm plate, grind beef with 3 mm plate and manually cut back fat into 5 mm pieces.

Mixing Mix meats with spices and back fat. Do not add water.

Stuffing Stuff into 55-60 mm beef middle casings. Do not add water. Make links 16-18" long. The ends tied up with a twine, 10-12 cm (4-5") hanging loop on one end.

Conditioning Hang for 4 days at 2-4°C (35-40°F), 85-90% humidity.

Aging and Drying Hang in a dark, slightly drafty area for 6-8 weeks, 10-12° C (50-54° F), 80-85% humidity. If wet mold appears,wash it off with warm, salty water, then wipe it dry with a clean cloth. When sausages loose about 30% weight and start developing dry mold, wipe them off and send for smoking.

Smoking Cold smoke with thin smoke for 4-6 days until dark red color is obtained. Store below 12° C (53° F).

Note Yield of a finished product in relation to the original weight - 63%.

Salmon Sausage
(Kiełbasa łososiowa)

There is no salmon in this recipe. In Poland certain high quality products carry the name "salmon" to imply that the product is of the high quality.

Pork class I, 800 g (1.76 lb)
Beef class II, 200 g (0.44 lb)

Ingredients for 1 kg (2.2 lb) of meat

Salt, 24 g (4 tsp)
Cure #1, 2.5 g (1/2 tsp)
Sugar, 1.0 g (1/2 tsp)
Pepper, 2.0 g (1 tsp)
Sweet paprika, 1.0 g (1/2 tsp)
Nutmeg, 1.0 g (1/2 tsp)
Garlic, 1.5 g (1/2 clove)

Curing	Cure meat, see page 44.
Grinding	Cut pork class I into 20 mm (3/4 ") pieces. grind beef class II through 3 mm plate.
Mixing	Mix ground meats with spices.
Stuffing	Stuff into 36 mm hog casings.
Conditioning	Hang at 2-4° C (35-40° F) 85-90% humidity for 4-6 days, then at 10-12° C (50-53° F), 75-80% humidity for 3-4 days.
Smoking	With cold smoke for 3-4 days until dark red color is obtained.
Drying	Cool and store sausages in air at 10-12° C (50-53° F) for about 6-8 days.

Smoked Frankfurters

(Frankfurterki wędzone)

Pork class I, 500 g (1.1 lb)
Pork class II, 500 g (1.1 lb)

Ingredients per 1 kg (2.2 lb) of meat

Salt, 21 g (3-1/3 tsp)
Cure #1, 2.5 g (1/2 tsp)
Sugar, 2.0 g (1/3 tsp)
Pepper, 1.5 g (3/4 tsp)
Nutmeg, 0.5 g (1/4 tsp)

Curing	Cure meat, see page 44.
Grinding	Grind pork through 8 mm plate.
Mixing	Mix pork with all ingredients until sticky.
Stuffing	Stuff into 22 mm or larger sheep casings. Form 15-18 cm (6-7”) links leaving them in a continuous coil.
Conditioning	Hang for 8 hours at 2-4° C (35-40° F), 85-90-% humidity or for 1 hour at room temperature.
Smoking	With cold smoke for 6-8 hours until light brown.
Drying	At 10-12° C (50-53° F) until test sausages display 84% yield.

Soft Servolatka

(Serwolatka miękka)

Beef class I, without connective tissue, 250 g (0.55 lb)
Beef class II, with connective tissue, 320 g (0.70 lb)
Beef class IV, 60 g (2.11 oz)
Beef class V, 20 g (0.70 oz)
Pork belly, skinless, 350 g (0.77 lb)

Ingredients per 1 kg (2.2 lb) of meat

Salt, 21 g (3-1/2 tsp)
Cure #1, 2.5 g (1/2 tsp)
Pepper, 1.5 g (3/4 tsp)
Coriander, 0.5 g (1/4 tsp)
Paprika, 1.0 g (1/2 tsp)

Curing Cure meat, see page 44.

Grinding Beef class I without connective tissue and pork belly through 5 mm plate.

Beef class I with connective tissue and beef class IV through 2-3 mm plate. Partially freeze and grind again.

Mixing Mix all meats with spices until sticky.

Stuffing Stuff firmly into 65 mm synthetic fibrous casings forming 25 cm (10”) links.

Conditioning Hang for 1-2 days at 2-4° C (35-40° F), 85-90% humidity.

Smoking With cold smoke for 1-2 days until brown.

Chapter 6

Long Lasting Hot Smoked Dry & Semi-Dry Sausages, Baked or Poached in Water

The advantage of hot smoke is that it can be produced at all climatic zones and in all different seasons of the year. Almost all meat products and fish are produced today with hot smoke. And if hot smoked sausages are submitted to an additional drying process which may take place at room temperatures, a very stable product can be obtained. In 1950-1970 when very few in Poland had their own refrigerators, these sausages hung from nails in most kitchens and were consumed on a need basis. Losing moisture in time they were turning into semi-dry and then into dry sausages.

Note: the sausage is done when cooked. The secondary smoking or additional drying increased the shelf life of the sausage so it could be kept at room temperature. You can simplify the manufacturing process and make it shorter. After stuffing, condition sausages (hang at room temperature) for 2 hours, apply hot smoke for 1-2 hours and cook the sausages to 68-70° C (154-158° F). Then cool and store them in a refrigerator.

Bałtycka Sausage
(Kiełbasa Bałtycka)

Popular sausage in the Northern-Baltic Sea area.

Pork class II from belly scraps, 400 g (0.88 lb)
Pork class III from belly scraps, 100 g (0.22 lb)
Beef class I or II, 400 g (0.88 lb)
Back fat, 100 g (0.22 lb)

Ingredients per 1 kg (2.2 lb.) of meat

Salt, 20 g (3-1/2 tsp)
Cure #1, 1.5 g (1/3 tsp)
Pepper, 2.0 g (1 tsp)
Marjoram, 1.0 g (1/2 tsp)
Garlic, 3.0 g (1 clove)
Sugar, 2.5 g (1/2 tsp)

Curing	Cure back fat and pure fat trimmings with salt only. Use salt and Cure #1 for beef and belly scraps with meat. Distribute salt proportionally. Cure for 72 hours. Meat plants cured back fat with salt only for 14-21 days.
Grinding	Pork class II (belly trimmings) ground through 13 mm plate. Pork class III (belly trimmings) ground through 2-3 mm. and then emulsified. ¼ of beef class I or II ground through 8 mm plate. 3/4 beef class I or II ground through 2-3 mm plate and then emulsified. Back fat pieces ground through 9 mm plate.
Emulsifying	Emulsify ¾ beef (class I or II) and pork class III adding 15-20% ice or cold water. Add spices during this step.
Mixing	Mix ¼ beef (not-emulsified) with pork class II until sticky. Add ground back fat and emulsified mixture and mix everything together.
Stuffing	Stuff into 36 mm hog casings. Form 50-70 cm (20-28") links and tie up ends making rings.
Conditioning	Hang for 12 hours at 2-6° C (35-43° F). Drying is also allowed at room temperature for 2-3 hours.
Smoking	With hot smoke for 120-150 min until brown color is obtained.

Poaching or Baking	Poach sausages in water at 72-75° C (161-167° F) for 25-35 min until internal temperature of the meat is 68-70° C (154-158° F). *Baked sausages,* in the last stage of smoking are baked for 30 min at 75-90° C (167-194° F) until internal meat temperature is 68-70° C (154-158° F).
Cooling	In air for 12 hours at temperatures below 18°C (64° F).
Secondary Smoking *(for poached sausages only)*	Poached sausages are submitted to a secondary smoking: • with cold smoke for 48 hours *OR* • with warm smoke (24-32° C, 75-90° F) for 24 hours until casings develop dark brown color.
Drying	For 7-12 days at 12-18° C (53-64° F), 75-80% humidity until sample sausages achieve 82% yield. If mold appears wipe it off with a cloth.

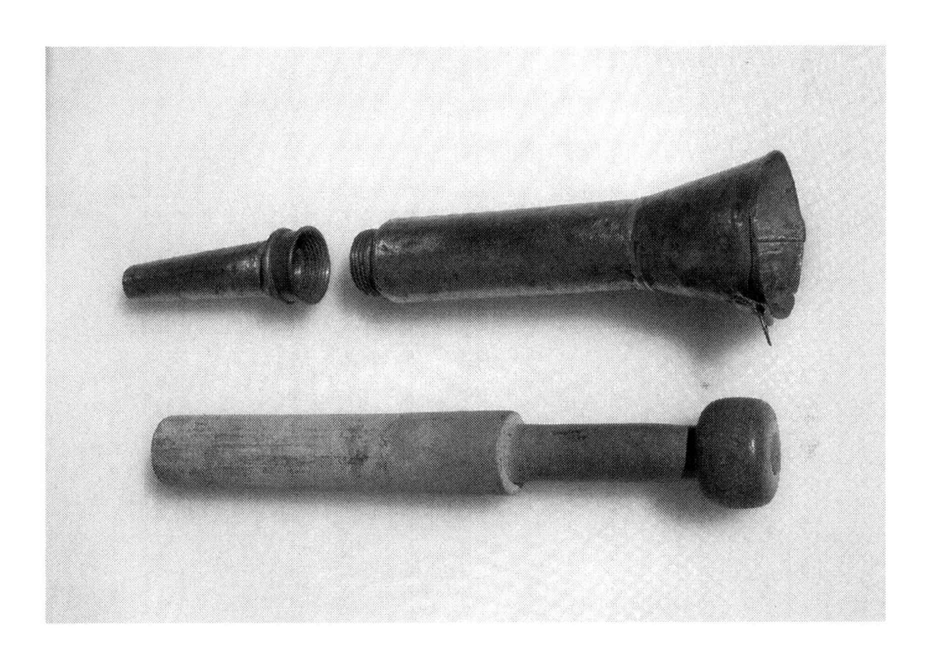

Photo 6.1 An old manual stuffer.

Beef Sausage

(Kiełbasa wołowa krajana pieczona)

All beef sausage with visible chunks of solid beef.

Beef class I without connective tissue, 500 g (1.10 lb)
Beef class I with connective tissue, 150 g (0.33 lb)
Beef class IV, 300 g (0.66 lb)
Beef class V, 50 g (0.11 lb)

Ingredients per 1 kg (2.2 lb) of meat

Salt,18 g (3-1/3 tsp)
Cure #1, 2.5 g (1/2 tsp)
Sugar, 1.0 g (1/5 tsp)
Pepper, 4.0 g (2 tsp)
Paprika, 1.0 g (1/2 tsp)
Garlic, 3.0 g (1 clove)

Curing Cut beef class I without connective tissue into 20 mm (3/4") cubes. Mix with 1/2 of salt and 1/2 Cure #1. Pack tightly in a container, cover with cloth and place in refrigerator for 3 days.

Grinding Grind:

- beef class IV through 8 mm plate.
- beef class I with connective tissue through 2-3 mm plate.
- beef class V through 2-3 mm plate.

Emulsifying Using food processor emulsify beef class I with connective tissue and beef class V with 20% cold water (40 ml, 1.35 oz fl). Add spices during this step.

Mixing Mix (knead) beef class I cubes until sticky. Add ground beef class IV and emulsified meat and mix all together.

Stuffing Stuff firmly into 55-65 mm synthetic fibrous casings making 40-45 cm (16-18") links. Make hanging loop.

Conditioning Hang for 12 hours in refrigerator or 3-4 hours at room temperature.

Smoking Apply hot smoke for 100 min until casings become brown with red tint. Increase temperature to 75-90° C (167-194° F) and bake sausages for 30-40 min until sausages reach 68-70° C (154-158° F) internal temperature. A very thin smoke is allowed during baking.

Cooling Cool in air.

Storing Keep refrigerated.

Beer Sausage

(Kiełbasa Piwna)

There is no beer in this recipe although the name may imply otherwise. The sausage derives its name from the final shape of its casing. Pork or beef bladders when stuffed with meat and sewn on both ends, resembled a little beer barrel and this is how the name was created.

Pork class I, 200 g (0.44 lb)
Pork class II, 200 g (0.44 lb)
Pork class III, 100 g (0.22 lb)
Beef class II or I, 200 g (0.44 lb)
Skinless jowls or hard fat 300 g (0.88 lb)

Ingredients per 1 kg (2.2 lb.) of meat

Salt, 20 g (3-1/3 tsp)
Cure # 1, 2.0 g (1/2 tsp)
Pepper, 2.0 g (1 tsp)
Paprika, 1.0 g (1/2 tsp)
Sugar, 1.0 g (1/2 tsp)
White mustard seeds, 0.5 g (1/4 tsp)

Curing Cure meat, see page 44.

Grinding Pork class I, II and fat ground through 8 mm plate. Beef class I, II and pork class III ground through 3 mm plate.

Mixing Mix pork class I and II with fat. Add beef class I, II and pork class III plus spices. Mix everything together.

Stuffing Stuff into large diameter casings. Originally, pork or beef bladders (sewn) 15-20 mm long and up to 100 mm were used. This created oval/egg shaped sausage, tied at one end and having 10-12 cm (4-5") hanging loop.

Conditioning Hang for 12 hours at 2-6° C (35-43° F). Drying is also allowed at room temperature for 2-3 hours.

Smoking Apply hot smoke for 100-125 min until light brown with red tint color is obtained.

Poaching or Baking Poach sausages in water at 72-75° C (161-167° F) for 70-100 min until internal temperature of the meat becomes 68-70° C (154-158° F). Baked sausages, in the last stage of smoking are baked for 40-45 min at 75-90° C (167-194° F) until the sausage reaches 68-70° C (154-158° F) temperature inside. *

Cooling For 12 hours at temperatures 18°C (64°F) or lower.

Smoking *(poached sausages only)* Poached sausages are submitted to a secondary smoking:

- with cold smoke for 24 hours.
- with warm smoke (24-32°C, 75-90°F) for 12 hours

until casings develop brown color with a red tint.

Drying For 4-6 days at 12-18°C (53-64°F), 75-80% humidity until sample sausages achieve 87% yield. If mold appears it should be wiped off with a cloth.

* The sausage is done when cooked. The additional steps increased the shelf life of the sausage so it could be kept at room temperature. Poached sausage may be cooled in water.

Beer Sausage with Goose Meat

(Kiełbasa piwna z gęsiną parzona podsuszana)

Beef class IV, 350 g (0.77 lb)
Goose meat (without fat and skin), 650 g (1.43 lb)

Ingredients per 1 kg (2.2 lb) of meat

Salt, 20 g (3-1/3 tsp)
Cure #1, 2.5 g (1/2 tsp)
Sugar, 1.0 g (1/5 tsp)
Pepper, 2.0 g (1 tsp)
Potato flour, 10 g (0.35 oz)

Curing	Cure meat, see page 44.
Grinding	Beef class IV - 5 mm plate. Goose meat - 3 mm.
Mixing	Add salt and Cure #1 to beef and goose meat and mix together until sticky. Then add spices and potato flour and mix again.
Stuffing	Stuff firmly into beef middles or 100 mm synthetic fibrous casings. Make 15-20 cm (6-8") long links. Make hanging loop.
Conditioning	Hang for 120 min at room temperature.
Smoking	Apply hot smoke for 80 - 100 minutes until casings develop light brown color with red tint.
Cooking	Cook in water at 75-78° C (167-172° F) for for 60-90 min until sausages reach 68-70° C (154-158° F) internal temperature.
Cooling	Cool in for 15 minutes in cold water, wipe off dry. The inside temperature of the sausage should be about 12° C (53° F).
Smoking	Apply *cold smoke* for 12 hours until sausages develop brown color with red tint.
Drying	Hang for 12 hours at 12-15° C (53-59° F). This may be accomplished in the smokehouse.
Notes	Originally the sausage was stuffed into pork or veal bladders.

Belzka

(Kiełbasa bełzka parzona podsuszana)

Beef class I (no connective tissue), 300 g (0.66 lb)
Beef, class I (with connective tissue), 400 g (0.88 lb)
Beef class IV, 300 g (0.66 lb)

Ingredients per 1 kg (2.2 lb) of meat

Salt, 20 g (3-1/3 tsp)
Cure #1, 2.5 g (1/2 tsp)
Pepper, 2.0 g (1 tsp)
Paprika, 2.0 g (1 tsp)
Marjoram, 1.0 g (1/2 tsp)
Sugar, 1.0 g (1/5 tsp)
Garlic, 2.5 g (1 clove)

Curing Cure meat, see page 44.

Grinding Beef class I (no connective tissue) - 5 mm plate.
Beef class I (with connective tissue) - 2-3 mm.
Beef class IV - 3 mm.

Mixing Mix (knead) beef class I (with connective tissue) with 5% (15 ml, 1 tablespoon) of cold water until sticky. Add other meats, salt, Cure #1, spices and mix everything together.

Stuffing Stuff firmly into beef middles or 60 mm synthetic fibrous casings. Form 25-30 cm.(12-14") links. Make a hanging loop.

Conditioning Hang for 2 hours at room temperature.

Smoking Apply hot smoke for 110-130 min until casings develop brown color with red tint.

Cooking Cook in water at 72-75° C (160-167° F) until sausages reach 68-70° C (154-158° F) internal temperature.

Cooling Cool in for 15 minutes in cold water.

Smoking Hang for 15 min in a warm smokehouse, then apply *cold smoke* for 12 hours.

Bialostocka

(Kiełbasa białostocka parzona podsuszana)

Beef class I or II (with connective tissue), 500 g (1.10 lb)
Beef class III, 300 g (0.66 lb)
Hard fat trimmings, 200 g (0.44 lb)

Ingredients per 1 kg (2.2 lb) of meat

Salt, 20 g (3-1/3 tsp)
Cure #1, 2.5 g (1/2 tsp)
Pepper, 2.0 g (1 tsp)
Paprika, 1.0 g (1/2 tsp)
Marjoram, 1.0 g (1/2 tsp)
Garlic, 3.0 g (1 clove)

Curing	Cure meat, see page 44.
Grinding	Grind beef class I or II with connective tissue through 3 mm plate. Grind beef class III through 5 mm plate. Grind fat through 8 mm.
Emulsifying	Using food processor emulsify ground beef class I or II adding 10% (50 ml or 1.76 oz fl) cold water. Add all ingredients and spices during this step.
Mixing	Mix (knead) beef class III until sticky. Add emulsified beef then ground fat. Mix everything together.
Stuffing	Stuff firmly into beef rounds or 40-50 mm hog casings. Make links but leave them in a continuous coil.
Conditioning	Hang for 120 min at room temperature.
Smoking	Apply hot smoke for 90-110 minutes until casings develop light brown color with a red tint.
Cooking	Cook in water at 72-75° C (160-167° F) for 30-40 min until sausages reach 68-70° C (154-158° F) internal temperature.
Cooling	Cool in air for 12 hours at 18° C (64° F) or lower or immerse in cold water for 20 minutes. Wipe off moisture.
Smoking	Apply cold smoke for 12 hours. Leave in smokehouse for 12 hours.
Drying	Leave in smokehouse for 12 hours at 12-15° C (53-59° F). Store at 12° C (53° F) or lower.

Bialostocka with Goose Fat

(Kiełbasa białostocka parzona podsuszana z gęsim tłuszczem)

Beef class I (with connective tissue), 500 g (1.10 lb)
Beef class IV, 300 g (0.66 lb)
Goose under skin fat, skin included, 200 g (0.44 lb)

Ingredients per 1 kg (2.2 lb) of meat

Salt, 20 g (3-1/3 tsp)
Cure #1, 2.5 g (1/2 tsp)
Sugar, 1.0 g (1/5 tsp)
Pepper, 2.0 g (1 tsp)
Paprika, 1.0 g (1/2 tsp)
Marjoram, 1.0 g (1/2 tsp)
Garlic, 3.0 g (1 clove)
Potato flour, 30 g (1 oz)

Curing Cure meat, see page 44.

Grinding Grind beef class I with connective tissue through 3 mm plate. Grind beef class IV through 5 mm plate. Grind partially frozen goose fat through 8 mm. The temperature of the goose fat should not be higher than 6° C (42° F).

Emulsifying Using food processor emulsify ground beef class I adding 20-30% (100 ml or 3 oz fl) cold water. Add all ingredients and spices during this step (except potato flour).

Mixing Mix (knead) beef class IV until sticky. Add emulsified beef then goose fat and potato flour. Mix everything together.

Stuffing Stuff firmly into beef rounds or 40-50 mm hog casings. Make rings. Tie the ends together.

Conditioning Hang for 120 min at room temperature.

Smoking Apply hot smoke for 90-110 minutes until casings develop light brown color with a red tint.

Cooking Cook in water at 72-75° C (160-167° F) until sausages reach 68-70° C (154-158° F) internal temperature.

Cooling Cool in air for 12 hours at 18° C (64° F) or lower or immerse in cold water for 20 minutes. Wipe off moisture.

Smoking Apply cold smoke for 12 hours. Leave in smokehouse for 12 hrs.

Drying Leave in smokehouse for 12 hours at 12-15° C (53-59° F). Store at 12° C (53° F) or lower.

Bielska

(Kiełbasa bielska)

Beef class I, 600 g (1.32 lb)
Beef class I with connective tissue, 100 g (0.22 lb)
Jowls, dewlap, skinless, 300 g (0.66 lb)

Ingredients per 1 kg (2.2 lb) of meat

Salt, 20 g (3-1/3 tsp)
Cure #1, 2.5 g (1/2 tsp)
Pepper, 1.5 g (1 tsp)
Garlic, 1.5 g (1/2 clove)

Curing	Cure meat, see page 44.
Grinding	Beef class I - 5 mm plate. Beef class I with connective tissue - 3 mm plate. 250 g jowls through 5 mm plate. 50 g jowls through 5 mm plate.
Emulsifying	Using food processor emulsify ground beef class I with connective tissue and 50 g jowls adding 10% (15 ml or 1 tablespoon) cold water. Add Cure #1 and spices during this step.
Mixing	Mix (knead) beef class I adding salt until sticky. Add emulsified meat then ground jowls. Mix everything together.
Stuffing	Stuff firmly into beef middles or 65 mm synthetic fibrous casings.
Conditioning	Hang for 120 min at room temperature.
Smoking	Apply hot smoke 45-80° C (113-176° F) for 90-110 minutes until casings develop brown color.
Cooking	Cook in water at 72-75° C (160-167° F) for 30-60 min until sausages reach 68-70° C (154-158° F) internal temperature.
Cooling	Immerse in cold water for 25 minutes. Wipe off moisture.
Smoking	Apply warm smoke 30° C (86° F) for 6 hours.
Drying	At 14-18° C (57-64° F) for 8-12 days until 70% yield is obtained.

Camp Sausage

(Kiełbasa wczasowa pieczona)

Pork class II, 150 g (0.33 lb)
Beef class I, II or III, 200 g (0.44 lb)
Lungs (pork, veal, beef, sheep), 200 g (0.44 lb)
Hearts (pork, veal, beef, sheep), 100 g (0.22 lb)
Jowls/dewlap, skinless, 250 g (0.55 lb)
Pork skins, pork class IV, veal class III, beef class V, 100 g (0.22 lb)

Ingredients per 1 kg (2.2 lb) of meat

Salt, 18 g (3-tsp)
Cure #1, 2.5 g (1/2 tsp)
Pepper, 1.5 g (3/4 tsp)
Ginger, 0.5 g (1/4 tsp)
Allspice, 0.5 g (1/4 tsp)
Garlic, 1.5 g (1/2 clove)

Curing Cure meat, see page 44.

Grinding
* 1/2 beef class I, II, or III (less connective tissue) - 5 mm plate.
* 1/2 beef class I, II, or III (more connective tissue)-3 mm plate.
* Pork class II - 8 mm plate.
* Hearts, jowls/dewlap - 5 mm plate.
* Lungs - 3 mm plate.
* Skins, pork class IV, veal class III, beef class V - 2-3 mm.

Emulsifying Using food processor emulsify:
ground beef class I, II, III (with connective tissue), pork skins, pork class IV, veal class III, beef class V with 30% (60 ml or 2 oz fl) cold water. Add salt, Cure #1 and spices during this step.

Mixing Mix pork class II with ground beef, fat and emulsified meats.

Stuffing Stuff firmly into 36 mm hog casings. Make 35-40 cm (14-16”) long links, keep in continuous coil.

Conditioning Hold for 30-60 min in refrigerator.

Smoking
- Drying - 20-30 min, thin smoke at 45-55° C (113-131° F).
- Smoking - 60 min, thick smoke at 45-55° C (113-131° F).
- Baking - 40-60 min, thin smoke at 75-90° C (167-194° F).

Total time about 120 minutes until sausages reach 68-70° C (154-158° F) internal temperature and dark brown color with red tint.

Cooling Cool in air. Keep refrigerated.

Debowiecka

(Kiełbasa dębowiecka)

Pork class I, 600 g (1.32 lb)
Pork class II, 300 g (0.66 lb)
Pork class III, 100 g (0.22 lb)

Ingredients per 1 kg (2.2 lb) of meat

Salt, 21 g (3-1/2 tsp)
Cure #1, 2.5 g (1/2 tsp)
Pepper, 2.0 g (1 tsp)
Sugar, 1.0 g (1/5 tsp)
Garlic, 2.5 g (1 clove)

Curing	Cut pork into 25 mm (1") cubes (keep pork classes separately). Mix with salt and Cure #1, estimate the amounts proportionally. Pack tightly in containers, cover with cloth and hold in refrigerator for 3 days.
Grinding	Pork class I - leave the way it is (25 mm cubes). Pork class II - 13 mm plate. Pork class III - 3 mm plate.
Emulsifying	In food processor emulsify pork class III adding 20-25% (20 ml, 0.7 oz fl) of cold water. Add sugar and spices during this step.
Mixing	Mix pork class I and II until sticky. Add emulsified meat and mix all together.
Stuffing	Stuff firmly into beef middles or 65 mm synthetic fibrous casings. Make links 40-45 cm (16-18") long, hanging loop at one end.
Conditioning	Hang for 120 min at room temperature.
Smoking	Apply hot smoke 45-80° C (113-176° F) for 110-130 minutes. Bake in smokehouse at 80-90° C (176-194° F) for 40-60 min (thin smoke allowed) until sausages reach 68-70° C (154-158° F) internal temperature.
Cooling	Cool in air to 12° C (53° F).
Smoking	Smoke with cold smoke - 22° C (71° F) for 12 hours OR with warm smoke - 24-32° C (75-90° F) for 6 hours.
Drying	At 12-18° C (53-64° F) for 2 days.
Cooling	Cool in air to 8-12° C (46-53° F).

Farmer Sausage

(Kiełbasa Wiejska)

"Wiejska" means rural, country area, away from the city limits. Some say it was smoked over an open fire. No matter what the origin of the name, the recipe contains quality meats and spices to make it a great sausage.

Pork class I, 800 g (1.76 lb)
Beef class I, 100 g (0.22 lb)
Fat pieces, 100 g (0.22 lb)

Ingredients per 1 kg (2.2 lb.) of meat

Salt, 18 g (3 tsp)
Cure # 1, 2.5 g (1/2 tsp)
Pepper, 2.0 g (1 tsp)
Garlic, 3.0 g (1 clove)
Sugar, 1.0 g

Curing	Cure meat, see page 44.
Grinding	Pork class I diced into 25-30 mm cubes. Beef class I ground through 2 mm plate. Fat pieces ground through 8 mm plate.
Emulsifying	Emulsify ground beef in a bowl cutter (food processor) adding 40% ice or cold water. Add remaining ingredients.
Mixing	Mix diced pork pieces with ground fat and add emulsified mixture. Mix everything well together.
Stuffing	Stuff into beef middles. Sausages formed into rings and shaped by the beef middle twist characteristics. Both ends tied together with a twine Outside diameter of the sausage ring 50-70 cm (20-28").
Conditioning	For 2-3 hours in a drafty area.
Smoking and Baking	Smoking is done in three steps: 1. Drying sausages using thin smoke, 45-55° C (113-131° F) for 20-30 min. 2. Proper smoking with a thick smoke, 45-55° C (113-131° F) for 40-60 min. 3. Baking with a thin smoke, 75-90° C (167-194° F) for 40-60 min. Total time 150 min until sausages reach 68-70° C (154-158° F) internal temperature and casings are dark brown with a reddish tint.
Cooling	Cool sausages in air to below 18° C (64° F).

Hunter's Sausage

(Kiełbasa Myśliwska)

Hunting always was a popular sport in Poland practiced originally by the nobility and even then by only well to do people. A hunter carried a big hunting bag where he kept the necessary tools and food that had to last for a number of days. Mysliwska Sausage was a relatively short, well smoked sausage that would make an ideal food or snack in those circumstances. Juniper gives this sausage its characteristic flavor and creates a special bond between the hunter and nature.

1. Pork class I, 400 g (0.88 lb)
2. Pork class II, 500 g (1.10 lb)
3. Beef class II or I, 100 g (0.22 lb)

Ingredients per 1 kg (2.2 lb.) of meat

Salt, 20 g (3-1/3 tsp)
Cure # 1, 2.5 g (1/2 tsp)
Pepper, 2.0 g (1 tsp)
Juniper, 1.5 g (1 tsp)
Garlic, 3.0 g (1 clove)
Sugar, 1.0 g (1/5 tsp)

Curing	Cure meat, see page 44.
Grinding	Grind pork class I through 13 mm plate and pork class II through 8 mm grinder plate. Grind beef through 3 mm plate and then emulsify in a bowl cutter (food processor).
Emulsifying	Beef should be emulsified for a short time and 20-25% cold water or flaked ice should be added. Add remaining salt and spices to beef during emulsifying.
Mixing	Mix pork class I and pork class II together until mixture feels gluey. Then add emulsified beef and mix everything together.
Stuffing	Stuff into 32 mm hog casings. Twist sausages into 18-20 cm (7-8") links leaving them in a continuous coil.
Drying	For 12 hours in a cooler at 2-6°C (35-43°F). Drying is also allowed at room temperature but for only 30-60 minutes.
Smoking and Baking	Hot smoke for 80-90 min followed by 25 minutes baking. Total time about 105-115 min. The casings should develop brown color and reach 68-70°C (154-158°F) internal temperature.

Cooling	Hold sausages at 18°C (64°F) or less.
Secondary Smoking	Cold smoke for 24 hours or warm smoke (24-32°C, 75-90°F) for 12 hours until casings develop dark brown color.
Drying	For 6-8 days at 12-18°C (53-64°F) and 75-80% humidity until sample sausages achieve 61% yield. If mold develops on casings wipe it off with a cloth.
Smoking	Place sausages in a warm smokehouse and smoke with warm smoke 24-32°C, (75-90°F) for 2-3 hours. This refreshes looks of the sausages.
Cooling	Cool sausages in air to 18° C (64° F) or lower and then divide links into pairs.
Notes	*To make a regular hot smoked sausage you may finish the process after the first smoking and baking.* The secondary smoking and drying were needed to make a dry version of the sausage that would last a long time at room temperature.

Husarska Sausage

(Kiełbasa husarska)

Beef class II (connective tissue allowed), 550 g (1.21 lb)
Back fat or hard fat trimmings, 350 g (0.77 lb)
Pork class III, 50 g (0.11 lb)
Beef class IV, 50 g (0.11 lb)

Ingredients per 1 kg (2.2 lb) of meat

Salt, 18 g (3 tsp)
Cure # 1, 2.5 g (1/2 tsp)
Pepper, 2.0 g (1 tsp)
White mustard seed (ground), 3.0 g (1-1/2 tsp)
Garlic, 3.0 g (1 clove)

Curing	Cure meat.
Grinding	Beef class II, ground through 8 mm plate. Pork class III and beef class IV ground through 3 mm plate. Fat ground through 8 mm plate.
Emulsifying	Using bowl cutter (food processor) emulsify beef class IV with pork class III adding 30-35% (30 ml or 1 oz fl) ice or cold water.
Mixing	Mix ground beef until sticky. Add emulsified mixture and ground fat and mix everything well together.
Stuffing	Stuff into beef middles or 65 mm synthetic fibrous casings.
Conditioning	Hang at room temperature for 2-3 hours.
Smoking and Baking	With hot smoke for 70-80 min, then baking for 30 min. Total time 100-110 minutes. The sausage is done when the meat reaches 68-70° C (154-158° F) internal temperature and casings develop light brown color.
Cooling	Cool sausages in air to 18° C (64° F) or lower. Keep refrigerated.
Poached Version	After smoking sausages may be cooked in water at 80° C (176° F) until meat reaches 68-70° C (154-158° F) internal temperature. Immerse (or shower) in cold water to lower sausage temperature to 12° C (53° F) or lower. Keep refrigerated.

Hutnicka

(Kiełbasa hutnicka parzona podsuszana)

Pork class II, 900 g (1.98 lb)
Beef class II, 100 g (0.322 lb)

Ingredients per 1 kg (2.2 lb) of meat

Salt, 18 g (3 tsp)
Cure #1, 2.5 g (1/2 tsp)
Pepper, 2.0 g 91 tsp)
Garlic, 3.0 g (1 clove)

Curing	Cure meat, see page 44.
Grinding	Grind pork through 10 mm plate. Grind beef through 3 mm plate.
Emulsifying	Using food processor emulsify ground beef adding 25-30% (30 ml or 1.35 oz fl) cold water. Add all ingredients and spices during this step.
Mixing	Mix (knead) pork until sticky. Add emulsified beef and mix everything together.
Stuffing	Stuff firmly into beef middles or 50 mm synthetic fibrous casings. Make 30-40 (12-16”) cm long links. Hanging loop at one end.
Conditioning	Hold for 60 min at room temperature.
Smoking	Apply hot smoke for 2 hours until casings become brown.
Cooking	Cook in water at 75-80° C (167-176° F) until sausages reach 68-70° C (154-158° F) internal temperature.
Cooling	Cool in for 15 minutes in cold water. Dry briefly and keep refrigerated.

Juniper Sausage

(Kiełbasa Jałowcowa)

Juniper sausage has a very characteristic look and flavor. Freshly crushed juniper berries are added to meat and then juniper twigs and branches are added to fire during smoking. This imparts a more pronounced juniper flavor and darker color when finished. It is always sold in the shape of a ring.

Pork class I, 200 g (0.44 lb)
Pork class II, 500 g (1.10 lb)
Pork class III, 100 g (0.22 lb)
Beef class II or I, 100 g (0.22 lb)
Hard fat pieces, 100 g (0.22 lb)

Ingredients per 1 kg (2.2 lb.) of meat

Salt, 20 g (3-1/3 tsp)
Cure # 1, 2.5 g (1/2 tsp)
Sugar, 1.0 g (1/2 tsp)
Pepper, 2.0 g (1 tsp)
Juniper, 3.0 g (1-1/2 tsp)

Curing Cure meat, see page 44.

Grinding Pork class I ground through 20 mm plate, pork class II and fat ground through 10 mm, pork class III and beef class I or II ground through 2 mm.

Emulsifying Beef class I or II and pork class III is emulsified in a bowl cutter adding 20-30% of crushed ice or cold water.

Mixing Mix pork class I with pork class II until sticky, then add fat and emulsified mixture of beef, pork, and spices. Mix everything well together.

Stuffing Stuff into 40 mm beef rounds and form rings. Sausage is formed into a ring by the natural properties (twist) of a beef middle, outside diameter 45-70 cm (17-27") depending on a size of the casing. Both ends tied together with a twine.

Drying For 12 hours at 2-6° C (35-43° F). Drying is also allowed at room temperature but for only 30-60 minutes.

Smoking and Baking With hot smoke for 90-100 min, then baking for 30 min. Total time 120-130 min until the internal meat temperature of 68-70° C (154-158° F) is reached and casings are brown. At the end of smoking juniper berries or twigs are added to wood chips for an extra flavor.

Cooling	Hold sausages at 18° C (64° F) or less for 12 hours.
Secondary Smoking	With cold smoke for about 24 hours or with warm smoke 24-32° C (75-90° F) for 12 hours until dark brown color is obtained.
Drying and Smoking	Dry for 5-8 days at 12-18° C (53-64° F) and 75-80% humidity until sample sausages achieve 71% yield. If mold develops on casings wipe it off with a cloth. Then place sausages in a warm smokehouse and smoke with warm smoke 24-32° C (75-90° F) for 2-3 hours. This refreshes looks of the sausages.
Cooling	Cool sausages in air to 18° C (64° F) or lower.
Note	Pork class II can be substituted with hard fat, Pork class III can be substituted with beef class I or II. *To make a regular hot smoked sausage you may finish the process after the first smoking and baking.* The secondary smoking and drying were needed to make a dry version of the sausage that would last a long time at room temperature.

Kabanosy

(Kabanosy)

The most popular Polish sausage and most likely the finest meat stick in the world. The name Kabanosy comes from the nickname "kabanek" given to a young fat pig no more than 120 kg in weight that was fed mainly potatoes in XIX Poland and on former Polish territories known today as Lithuania (Litwa before).

Pork class I, 400 g (0.88 lb)
Pork class II, 600 g (1.32 lb)

Ingredients per 1 kg (2.2 lb.) of meat

Salt, 18 g (3 tsp)
Cure # 1, 2.5 g (1/2 tsp)
Pepper, 2.0 g (1 tsp)
Nutmeg, 1.0 g (1/2 tsp)
Sugar, 1.0 g (1/5 tsp)
Caraway, 1.0 g (1/2 tsp)

Curing Cure meat, see page 44.

Grinding Grind pork class I through 8 mm plate and pork class II through 5 mm grinder plate.

Mixing Mix pork class I and class II together, add remaining salt and spices and mix all well together.

Stuffing Stuff into 22 mm sheep casings, forming 60-70 cm (23-27") links. Hang in the middle on a smoking stick. Leave sausage links in a continuous coil.

Conditioning For 12 hours in a cooler at 2-6°C (35-43°F). Drying is also allowed at room temperature but for only 30-60 minutes.

Smoking and Baking Hot smoke for 50-60 min followed by 20 minutes baking. Total time about 70-90 min. The casings should develop dark brown color and the sausage should reach 68-70° C (154-158° F) inside.

Drying For 5-7 days at 12-18 °C (53-64 °F), 75-80% humidity until sample sausages would demonstrate 55% yield. Then the sausages are divided into previously twisted links. If mold develops on outside, it should be wiped off with a clean cloth.

Notes Nutmeg may be substituted with double amount of white mustard seeds.
One gram (1/2 clove) of garlic may be added.

The majority of sausages after smoking are cooked in water; Kabanosy is baked in a smokehouse.

Originally, Kabanosy was dried after smoking to produce a semi-dry sausage that could be kept without refrigeration. Usually, the sausage was hung on a nail and consumed as needed. Today, Kabanosy is hot smoked, baked and kept in a refrigerator where it will dry more. Thus, the process may be ended after smoking and baking. However, Kabanosy may be kept at room temperature as long as the temperature will remain below 20° C (68° F). It will keep on losing moisture and will become a meat stick.

Photos 6.2 and **6.3** Kabanosy.

Photos courtesy Marcin Klessa vel Oli.

Knyszynska

(Kiełbasa knyszyńska)

Pork class I, 200 g (0.44 lb)
Pork class II, 500 g (1.10 lb)
Beef class I, no connective tissue, 200 g (0.44 lb)
Beef class I or II with connective tissue, 100 g (0.22 lb)

Ingredients per 1 kg (2.2 lb) of meat

Salt, 20 g (3-1/3 tsp)
Cure #1, 2.5 g (1/2 tsp
Pepper, 1.5 g (1 tsp)
Juniper, 1.0 g 91/2 tsp)
Sugar, 1.0 g (1/5 tsp)
Garlic, 1.5 g (1/2 clove)
Water, 20 ml (3/4 oz fl)

Curing	Cure meat, see page 44.
Grinding	Pork class I ground through 13 mm plate, pork class II ground through 8 mm plate, beef class I and II ground through 2-3 mm and then emulsified.
Emulsifying	Using bowl cutter (food processor) emulsify beef ading 30 ml (1 oz fl) of crushed ice or cold water. Add spices at this stage.
Mixing	Mix pork class I with pork class II until sticky. Add emulsified mixture and mix with all ingredients well together.
Stuffing	Stuff into 32-36 mm hog casings. Form 18-20 cm (7-8") links leaving them in a continuous coil.
Conditioning	Hang for 12 hours at 2-6° C (35-43° F). Drying is also allowed at room temperature for 2-3 hours.
Smoking and Baking	With hot smoke for 70-80 min, then baking for 30 min. Total time 100-110 min until the internal meat temperature is 68-70° C (154-158° F) and casings develop light brown color.
Cooling	Cool to 10° C (50° F) and divide into pairs. Keep refrigerated.

Krakowska Cut Sausage

(Kiełbasa Krakowska Krajana)

This sausage has always been one of the top sellers in Poland. The name relates to the city of Krakow, one of the oldest cities in Europe. The middle part of the name "krajana" explains that the meat was manually cut into pieces. If you follow the recipe you will see that the sliced sausage will have visible chunks of meat (2") in it. The reason being that lean pork (class I) was never ground with a grinder.

Pork class I, 900 g (1.98 lb)
Pork class III, 100 g (0.22 lb)

Ingredients per 1 kg (2.2 lb.) of meat

Salt, 18 g (3 tsp)
Cure # 1, 2.5 g (1/2 tsp)
White pepper, 2.0 g (1 tsp)
Nutmeg, 0.5 g (1/4 tsp)
Sugar, 1.0 g (1/4 tsp)

Curing Cure meat, see page 44.

Grinding Pork class I cut manually into 4-5 cm (2") pieces. Pork class III ground through 2-3 mm plate and then emulsified.

Emulsifying Emulsify pork class III in a bowl cutter (food processor) adding 25-30% ice or cold water. Add remaining ingredients.

Mixing Mix pork class I until sticky. Add emulsified pork class III and mix everything together.

Stuffing Stuff into 75 mm synthetic fibrous casings. Form 40-45 cm (16-18") links and tie up both ends. Made at one end loop for hanging.

Drying For 2-4 hours in a drafty area.

Smoking and Baking Smoking is done in three steps:
1. Drying sausages using thin smoke, 45-55° C (113-131° F) for 20 min.
2. Proper smoking with a thick smoke, 45-55° C (113-131° F) for 150 min.
3. Baking with a thin smoke, 75-90° C (167-194° F) for 20-30 min.
Total time about 3 hours until the internal meat temperature is 68-70° C (154-158° F) and casings are dark brown. Re-arrange smoke sticks or smoke carts during smoking.

Cooling Cool sausages in air to 18° C (64° F) or lower.

Note: Nowadays, Krakowska Sausage is usually not baked, but cooked in water 80° C (176° F) after smoking. The baking step is eliminated. After cooking, the sausage is cooled in cold water, briefly dried and placed in a refrigerator.

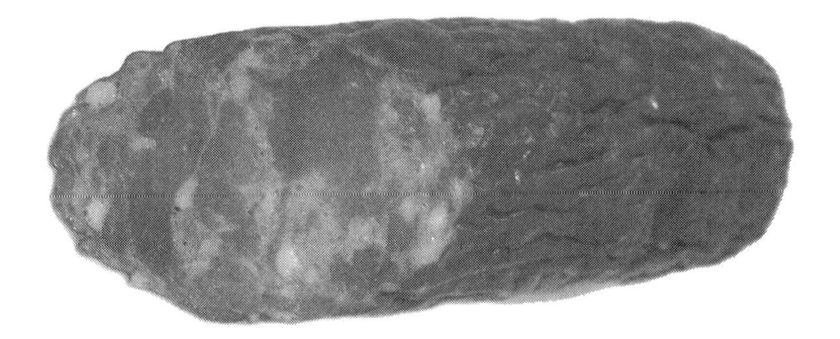

Photo 6.4 Krakowska Sausage.

Photo 6.5 Visible chunks of manually cut meat.
Photo by Szczepan

Krakowska Dry Sausage

(Kiełbasa krakowska trwała)

This sausage has been always one of the top sellers in Poland. The name relates to the city of Krakow, one of the oldest cities in Europe. If you follow the recipe you will see that the sliced sausage will have visible chunks of meat (¾") in it. This is due to lean pork (type I) being ground with a ¾" plate. This is a dry sausage, you can see the instructions require three smoking sessions and extensive drying. The final yield is only 65% and that means that sausage has lost a lot of moisture.

Pork class I, 650 g (1.43 lb)
Pork class II, 150 g (0.33 lb)
Pork class III, 50 g (0.11 lb)
Beef class II, 50 g, (0.11 lb)
Back fat, 100 g (0.22 lb)

Ingredients per 1 kg (2.2 lb.) of meat

Salt, 21 g (3-1/2 tsp)
Cure # 1, 2.5 g (1/2 tsp)
White pepper, 2.0 g
Nutmeg, 0.5 g (1/4 tsp)
Garlic, 1.5 g (1/2 clove)

Curing Cure meat, see page 44.

Grinding Pork class I ground through 20 mm plate, pork class II ground through 13 mm plate, pork class III and beef class II ground through 2 mm plate. Fatback diced through the machine or manually cut into 12 mm cubes. *The whole sausage (all meats and fat) can be manually cut with a knife.*

Emulsifying Emulsify ground beef class II and ground pork class III in a bowl cutter (food processor) adding 20-25% ice or cold water. Add spices at this stage.

Mixing Mix pork class I with pork class II until sticky, then add back fat and emulsified mixture. Mix everything well together.

Stuffing Stuff into 50-60 mm beef middles or 65 mm synthetic fibrous casings. Form 40-45 cm (16-18"). links. Tie up ends with a twine, make a hanging loop.

Drying For 12 hours at 2-6° C (35-43° F). Drying is also allowed at room temperature for 3-5 hours.

Smoking	With hot smoke for 110-130 min until casings develop brown color. Re-arrange smoke sticks or smoke carts during smoking.
Poaching or Baking	Poach sausages in water at 72-75° C (161-167° F) until internal temperature of the meat is 68-70°C (154-158°F). Baked sausages are baked in the last stage of smoking for 30-40 min at 75-90° C (167-194° F) until internal meat temperature is 68-70°C (154-158° F).
Cooling	For 12 hours at temperature of 18°C (64°F) or less.
Secondary Smoking *(poached sausages only)*	*Poached* sausages are submitted to a secondary smoking: • with cold smoke for 24 hours *OR* • with warm smoke 24-32° C (75-90° F) for 12 hours until casings develop dark brown color.
Drying	For 10-16 days at 12-18° C (53-64° F), 75-80% humidity until sample sausages achieve 67% yield. If a mold appears on the sausages, it should be wiped off with a cloth. Then they are smoked with warm smoke 24-32° C (75-90° F) for 2-3 hours.
Cooling	Cool sausages in air to 18°C (64°F) or lower.
Notes	Pork class III may be substituted with beef class II.

Kujawska

(Kiełbasa kujawska parzona podsuszana)

Pork class II, cured and smoked, 700 g (1.54 lb)
Pork class III, cured and smoked, 100 g (0.22 lb)
Beef, class III or II, not cured, 100 g (0.22 lb)
Jowls/dewlap or hard fat trimmings, 100 g (0.22 lb)

Note: the source of cured and smoked pork meat used in this sausage were the meat trimmings left over from canning hams, butts and loins.

Ingredients per 1 kg (2.2 lb) of meat

Salt, 20 g (3-1/3 tsp)
Cure # 1, 2.5 g (1/2 tsp)
Pepper, 2.0 g (1 tsp)
Paprika, 1.0 g (1/2 tsp)
Garlic, 1.5 g (1/2 clove

Curing Cure meat, see page 44.

Grinding Pork class II - 5 mm plate.
Jowls or fat trimmings - 5 mm plate.
Pork class III with 2-3 mm plate.
Beef through 2-3 mm plate.

Emulsifying Using food processor emulsify pork class III adding 20-30% (30 ml or 1.35 oz fl) cold water. Add all ingredients and spices during this step.

Mixing Mix pork class II with fat, add beef, emulsified meat and mix everything together.

Stuffing Stuff firmly into beef middles or 65 mm synthetic fibrous casings. Make links 40-45 cm (16-18") long. Tie the ends together and make a hanging loop.

Conditioning Hang for 120 min at room temperature.

Smoking Apply hot smoke for 90-120 minutes until casings develop light brown color.

Cooking Cook in water at 72-75° C (160-167° F) for 50-70 min until sausages reach 68-70° C (154-158° F) internal temperature.

Cooling Cool for 15 minutes in cold water.

Drying For 1-2 days at 12-18°C (53-84°F), 75-80% humidity. Store at 12° C (53° F) or lower.

Limanowska Sausage
(Kiełbasa Limanowska)

Sausage from the Limanowa area (Ziemia Limanowska), located high in the mountains, in the Southern part of the country.

Pork class III, 50 g (0.11 lb)
Veal class I, 800 g (1.76 lb)
Veal class II, 100 g (0.22 lb)
Pieces of hard fat, 50 g (0.11 lb)

Ingredients per 1 kg (2.2 lb.) of meat

Salt, 20 g (3-1/3 tsp)
Cure # 1, 2.5 g (1/2 tsp)
Pepper, 2.0 g (1 tsp)
Coriander, 0.5 g (1/4 tsp)

Curing	Cure meat, see page 44.
Grinding	Pork class III ground through 2 mm plate and then emulsified. Veal class I diced or manually cut into 5-6 cm (2") pieces, veal class II ground through 10 mm plate, fat pieces through 8 mm plate.
Emulsifying	Pork class III is emulsified in a bowl cutter (food processor) adding 20-30% of crushed ice or cold water. Add remaining salt and spices at this stage.
Mixing	Mix veal class I with veal class II until sticky, then add emulsified mixture and mix everything together.
Stuffing	Stuff into beef bungs or 55-65 mm cellulose casings. Form links about 40-45 cm (16-18") long, on one end loop 10-12 cm (4-5") for hanging.
Conditioning	For 12 hours at 2-6° C (35-43° F). Drying is also allowed at room temperature for 3-4 hours.
Smoking	With hot smoke for 90-100 min, then baking for 40 min. Total time 130-150 min until sausages reach 68-70° C (154-158° F) internal temperature.
Drying	For 1-2 days at 12-18° C (53-84° F), 75-80% humidity until 84% yield is achieved.

Lithuanian Sausage

(Kiełbasa Litewska)

Polish version of Lithuanian sausage.

Pork class II, 200 g (0.44 lb)
Beef class II or III, 300 g (0.66 lb)
Hard fat trimmings, 200 g (0.44 lb)
Cured parts: hearts, tongues, bloody scraps of meat, beef head meat, lean pork head meat, 300 g (0.66 lb)

Ingredients per 1 kg (2.2 lb.) of meat

Salt, 20 g (3-1/3 tsp)
Cure # 1, 2.5 g (1/2 tsp)
Pepper, 1.0 (1/2 tsp)
Paprika, 1.0 g (1 tsp)
Allspice, 0.5 g (1/4 tsp)
Garlic, 3.0 g (1 clove)

Curing and Grinding	Cure meat. Pork class II and fat trimmings ground through 8 mm plate. Beef class II or III and other meats ground through 2 mm plate and emulsified.
Emulsifying	Emulsify beef class II or III and offal meats adding 20% ice or cold water. Add spices.
Mixing	Mix pork class II , ground fat and emulsified meats well together.
Stuffing	Stuff into 32 mm hog casings. Form 25-28 cm (10-11”) links and divide into pairs.
Conditioning	Hang for 12 hours at 2-6° C (35-43° F). Drying is also allowed at room temperature for 1-2 hours.
Smoking	With hot smoke for 80-100 min until light brown.
Poaching or Baking	Poach sausages in water at 72-75° C (161-167° F) for 25-35 min until internal temperature of the meat becomes 68-70° C (154-158° F). Baked sausages, in the last stage of smoking are baked for about 30 min at 75-90° C (167-194° F) until sausages reach 68-70° C (154-158° F) internal temperature.
Cooling	For 12 hours at temperatures below 18°C (64°F).
Smoking *(poached sausages only)*	Poached sausages are submitted to a secondary smoking: • with cold smoke for 12 hours • with warm smoke (24-32°C, 75-90° F) for 6 hours
Drying	For 2-3 days at 12-18°C (53-64°F), 75-80% humidity until sample sausages achieve 86% yield. If mold appears wipe it off.

Loin Sausage

(Kiełbasa polędwicowa pieczona)

Baked loin sausage with visible chunks of meat held together by emulsified beef.

Pork class I (loin), 900 g (1.98 lb)
Beef, class I, 100 g (0.22 lb)

Ingredients per 1 kg (2.2 lb) of meat

Salt, 18 g (3 tsp)
Cure #1, 2.5 g (1/2 tsp)
Pepper, 2.0 g (1 tsp)
Nutmeg, 0.3 g (1/5 tsp)

Curing	Remove from loin any connective tissue and silver screen. Cut loin into 4 x 4 cm (1.5”) cubes. Mix with 90% of salt and Cure #1. Cut beef into 5 cm (2”) pieces and mix with remaining 10% of salt and cure #1. Pack tightly in separate containers, cover with cloth and hold for 3 days in refrigerator.
Grinding	Grind beef through 3 mm plate.
Emulsifying	Using food processor emulsify beef adding 25-30% (30 ml or 1 oz fl) cold water and spices.
Mixing	Mix (knead) loin until sticky. Add emulsified beef and mix everything together.
Stuffing	Stuff firmly into 55-65 mm beef middles or synthetic fibrous casings making 35-45 cm (14-18”). Make hanging loop.
Conditioning	Hang for 2 hours at room temperature.
Smoking	Apply hot smoke for 60-80 minutes, increase temperature to 80-90° C (176-194° F) and bake for 2.5-3 hours. Total time of smoking and baking 3-4 hours, until sausages reach 68-70° C (154-158° F) internal temperature.
Cooling	Cool in air.
Storing	Keep refrigerated.

Lowiecka Sausage

(Kiełbasa łowiecka pieczona)

This sausage belongs to the hunter type of sausages like Myśliwska Sausage. The word "łowić" or "polować" means to hunt in Polish. The sausage keeps well, that is why it was carried on hunting trips.

Pork class I, 500 g (1.10 lb)
Pork class II, 350 g (0.77 lb)
Beef class I, 150 g (0.33 lb)

Ingredients per 1 kg (2.2 lb) of meat

Salt, 20 g (3-1/3 tsp)
Cure #1, 2.5 g (1/2 tsp)
Sugar, 1.0 g (1/5 tsp)
Garlic, 1.5 g (1/2 clove)

Curing	Cure meat, see page 44.
Grinding	Cut pork class I into 25 mm (1") cubes. Grind pork class II through 13 mm plate. Grind beef class I through 2-3 mm plate.
Emulsifying	Using food processor emulsify beef class I with 25% (37 ml, about 1 fl oz) of water adding spices during the process.
Mixing	Mix all pork until sticky. Add emulsified beef and mix everything together.
Stuffing	Stuff firmly into 36-40 mm beef rounds or hog casings forming rings. Tie the ends together.
Conditioning	Hang for 2 hours at room temperature.
Smoking	With hot smoke for 80-100 minutes until brown. Increase the temperature and bake for about 60-80 minutes until sausages reach 68-70° C (154-158° F) internal temperature.
Cooling	Cool in air.
Storing	Keep refrigerated. The sausage may be hung at 10-12° C (50-53° F). The sausage will lose moisture becoming a semi-dry, then a dry sausage.

Olawska

(Kiełbasa oławska)

Pork class I, 650 g (1.43 lb)
Pork class II, 150 g (0.33 lb)
Pork class III, 100 g (0.22 lb)
Pork hard fat trimmings, 100 g (0.22 lb)

Ingredients per 1 kg (2.2 lb) of meat

Salt, 18 g (3 tsp)
Cure #1, 2.5 g (1/2 tsp)
Pepper, 1.5 g (1 tsp)
Garlic, 1.0 g (1/3 clove)
Caraway, 0.3 g (1/5 tsp)

Curing	Cure meat, see page 44.
Grinding	Pork class I ground through 13 mm plate, pork class II ground through 8 mm plate, pork class III ground through 2 mm and then emulsified.
Emulsifying	Using bowl cutter (food processor) emulsify pork class III adding 15 ml (1 tablespoon) of crushed ice or cold water. Add spices at this stage.
Mixing	Mix pork class I with pork class II until sticky. Add emulsified mixture and mix everything well together.
Stuffing	Stuff firmly into 36-40 mm, hog casings. Form 18-20 cm (7-8”) links. leaving them in a continuous coil.
Conditioning	Hang for 12 hours at 2-6° C (35-43° F). Drying is also allowed at room temperature for 2-3 hours.
Smoking and Baking	With hot smoke for 70-80 min, then baking for 30 min. Total time 100-110 min until sausages reach 68-70° C (154-158° F) internal temperature and casings develop light brown color.
Cooling	Cool in air to 12° C (53° F).

Podhalanska Sausage

(Kiełbasa Podhalańska)

This sausage originates in Poland's most southern region, often referred as the "Polish highlands". The region is located at the foothills of the Tatry Mountains which are the highest mountains in Poland. A sheep is the most popular animal in the hilly areas and this is also reflected in this recipe that calls for lamb meat.

Pork class II, 300 g (0.66 lb)
Lamb class I, 200 g (0.44 lb)
Lamb class II, 400 g (0.88 lb)
Hard fat trimmings, 100 g (0.22 lb)

Ingredients per 1 kg (2.2 lb.) of meat

Salt, 20 g (3-1/3 tsp)
Cure # 1, 2.5 g (1/2 tsp)
Pepper, 1.0 g (1/2 tsp)
Allspice, 0.5 g (1/4 tsp)
Marjoram, 1.0 g (1/2 tsp)
Garlic, 3.5 g (1 clove)

Curing Cure meat, see page 44.

Grinding Pork class II and fat trimmings ground through 10 mm plate. Lamb class I ground through 13 mm plate, lamb class II ground through 2 mm plate and then emulsified.

Emulsifying Using food processor emulsify lamb class II adding 30% ice or cold water. Add spices.

Mixing Mix lamb class I with pork class II until sticky. Add ground fat and emulsified meat and mix everything together.

Stuffing Stuff into 32-36 mm hog casings. Form 30-35 cm (12-14") links and divide into pairs. Leave in a continuous coil.

Conditioning Hang for 12 hours at 2-6° C (35-43° F). Drying is also allowed at room temperature for 1-2 hours.

Smoking With hot smoke for 80-100 min until light brown color is obtained.

Poaching or Baking Poach sausages in water at 72-75° C (161-167° F) for 25-35 min until meat reaches 68-70° C (154-158° F) internal temperature. Baked sausages, in the last stage of smoking are baked for about 30 min at 75-90° C (167-194° F) until until meat reaches 68-70° C (154-158° F) internal temperature.

Cooling	Hold for 12 hours at 18° C (64° F) or lower.
Smoking *(poached sausages only)*	Poached sausages are submitted to a secondary smoking: • with cold smoke for 12 hours *OR* • with warm smoke (24-32° C, 75-90° F) for 6 hours until casings develop brown color.
Drying	For 2-3 days at 12-18° C (53-64° F), 75-80% humidity until sample sausages achieve 86% yield. If mold appears wipe it off. Divide linked sausages into separate pairs.

Podkarpacka

(Kiełbasa podkarpacka pieczona półtrwała)

Pork class I, 750 g (1.65 lb)
Pork class II, 100 g (0.22 lb)
Beef class I, 150 g (0.33 lb)

Ingredients per 1 kg (2.2 lb) of meat

Salt, 18 g (3 tsp)
Cure #1, 2.5 g (1/2 tsp)
Pepper, 2.0 g (1 tsp)
Nutmeg, 0,5 g (1/4 tsp)

Curing	Cure meat, see page 44.
Grinding	Cut pork class I and II into 3-5 cm (1-2”) pieces. Grind beef class I through 2-3 mm plate.
Emulsifying	Using food processor emulsify beef class I with 30% (50 ml or 1/5 cup) of water adding spices during the process.
Mixing	Mix all pork until sticky. Add emulsified beef and mix everything together.
Stuffing	Stuff firmly into 110-120 mm synthetic fibrous casings making 35-45 cm (1-1.5 foot). Tie the ends together.
Conditioning	Hang for 1-2 hours at room temperature.
Smoking	Drying for 20-30 min with thin smoke at 50-60° C (122-140° F). Smoking for 90 min at 70° C (158° F). Baking for 70-120 min in thin smoke at 80-90° C (176-194° F). Total time about 3-4 hours until sausages reach 68-70° C (154-158° F) internal temperature.
Cooling	Cool in air.
Storing	Keep refrigerated. The sausage may be hung at 10-12° C (50-53° F). The sausage will lose moisture becoming a semi-dry, then a dry sausage.

Rzeszowska Sausage

(Kiełbasa Rzeszowska)

Name of this sausage originates in the city of Rzeszow, located in the South-Eastern region of Poland.

Pork class I, 450 g (0.99 lb)
Pork class II, 350 g (0.77 lb)
Pork class III, 100 g 0.22 lb)
Beef class I, 100 g (0.22 lb)

Ingredients per 1 kg (2.2 lb.) of meat

Salt, 18 g (3 tsp)
Cure # 1, 2.5 g (1/2 tsp)
Pepper, 2.0 g (1 tsp)
Cardamom, 0.5 g (1/4 tsp)
Garlic, 3.0 g (1 clove)

Curing	Cure meat, see page 44.
Grinding	Pork class I ground through 13 mm plate, pork class II ground through 8 mm plate, pork class III and beef class I ground through 2 mm and then emulsified.
Emulsifying	Using bowl cutter (food processor) emulsify beef class I with pork class III adding 30-35% ice or cold water. Add spices at this stage.
Mixing	Mix pork class I with pork class II until sticky. Add emulsified mixture and mix everything well together.
Stuffing	Stuff into 32-36 mm hog casings. Form 18-20 cm (7-8") links leaving them in a continuous coil.
Conditioning	For 12 hours at 2-6° C (35-43° F). Drying is also allowed at room temperature for 2-3 hours.
Smoking and Baking	With hot smoke for 70-80 min, then baking for 30 min. Total time 100-110 min until sausages reach 68-70° C (154-158° F) internal temperature and casings develop light brown color.
Cooling	Cool sausages in air to 18° C (64° F) or lower.

Salami Krakowskie

(Salami krakowskie pieczone suche)

Although salami is of Italian origin, almost every country has its own version and Poland is no exception. Salami Krakowskie owes its name to the city of Krakow, one of the oldest cities in Europe.

Pork, class I and II from ham and butt leftovers, best from older animals with darker meat color, 770 g, (1.70 lb)
Fat trimmings from hams and butts, 230 g (0.50 lb)

I*ngredients per 1 kg (2.2 lb.) of meat*

Salt, 18 g (3 tsp)
Cure # 1, 2.5 g (1/2 tsp)
Pepper, 4.0 g (2 tsp)
Garlic, 3.5 g (1 clove)

Grinding	Cut meat and fat into 5-6 cm (1 inch) pieces and mix well with salt, Cure #1 and spices. Grind through 4 mm plate (1/8").
Curing	Place ground mixture in a food grade container, pack tightly, stuff tightly to eliminate pockets of air and cover with butcher paper or cellophane foil. Cure for 7 days at 2-4° C (35-40° F).
Stuffing	Stuff firmly into 55-65 mm beef middles or synthetic cellulose or fibrous casings. Natural casings-straight links 40-45 cm (16-18") long. Synthetic casings-straight links 55-65 cm (21-25") long. Ends tied up with a twine, 10-12 cm (4-5") loop on one end. Prick any visible air pockets with a needle.
Conditioning	Hang in a drafty area for 2 hours.
Smoking	1. Drying sausages with thin smoke, 45-50° C (113-122° F) for 20-40 min. 2. Smoking with a thick smoke, 40-50° C (104-122° F) for 90-140 min. 3. Baking with a thin smoke, 75-90° C (167-194° F) for 70-100 min.
Aging and Drying	In a dark, lightly drafty area at 10-12° C (50-53° F), humidity 80-85% for 4-6 weeks until salami develops white, dry mold on outside. If moist green mold appears it must be washed with warm salty water and wiped off. Then continue drying. The product is done when its yield is 65%.

Serbian Sausage

(Kiełbasa serbska parzona)

Beef class I or II, 400 g (0.88 lb)
Pork back fat, 600 g (1.32 lb)

Ingredients per 1 kg (2.2 lb) of meat

Salt for salting back fat, as needed.
Salt, 18 g (3 tsp)
Cure #1, 1.5 g (1/4 tsp)
Pepper, 2.0 g (1 tsp)
Paprika, 2.0 g (1 tsp)

Curing and Salting	Cure meat. Cut back fat into 15 x 15 mm (1/2") strips. Rub salt into the strips all around and place them in refrigerator for 12 days.
Grinding	Cut back fat into 15 x 15 mm (1/2") cubes. Grind beef through 2-3 mm plate.
Mixing	Mix (knead) beef with salt (12 g) until sticky. Add Cure #1, spices and mix everything together. Mix back fat cubes with paprika. Mix everything together.
Stuffing	Stuff firmly into beef rounds or 36-40 mm hog casings. Make rings, tie the ends together.
Conditioning	Hang for 12 hours in refrigerator or leave for 2-3 hours at room temperature.
Smoking	Apply warm smoke for 3 hours until casings develop yellow color with red spots.
Cooking	Cook in water at 72-75° C (160-167° F) until sausages reach 68-70° C (154-158° F) internal temperature.
Cooling	Cool for 15 minutes in cold water.

Servolatka

(Serwolatka pieczona)

Beef class I, little connective tissue, 250 g (0.55 lb)
Beef class I, rich in connective tissue, 320 g (0.70 lb)
Beef class IV, 60 g (0.13 lb)
Beef class V, 20 g (0.70 oz)
Pork belly, skinless, 350 g (0.77 lb)

Ingredients per 1 kg (2.2 lb.) of meat

Salt, 18 g (3 tsp)
Cure #1, 2.5 g (1/2 tsp)
Pepper, 2.0 g (1 tsp)
Coriander, 0.5 g (1/4 tsp)
Paprika, 0.5 g (1/4 tsp)

Curing Cure meat, see page 44.

Grinding Grind:

- Beef class I (little connective tissue) - 5 mm plate.
- Beef class I (rich in connective tissue), beef class IV and V - 2-3 mm plate.
- Pork belly - 5 mm plate.

Emulsifying Using food processor emulsify ground beef class I (rich in connective tissue), IV, and V adding 10% (40 ml or 1.35 oz fl) cold water. Add all ingredients and spices during this step.

Mixing Mix beef class I (little connective tissue) with ground belly until sticky. Add emulsified meats and mix all together.

Stuffing Stuff firmly into 65 mm synthetic fibrous. Make 25 cm (10”) long links. Hanging loop at one end.

Conditioning Hold for 60 min at room temperature.

Smoking

- Drying - 20-30 min, thin smoke at 45-55° C (113-131° F).
- Smoking - 80 min, thick smoke at 45-55° C (113-131° F).
- Baking - 40-60 min, thin smoke at 75-90° C (167-194° F).

Total time about 150 minutes until sausages reach 68-70° C (154-158° F) internal temperature and dark brown color with red tint.

Cooling Cool in air. Keep refrigerated.

Tarnogorska Sausage

(Kiełbasa tarnogórska parzona podsuszana)

Pork class II, 250 g (0.55 lb)
Beef class I, with connective tissue, 400 g (0.88 lb)
Jowls/dewlap or hard fat trimmings, 350 g

Ingredients per 1 kg (2.2 lb) of meat

Salt, 20 g (3-1/3 tsp)
Cure #1, 2.0 g (1/3 tsp)
Pepper, 2.0 g (1 tsp)
Paprika, 2.0 g (1 tsp)
Marjoram, 1.0 g (1/2 tsp)
Sugar, 1.0 g (1/5 tsp)

Grinding	Pork class II - 3 mm plate. Jowls or fat trimmings - cut manually or grind with 5 mm plate. Beef through 2-3 mm plate.
Mixing	Mix pork class II with beef adding salt, Cure #1 and spices until the mass feels sticky. Add fat and mix again. Pack in container and place for 24 hours in refrigerator. Remix before stuffing.
Stuffing	Stuff firmly into beef rounds or large hog casings. Make rings, tie the ends together.
Conditioning	Hang for 120 min at room temperature.
Smoking	Apply hot smoke for 80 - 100 minutes until casings develop light brown color.
Cooking	Cook in water at 72-75° C (160-167° F) for 40-60 min until sausages reach 68-70° C (154-158° F) internal temperature.
Cooling	Cool for 15 minutes in cold water.
Drying	Hang for 2-3 days at 12-15° C (53-59° F), 75-80% humidity until 87% yield is obtained.

Tarnowska Sausage

(Kiełbasa cielęca tarnowska pieczona)

Veal class II, 500 g (1.1 lb)
Veal class III, 200 g (0.44 lb)
Pork class II, 200 g (0.44 lb)
Hard fat trimmings, 100 g

Ingredients per 1 kg (2.2 lb) of meat

Salt, 18 g (3 tsp)
Cure #1, 2.5 g (1/2 tsp)
Pepper, 1.0 g (1/2 tsp)
Garlic,1.5 g (1/2 clove)

Curing	Cure meat, see page 44.
Grinding	4/5 veal class II (400 g) ground through 8 mm plate. 1/5 veal class II (100 g) ground through 2-3 mm plate. Veal class III ground through 2-3 mm plate. Pork class II ground through 8 mm plate. Fat trimmings ground through 8 mm plate.
Emulsifying	Using food processor emulsify veal class III, 1/5 veal class II (100 g) adding 35-40% (100 ml or 5/8 cup) of water adding spices during the process.
Mixing	Mix ground veal class II with ground pork class II until sticky. Add emulsified meat and ground fat. Mix everything together.
Stuffing	Stuff firmly into 32-36 mm hog or synthetic fibrous casings making 35-45 cm (1-1.5 foot) links. Make hanging loop.
Conditioning	Hang for 2 hours at room temperature.
Smoking	Drying for 15-20 min with thin smoke at 45-55° C (113-131° F). Smoking for 120 min at 45-55° C (113-131° F). Baking in thin smoke for 30 min at 75-90° C (167-194° F). Total time about 170 minutes until sausages reach 68-70° C (154-158° F) internal temperature and light brown color.
Cooling	Cool in air.
Storing	Keep refrigerated.

Torunska

(Kiełbasa toruńska parzona podsuszana)

Pork class II, 800 g (1.76 lb)
Pork class III, 200 g (0.44 lb)

Ingredients per 1 kg (2.2 lb) of meat

Salt, 18 g (3 tsp)
Cure #1, 2.5 g (1/2 tsp)
Pepper, 2.0 g (1 tsp)Sugar, 1.0 g (1/5 tsp)
Garlic, 1.5 g (1/2 tsp)

Curing	Cure meat, see page 44.
Grinding	Pork class II - 8 mm plate. Pork class III - 2-3 mm.
Emulsifying	In food processor emulsify pork class III adding 20-25% (40 ml or 1.41 oz fl) cold water. Add salt, Cure #1 and spices during this step.
Mixing	Mix pork class II with emulsified meat.
Stuffing	Stuff firmly into 32-36 mm hog casings. Form 25-30 cm (12-14”) links leaving them in a continuous coil.
Conditioning	Hang for 60 min at room temperature.
Cooking	Cook in water at 72-75° C (160-167° F) until sausages reach 68-70° C (154-158° F) internal temperature.
Cooling	Cool for 15 minutes in cold water.
Smoking	Hang for 15 min in a warm smokehouse, then apply *cold smoke* for 12 hours. until 84% yield is obtained.

Tourist Sausage

(Kiełbasa turystyczna pieczona)

Pork class II, 500 g (1.10 lb)
Beef class I, II or III, 200 g (0.44 lb)
Hearts (pork, veal, cow, sheep), 100 g (0.33 lb)
Pork skins, 100 g (0.22 lb)
Veal class III, pork class IV, udders, head meat (optional), 100 g (0.22 lb)

Ingredients per 1 kg (2.2 lb) of meat

Salt, 18 g (3 tsp)
Cure #1, 2.5 g (1/2 tsp)
Pepper, 1.5 g (3/4 tsp)
Nutmeg, 0.5 g (1/4 tsp)
Ginger, 0.5 g (1/4 tsp)

Curing Cure meat, see page 44.

Grinding Grind:

- Pork class II - 10 mm plate.
- Beef class I, II or III - 2-3 mm plate.
- Hearts - 5 mm plate.
- Skins, veal class III, pork class IV, udders -2-3 mm.

Emulsifying Using food processor emulsify ground beef class I, II, III adding 20% (40 ml or 1.35 oz fl) cold water. Add pork skins, pork class IV, veal class III, udders and head meat (if used). Add all ingredients and spices during this step.

Mixing Mix pork class II with ground hearts and emulsified meats.

Stuffing Stuff firmly into 36 mm hog casings. Make 35-40 cm (14-16") long links, keep in continuous coil.

Conditioning Hold for 30-60 min in refrigerator.

Smoking

- Drying - 20-30 min, thin smoke at 45-55° C (113-131° F).
- Smoking - 60 min, thick smoke at 45-55° C (113-131° F).
- Baking - 40-60 min, thin smoke at 75-90° C (167-194° F).

Total time about 120 minutes until sausages reach 68-70° C (154-158° F) internal temperature and dark brown color with red tint.

Cooling Cool in air. Keep refrigerated.

Tuchowska Sausage
(Kiełbasa Tuchowska)

The origin of this sausage is Tuchow, the city with long tradition in making quality sausages. It lies about 80 km (50 miles) from Krakow, at the foothills of Carpathian Mountains (Karpaty).

Pork class I. 600 g (1.32 lb)
Beef class I, 200 g (0.44 lb)
Hard fat trimmings, 200 g (0.44 lb)

Ingredients per 1 kg (2.2 lb.) of meat

Salt, 20 g (3-1/3 tsp)
Cure # 1, 2.5 g (1/2 tsp)
Pepper, 2.0 g (1 tsp)
Garlic, 3.0 g (1 clove)

Curing Cure meat, see page 44.

Grinding Pork class I ground through 8 mm plate, beef class I ground through 2 mm plate and then half of the beef emulsified in a bowl cutter (food processor). Hard fat trimmings ground through 10 mm plate.

Emulsifying Emulsify half of class I beef (10% of the meat total) adding 30-35% ice or cold water. Add spices at this stage.

Mixing Mix remaining half of beef class I with pork class I until mixture feels sticky. Add fat and emulsified mixture and mix everything well together.

Stuffing Stuff into 36 mm or larger hog casings. Form straight links 80-100 cm (30-40") long, both ends tied with twine. Sausages hung on smoke sticks in the middle on themselves.

Drying For 12 hours at 2-6° C (35-43° F). Drying is also allowed at room temperature for 2-3 hours.

Smoking and Baking With hot smoke for 120-140 min, then baking for 30 min. Total time 150-170 min until sausages reach 68-70° C (154-158° F) internal temperature and casings develop brown color.

Cooling For 12 hours below 18° C (64° F).

Smoking With cold smoke for about 12 hours or with warm smoke (24-32° C, 75-90° F) for about 6 hours until dark brown color is obtained.

Cooling Cool sausages in air to 18° C (64° F) or lower.

Ukrainian Sausage
(Kiełbasa Ukraińska)

Polish sausage with Ukrainian name.

Beef class I, II or III, 700 g (1.54 lb)
Skinless jowls, 300 g (0.66 lb)

Ingredients per 1 kg (2.2 lb.) of meat

Salt, 20 g (3-1/3 tsp)
Cure # 1, 2.5 g (1/2 tsp)
Pepper, 1.0 g
Paprika, 1.0 g
Allspice, 0.5 g
Marjoram, 0.5 g
Garlic, 3.0 g (1 clove)

Curing	Cure meat, see page 44.
Grinding	Beef class I and II ground through 5 mm plate. Beef class IIII with connective tissue ground through 2 mm plate and emulsified. Jowls ground through 10 mm plate.
Emulsifying	Emulsify beef class III adding 25% ice or cold water. Add spices.
Mixing	Mix beef class I and II until sticky. Add ground jowls and emulsified mixture and mix everything together.
Stuffing	Stuff into 36 mm beef rounds and tie up ends. Sausage shaped into rings dependent on a natural twist of beef rounds. Outside diameter of the rings 45-70 cm (18-28").
Drying	For 12 hours at 2-6° C (35-43° F). Drying is also allowed at room temperature for 2-3 hours.
Smoking	With hot smoke for 90-110 min until light brown with a tint of red color is obtained.
Cooking	Poach in water at 72-75° C (161-167° F) for 30-40 min until sausages reach 68-70° C (154-158° F) internal temperature.
Cooling	For 12 hours at temperatures below 18°C (64°F).
Secondary Smoking	• with cold smoke for 24 hours *OR* • with warm smoke (24-32°C, 75-90°F) for 12 hours
Drying	For 2-4 days at 12-18° C (53-64° F), 75-80% humidity until 82% yield is obtained. If a mold appears wipe it off.

Village Sausage
(Kiełbasa wiejska)

Pork class I, 800 g (1.76 lb)
Beef class I, 100 g (0.22 lb)
Hard fat trimmings, 100 g (0.33 lb)

Ingredients per 1 kg (2.2 lb) of meat

Salt, 18 g (3 tsp)
Curc # 1, 2.5 g (1/2 tsp)
Sugar, 1.0 g (1/5 tsp)
Pepper, 2.0 g (1 tsp)
Garlic, 3.0 g (1 clove)

Curing	Cut pork class I into 25 mm (1 inch) cubes. Mix with salt and Cure #1, pack tightly in container, cover with cloth and hold for 48 hours in refrigerator. Follow the same procedure with beef, but in a separate container. Allocate salt and Cure #1 proportionally with pork getting most of it.
Grinding	Grind beef through 2-3 mm plate. Grind fat through 8 mm plate.
Emulsifying	Using food processor emulsify beef with 25-30% cold water (30 ml, 1 oz fl). Add spices during this step.
Mixing	Mix pork cubes with ground fat, then add emulsified beef and mix all together.
Stuffing	Stuff firmly into beef rounds or 36 mm hog casings. Form rings.
Conditioning	Hang for 2-3 hours at room temperature.
Smoking	• Drying - 20-30 min, thin smoke at 45-55° C (113-131° F). • Smoking - 80 min, thick smoke at 45-55° C (113-131° F). • Baking - 40-60 min, thin smoke at 75-90° C (167-194° F). Total time about 150 minutes until sausages reach 68-70° C (154-158° F) internal temperature and dark brown color with red tint.
Cooling	Cool in air.
Storing	Keep refrigerated.

Zulawska Sausage

(Kiełbasa żuławska pieczona)

Pork class II, 620 g (1.36 lb)
Beef class I, 300 g (0.66 lb)
Beef class IV, 60 g (0.13 lb)
Beef class V, 20 g (0.70 oz)

Ingredients per 1 kg (2.2 lb) of meat

Salt, 18 g (3 tsp)
Cure #1, (1/2 tsp)
Pepper, 1.0 g (1/2 tsp)
Hot paprika, 0.5 g (1/4 tsp)
Allspice, 0.5 g (1/4 tsp)
Marjoram, 0.3 g (1/5 tsp)

Curing Cure meat, see page 44.

Grinding Grind:
- Pork class II - 8 mm plate
- Beef class I, IV and V - 2-3 mm plate

Emulsifying Using food processor emulsify ground beef class I, IV, and V adding 10% (40 ml or 1.35 oz fl) cold water. Add all ingredients and spices during this step.

Mixing Mix pork class II with emulsified meats.

Stuffing Stuff firmly into beef rounds or 36 mm hog casings. Make rings and the ends together.

Conditioning Hold for 120 min at room temperature.

Smoking
- Drying - 20-30 min, thin smoke at 45-55° C (113-131° F).
- Smoking - 80 min, thick smoke at 45-55° C (113-131° F).
- Baking - 40-60 min, thin smoke at 75-90° C (167-194° F).

Total time about 150 minutes until sausages reach 68-70° C (154-158° F) internal temperature and dark brown color with red tint.

Cooling Cool in air. Keep refrigerated.

Zywiecka Sausage

(Żywiecka Sausage)

The name originates in the city of Żywiec, the same place where most popular Polish beer called "Żywiec" is made.

Pork class I, 400 g (0.88 lb)
Pork class II, 200 g (0.44 lb)
Pork class III, 100 g (0.22 lb)
Beef class II, 150 g (0.33 lb)
Hard fat trimmings, 150 g (0.33 lb)

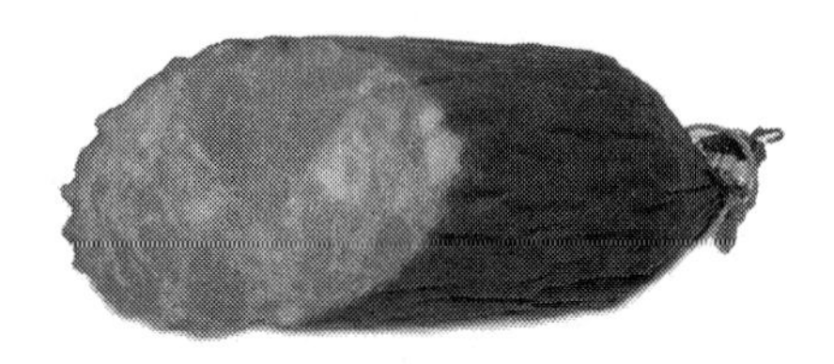

Photo 6.6 Zywiecka Sausage.

Ingredients per 1 kg (2.2 lb.) of meat

Salt, 20 g (3-1/3 tsp)
Cure # 1, 2.5 g (1/2 tsp)
Pepper, 2.0 g
Garlic, 3.0 g (1 clove)
Sugar, 1.0 g (1/5 tsp)

Curing Cure meat, see page 44.

Grinding Pork class I ground (or manually diced) through 20 mm plate, pork class II and fat trimmings ground through 10 mm plate. Pork class III and beef class II ground through 2 mm plate and then emulsified.

Emulsifying Emulsify beef class II with pork class III adding 25% ice or cold water. Add spices.

Mixing Mix pork class I until meat feels sticky, then add pork class II and continue mixing. Add fat and emulsified mixture and mix everything well together.

Stuffing Stuff into beef middles of any size, synthetic cellulose or fibrous casings. Form 35-40 cm (14-16") straight links. The ends tied with a twine, hanging loop on one end.

Drying For 12 hours at 2-6° C (35-43° F). Drying is also allowed at room temperature for 3-4 hours.

Smoking With hot smoke for 110-130 min until brown color with a tint of red is obtained.

Poaching or Baking Poach in water at 72-75° C (161-167° F) for 30-40 min until internal temperature of the meat becomes 68-70° C (154-158° F). Baked sausages-in the last stage of smoking are baked for 30-40 min at 75-90° C (167-194° F) until sausages reach 68-70° C (154-158° F) internal temperature.

Cooling	For 12 hours at 18°C (64°F) or lower.
Smoking *(poached sausages only)*	Poached sausages are submitted to a secondary smoking: • with cold smoke for 24 hours *OR* • with warm smoke (24-32° C, 75-90° F) for 12 hours.
Drying	For 2-3 days at 12-18° C (53-64° F), 75-80% humidity until sample sausages achieve 83% yield. If a mold starts to appear on the sausages, it should be wiped off with a cloth.

Chapter 7

Hot Smoked Sausages, Coarse and Medium Ground, With Limited Shelf Life

This is the group of smoked sausages most people are familiar with. After smoking they are usually cooked in water. Many recipes called for lean meat to be either cut manually into larger chunks or ground with a large plate. Such chunks must be cured to develop a solid pink color as they become the showpiece of the sliced sausage and should stand out. Sausages with solid meat chunks have a wonderful flavor because the meat still contains its original juices and flavor.

Photo 7.1 Polish Sausages can be found everywhere. Wiktor Minkiewicz makes and sells his products in Johannesburg, South Africa.

Beef Ham Sausage

(Kiełbasa szynkowa wołowa)

Called ham sausage because solid chunks of beef ham are imbedded in its texture.

Beef class I, 800 g (1.76 lb)
Beef class III, 200 g (0.44 lb)

Salt, 18 g (3 tsp)
Cure # 1, 2.5 g (1/2 tsp)
Pepper, 2.0 g
Nutmeg, 0.5 g
Sugar, 1.0 g

Photo 7.2 Meat chunks are highly visible.

Curing	Cure meat, see page 44.
Grinding	Cut beef class I (little connective tissue) into 3-4 cm (1¼ - 1¾") chunks. Grind beef class I (with connective tissue) through 2 mm plate and emulsify.
Emulsifying	Using bowl cutter (food processor) emulsify ground beef class I (with connective tissue) adding 50 % ice or cold water. Add spices when emulsifying.
Mixing	Mix beef class I chunks with emulsified meat.
Stuffing	Stuff into beef bungs or 100-120 mm synthetic fibrous casings. Sausage in beef bungs 35-50 cm (14-20") long and laced up with twine. Two loops lengthwise and loops across the bung every 4-6 cm (1.5-2 1/4"). Fibrous casings: 35 cm-40 cm (14-16") long and laced up with twine. Two loops lengthwise and loops across the casings every 4-5 cm (1.5-2").The ends tied up with twine, hanging loop 10-12 cm (4-5") on one end.
Conditioning	For 1-2 hours.
Smoking	With hot smoke for 120-150 min until casings develop light brown color with a pink tint.
Cooking	In water at 72-75° C (161-167° F) for 100-130 min until the sausages reach 68-70° C (154-158° F) internal temperature.
Cooling	Immerse (or shower) in cold water to cool sausages to 12° C (53° F) or lower. Keep refrigerated.

Bieszczadzka

(Kiełbasa bieszczadzka parzona)

Beef class I (no connective tissue), 750 g (1.65 lb)
Beef class I (with connective tissue), 150 g (0.33 lb)
Hard fat trimmings, 100 g (0.22 lb)

Ingredients per 1 kg (2.2 lb) of meat

Salt, 18 g (3 tsp)
Cure # 1, 2.5 g (1/2 tsp)
Pepper, 2.0 g (1 tsp)
Garlic, 2.0 g (1/2 clove)

Curing	Cut beef class I (with no connective tissue) into 5 cm (2”) pieces and mix with 3/4 (2.0 g) Cure #1 and 2 tsp of salt. Pack tightly in a container, cover with cloth and hold for 3 days in refrigerator.
Grinding	Cut cured beef class I into 20 mm (3/4”) cubes. Grind beef class I (with connective tissue) through 2-3 mm plate. Grind fat trimmings through 8 mm plate.
Emulsifying	In food processor emulsify ground beef adding 50% (75 ml, 2.5 oz fl) of water. Add remaining salt, Cure #1 and spices during this step.
Mixing	Mix everything together.
Stuffing	Stuff firmly into beef rounds or 36-40 mm hog casings. Make rings, tie the ends together.
Conditioning	Hang for 60 min at room temperature.
Smoking	Apply hot smoke for 110-130 min until casings develop brown color with red spots.
Cooking	Cook in water at 72-75° C (160-167° F) for 40-50 min until sausages reach 68-70° C (154-158° F) internal temperature.
Cooling	Cool in for 15 minutes in cold water. Wipe off moisture and refrigerate.

Bydgoska Sausage
(Kiełbasa bydgoska)

The sausage name implies that it originated in the city of Bydgoszcz.

Beef class I, II or III (without connective tissue), 400 g (0.88 lb)
Beef class III (with connective tissue), 200 g (0.44 lb)
Fat trimmings, 300 g (0.66 lb)
Veal class III or beef class V (with connective tissue), pork skins, 100 g (0.22 lb)

Ingredients per 1 kg (2.2 lb.) of meat

Salt, 18 g (3 tsp)
Cure # 1, 2.0 g (1/2 tsp)
Pepper, 1.5 g
Garlic, 1.5 g (1/2 clove)

The original recipe allowed replacing the natural pepper with a double amount of herbal pepper (white mustard seed, caraway, marjoram, chili, hot and sweet paprika, bay leaf).

Curing Cure meat, see page 44.

Grinding Grind 2/3 beef class III, II or I (without connective tissue) through 5 mm plate. Grind remaining 1/3 beef class III, II or I (with connective tissue) through 2 mm plate and then emulsify. Veal class III, beef type V (without blood) or boiled skins ground twice through 1-2 mm plate and then emulsified. Fat trimmings ground through 8 mm plate.

Emulsifying Add equal amount of water to beef class V and veal class III and skins. Boil at 95° C (203° F) until soft and grind when still hot through 2 mm plate. Then emulsify them with a little of leftover stock from boiling. Then pour the mixture into shallow pans to cool. In food processor emulsify beef class III, II or I (with connective tissue) adding 50% ice or cold water. Add spices when emulsifying. Lastly add previously emulsified mixture (beef class V, veal class III and skins) and emulsify everything together.

Mixing Mix ground beef without connective tissue (class III, II or I) with fat. Then add emulsified meat mixture and mix everything together.

Stuffing Stuff into 60-70 mm synthetic fibrous casings. Sausage in straight links, 40-45 cm (16-18 ") long. The ends tied with a twine, hanging loop (10-12 cm, 4-5") on one end.

Conditioning	For 30-60 min.
Smoking	With hot smoke for 100-120 min.
Cooking	In water at 72-75° C (161-167° F) for 50-70 min until the sausages reach 68-70° C (154-158° F) internal temperature.
Cooling	Immerse (or shower) in cold water to cool sausages to 12° C (53° F) or lower. Keep refrigerated.

Caraway Sausage

(Kiełbasa kminkowa)

This sausage gets its characteristic flavor and aroma from caraway. Caraway is a popular spice often added to rye bread for this extra flavor. It is also used with dill and garlic for making pickles.

Pork class I, 400 g (0.88 lb)
Pork class II, 500 g (1.10 lb)
Beef class II or I, 100 g (0.22 lb)

Ingredients per 1 kg (2.2 lb.) of meat

Salt, 18 g (3 tsp)
Cure # 1, 2.5 g (1/2 tsp)
Pepper, 2.0 g (1 tsp)
Caraway, 2.0 g (1 tsp)
Onion, 5.0 g (1 tsp)

Curing Cure meat, see page 44.

Grinding Grind beef through 2 mm plate. Grind pork class I through 16 mm plate. Grind pork class II through 10 mm plate.

Emulsifying Using bowl cutter (food processor) emulsify ground beef adding 25 % ice or cold water. Add spices when emulsifying.

Mixing Mix pork class I and pork class II with emulsified meat.

Stuffing Stuff into beef middles of any size. Sausage in straight links, 30-35 cm (12-14 ") long. The ends tied with a twine, hanging loop (10-12 cm, 4-5") on one end.

Conditioning For 30-60 min.

Smoking With hot smoke for 90-120 min until casings develop light brown color.

Cooking In water at 72-75° C (161-167° F) for 45-60 min until sausages reach 68-70° C (154-158° F) internal temperature.

Cooling Immerse (or shower) in cold water to cool sausages to 12° C (53° F) or lower. Keep refrigerated.

Garlic Sausage

(Kiełbasa czosnkowa)

Garlic is the dominant spice in this sausage. There are garlic lovers everywhere and each country has its own version, for example German "Knoblauchwurst."

Pork class I, 350 g (0.77 lb)
Pork class II, 200 g (0.44 lb)
Beef class I or II, 250 g (0.55 lb)
Hard fat trimmings, 200 g (0.44 lb)

Ingredients per 1 kg (2.2 lb.) of meat

Salt, 18 g (3 tsp)
Cure #1, 2.5 g (1/2 tsp)
Pepper, 3.0 g (1-1/2 tsp)
Coriander, 1.0 g (1.2 tsp)
Paprika, 2.0 g (1 tsp)
Marjoram, 2.0 g (1 tsp)
Garlic, 10 g (3 cloves)

Curing	Cure meat, see page 44.
Grinding	Grind pork class I through 20 mm plate, pork class II and hard fat ground through 10 mm plate. Beef class I or II ground through 2 mm plate and emulsified.
Emulsifying	Emulsify beef class I or II adding 50-60% ice or cold water. Add spices at this stage.
Mixing	Mix pork class I, pork class II, fat and emulsified meat well together.
Stuffing	Stuff into 40 mm beef rounds and form rings. Sausage formed into a ring by the natural properties (twist) of a beef middle, outside diameter 50-70 cm (20-27") depending on a size of the casing. Both ends tied together with a twine.
Conditioning	Hang for 30-60 minutes at room temperature.
Smoking	With hot smoke for 110-130 min until casings develop brown color with a red tint.
Cooking	Poach sausages in water at 72-75° C (161-167° F) for 25-35 min until the sausage reaches 68-70° C (154-158° F) internal temperature.
Cooling	Immerse sausages in cold water to cool sausages to 12° C (53° F) or lower. Keep refrigerated.

Glogowska

(Kiełbasa głogowska)

Pork class I, 350 g (0.77 lb)
Pork class II, 550 g (1.22 lb)
Pork class III, 100 g (0.22 lb)

Ingredients per 1 kg (2.2 lb) of meat

Salt, 18 g (3 tsp)
Cure #1, 2.5 g (1/2 tsp)
Pepper, 2.0 g (1 tsp)
Garlic, 3.0 g (1 clove)

Curing	Cut pork class into 20 mm cubes. Mix with 1/3 of salt and 1/3 of Cure #1. Pack tightly in a container, cover with cloth and hold in refrigerator for 3 days.
Grinding	Pork class II - 10 mm plate. Pork class III - 3 mm plate.
Emulsifying	Using food processor emulsify ground pork class III adding 5% (5 ml or 1 teaspoon) of cold water. Add remaining salt, Cure #1 and spices during this step.
Mixing	Mix everything together.
Stuffing	Stuff firmly into 32-36 mm hog casings.
Conditioning	Hang for 120 min at room temperature.
Smoking	Apply hot smoke 45-80° C (113-176° F) for 90 min until casings develop brown color.
Baking	Bake in smokehouse (thin smoke allowed) at 85° C (185° F) for 30 min until sausages reach 68-72° C (154-160° F) internal temperature.
Cooling	Cool in air to 15° C (59° F) or lower temperature.

Gniezno Sausage

(Kiełbasa gnieźnieńska)

The name of the sausage implies that it originated in Gniezno, the first Polish capital and the scene of coronation of many Polish Kings.

Pork class II, 500 g (1.10 lb)
Veal class II, 500 g (1.10 lb)

I*ngredients per 1 kg (2.2 lb.) of meat*

Salt, 18 g (3 tsp)
Cure # 1, 2.5 g (1/2 tsp)
Pepper, 2.0 g (1 tsp)
White mustard seeds, 0.5 g (1/4 tsp)
Garlic, 2.5 g (1 clove)

Curing	Cure meat, see page 44.
Grinding	Grind pork class II through 8 mm plate. Grind veal class II through 2 mm plate and then emulsify.
Emulsifying	Using bowl cutter (food processor) emulsify veal adding 30 % ice or cold water. Add spices when emulsifying.
Mixing	Mix pork class II with emulsified meat.
Stuffing	Stuff into beef middles of any size. Sausage in straight links, 30-35 cm (12-14 ") long. The ends tied with a twine, hanging loop (10-12 cm, 4-5") on one end.
Conditioning	For 30-60 min.
Smoking	With hot smoke for 90-110 min.
Cooking	In water at 72-75° C (161-167° F) for 30-40 min the sausages reach 68-70° C (154-158° F) internal temperature.
Cooling	Immerse (or shower) in cold water to cool sausages to 12° C (53° F) or lower. Keep refrigerated.

The original recipe allowed replacing the natural pepper with a double amount of herbal pepper (white mustard seed, caraway, marjoram, chili, hot and sweet paprika, bay leaf).

Ham Sausage

(Kiełbasa szynkowa)

Called ham sausage because solid chunks of ham cubes are imbedded in its texture.

Pork class I, 850 g (1.87 lb)
Pork class III, 150 g (0.33 lb)

Ingredients per 1 kg (2.2 lb.) of meat

Salt, 18 g (3 tsp)
Cure # 1, 2.5 g (1/2 tsp)
Pepper, 2.0 g (1 tsp)
Coriander, 0.5 g (1/4 tsp)
Nutmeg, 0.5 g
Sugar, 1.0 g

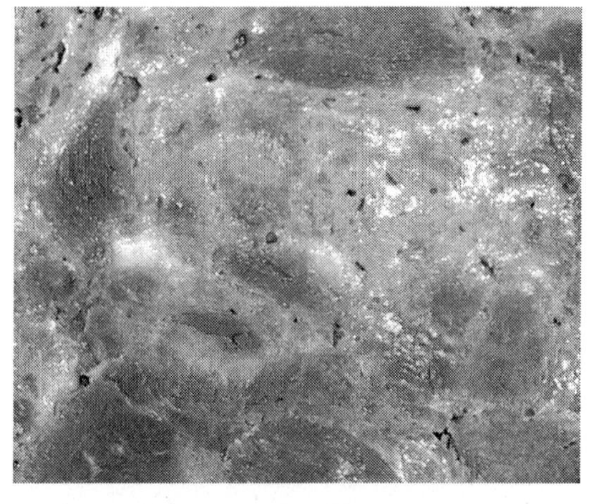

Photo 7.3 Visible chunks of lean meat.
Photo by Szczepan

Curing Cure meat. *Pork class I must come from hams and butts only.*

Grinding Pork class I cut manually into 4-5 cm (1 1/5 - 2”) pieces. Pork class III ground through 2 mm plate and emulsified.

Emulsifying Using bowl cutter (food processor) emulsify pork class III adding 50-60 % ice or cold water. Add spices when emulsifying.

Mixing Mix pork class I until sticky, then add emulsified meat and mix everything well together.

Stuffing Stuff casings into beef bungs or 100-120 mm synthetic fibrous casings. Sausage in 35-60 cm (14-24”) lengths and laced up with twine. Two loops lengthwise and loops across the bung every 4-6 cm (1.5-2 1/4”). Fibrous casings: 35 cm-40 cm (14-16”) lengths and laced up with twine. Two loops lengthwise and loops across the casings every 4-5 cm (1.5-2”).The ends tied up with twine, hanging loop 10-12 cm (4-5”) on one end.

Conditioning For 1-2 hours.

Smoking With hot smoke for 120-150 min until casings develop light brown color with a pink tint.

Cooking In water at 72-75° C (161-167° F) for 80-110 min until sausages reach 68-70° C (154-158° F) internal temperature.

Cooling Immerse (or shower) in cold water to cool sausages to 12° C (53° F) or lower. Keep refrigerated.

Kolska

(Kiełbasa kolska)

Pork class I, 650 g (1.43 lb)
Pork class II, 200 g (0.44 lb)
Pork class III, 150 g (0.33 lb)

Ingredients per 1 kg (2.2 lb) of meat

Salt, 18 g (3 tsp)
Cure #1, 2.5 g (1/2 tsp)
Pepper, 2.0 g (1 tsp)
Sweet paprika, 2.5 g (1 tsp)
Garlic, 3.0 g (1 clove)

Curing	Cut pork into 25 mm (1") cubes (keep pork classes separately). Mix with salt and Cure #1, estimate the amounts proportionally. Pack tightly in containers, cover with cloth and hold in refrigerator for 3 days.
Grinding	Pork class I - leave the way it is (25 mm cubes). Pork class II - 13 mm plate. Pork class III - 3 mm plate.
Emulsifying	In food processor emulsify pork class III adding 50% (60 ml, 2 oz fl) of cold water. Add sugar and spices during this step.
Mixing	Mix pork class I and II until sticky. Add emulsified meat and mix all together.
Stuffing	Stuff firmly into beef middles or 75-80 mm synthetic fibrous casings. Make links 40-45 cm (16-18") long, hanging loop at one end.
Conditioning	Hang for 30 min at room temperature.
Smoking	Apply hot smoke 45-80° C (113-176° F) for 110-130 minutes.
Cooking	Cook in water at 80° C (176° F) until sausages reach 68-70° C (154-158° F) internal temperature.
Cooling	Immerse for 15 min in cold water. Wipe off moisture and dry briefly.
Cooling	Keep refrigerated.

Krakowska Sausage

(Kiełbasa krakowska)

This sausage has always been one of the top sellers in Poland. The name relates to the city of Krakow, one of the oldest cities in Europe. The middle part of the name "krajana" explains that the meat was manually cut into pieces. If you follow the recipe you will see that the sliced sausage will have visible chunks of meat (2") in it. The reason being that lean pork (class I) was never ground with a grinder. This popular sausage is made in different forms: dry sausage, semi-dry sausage and this version which would be considered as a regular hot smoked sausage.

Pork class I, 450 g (0.99 ;b)
Pork class II, 350 g (0.77 lb)
Pork class III, 100 g (0.22 lb)
Beef class II or I, 100 g (0.22 lb)

Ingredients per 1 kg (2.2 lb.) of meat

Salt, 18 g (3 tsp)
Cure # 1, 2.5 g (1/2 tsp)
White pepper, 2.0 g
Coriander, 0.5 g (1/4 tsp)
Garlic, 2.5 g (1 clove)

Curing Cure meat, see page 44. Solid chunks of meat must be cured for 3 days in order to develop a solid pink color.

Grinding Pork class I cut into 5-6 cm (2") pieces. Pork class II ground through 20 mm (3/4") plate. Pork class III and beef class I or II ground through 2 mm plate and then emulsified.

Emulsifying Using bowl cutter (food processor) emulsify pork class III and beef class I or II adding 40-50 % ice or cold water. Add spices when emulsifying.

Mixing Mix pork class I and class II with emulsified meat.

Stuffing Stuff into 75 mm synthetic fibrous casings. Form 35-40 cm (14-16") links and tie the ends with twine forming a hanging loop on one end.

Conditioning For 30-60 minutes.

Smoking With hot smoke for 110-130 min.

Cooking In water at 72-75° C (161-167° F) for 55-75 min until internal temperature of the meat becomes 68-70° C (154-158° F).

Cooling Immerse (or shower) in cold water to cool sausages to 12° C (53° F) or lower. Keep refrigerated.

The original recipe allowed replacing the natural pepper with a double amount of herbal pepper (white mustard seed, caraway, marjoram, chili, hot and sweet paprika, bay leaf).

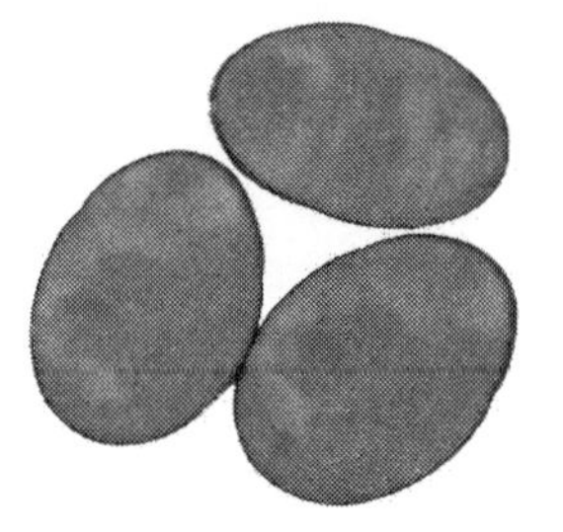

Photo 7.4 and 7.5 Krakowska Sausage. *Photos by Andrzej Piątek "Bagno"*

Krolewiecka

(Kiełbasa królewiecka parzona)

Pork class II, 400 g (0.88 lb)
Beef class I, II or III, 200 g (0.44 lb)
Pork head meat, 200 g (0.44 lb)
Pork skins, 100 g (0.22 lb)
Veal class III, pork class IV, beef class IV, udders, 100 g (0.33 lb)
Beef class I, II or III can be partially or wholly substituted with pork class III.

Ingredients per 1 kg (2.2 lb) of meat

Salt, 18 g (3 tsp)
Cure #1, 2.5 g (1/2 tsp)
Pepper, 1.0 g (1/2 tsp)
Whole mustard seeds, 1.5 g (1-1/2 tsp)
Garlic, 1.5 g (1/2 clove)

Curing	Cure meat, see page 44.
Grinding	Pork class II - 13 mm plate. Beef class I, II or III, pork head meat - 3 mm plate. Pork skins, veal class IV, pork class IV, beef class V, udders - 2-3 mm plate.
Emulsifying	In food processor emulsify ground beef class I, II or III, and pork head meat adding 30% (120 ml, 1/2 cup) of water. Then ground pork skins, veal class IV, pork class IV, beef class V and udders. Add salt, Cure #1 and spices during this step.
Mixing	Mix everything together.
Stuffing	Stuff firmly into beef middles or 65 mm synthetic fibrous casings. Make links 40-45 cm (16-18") long, hanging loop at one end.
Conditioning	Hang for 30-60 min at room temperature.
Smoking	Apply hot smoke for 100-120 minutes.
Cooking	Cook in water at 72-75° C (160-167° F) for 50-70 min until sausages reach 68-70° C (154-158° F) internal temperature.
Cooling	Cool in for 15 minutes in cold water. Wipe off moisture and refrigerate.

Lemon Sausage

(Kiełbasa Cytrynowa)

It is called lemon flavored sausage because very often the rind of the lemon was ground and added to meat for flavoring or citric acid powder was used for the same purpose.

Pork class I, 450 g
Pork class II, 450 g
Pork class III, 50 g (0.11 g)
Beef class I or II, 50 g (0.11 g)

Ingredients per 1 kg (2.2 lb.) of meat

Salt, 18 g (3 tsp)
Cure # 1, 2.5 g (1/2 tsp)
Pepper, 2.0 g (1 tsp)
Nutmeg, 0.5 g (1/2 tsp)
Sugar, 2.0 g (1/2 tsp)

Curing Cure meat, see page 44.

Grinding Pork class I or II diced into 3-4 cm (1 1/4 - 1 1/5") pieces. Pork class III and beef class I or II ground through 2 mm plate.

Emulsifying Using bowl cutter (food processor) emulsify pork class III and beef class I or II adding 40-50 % ice or cold water. Add spices when emulsifying.

Mixing Mix pork class I and class II until sticky, then add emulsified meat and mix everything well together.

Stuffing Stuff into beef bungs or 85-95 mm synthetic fibrous casings. Beef bungs: 35-60 cm (14-24") lengths and laced up with twine. Two loops lengthwise and loops across the bung every 4-6 cm (1.5-2 1/4"). Fibrous casings: 35 cm-40 cm (14-16") lengths and laced up with twine. Two loops lengthwise and loops across the casings every 4-5 cm (1.5-2"). The ends tied up with twine, hanging loop 10-12 cm (4-5") on one end.

Conditioning For 1-2 hours.

Smoking With hot smoke for 130-160 min.

Cooking In water at 72-75°C (161-167°F) for 90-120 min until the sausages reach 68-70°C (154-158°F) internal temperature.

Cooling Immerse (or shower) in cold water to cool sausages to 12° C (53° F) or lower. Keep refrigerated.

Pork class III and beef class II or I may be substituted with veal class II. Pork class I may be substituted with pork class II. Pork class III may be substituted with beef or veal.

Lubuska

(Kiełbasa lubuska)

Pork class I, 300 g (0.66 lb)
Pork class II, 500 g (1.10 lb)
Beef class I, no connective tissue, 200 g (0.44 lb)

Ingredients per 1 kg (2.2 lb) of meat

Salt, 18 g (3 tsp)
Cure #1, 2.5 g (1/2 tsp)
Pepper, 1.5 g (1 tsp)
Marjoram, 0.5 g (1/4 tsp)
Sugar, 1.0 g (1/5 tsp)
Garlic, 1.5 g (1/2 clove)

Curing	Cure meat, see page 44.
Grinding	Pork class I - 8 mm plate. Pork class II - 8 mm plate. Beef class I - 3 mm plate.
Mixing	Mix meats and spices together until sticky.
Stuffing	Stuff firmly into 32-36 mm hog casings. Form 25-30 cm (12-14”) links leaving them in a continuous coil.
Conditioning	Hang for 60 min at room temperature.
Smoking	Apply hot smoke 45-80° C (113-176° F) for 80 min until casings develop brown color.
Cooking	Cook in water at 72-75° C (160-167° F) for 30-60 min until sausages reach 68-72° C (154-160° F) internal temperature.
Cooling	Cool in air to 30° C (86° F) internal temperature or immerse sausages in cold water for 20 minutes. Wipe off moisture. Cool to 10° C (50° F) and divide into pairs. Keep refrigerated.

Opolska

(Kiełbasa opolska)

The sausage comes from Opole region. The city of Opole is known for the national music festival.

Pork class I, 200 g (0.44 lb)
Pork class II, 190 g (0.42 lb)
Beef class I, 100 g (0.22 lb)
Beef class II, 200 g (0.44 lb)
Pork class III, 90 g (0.19 lb)
Hard fat trimmings, 100 g (0.22 lb)
Blood, 120 g (0.26 lb)

Ingredients per 1 kg (2.2 lb) of meat

Salt, 18 g (3 tsp)
Cure #1, 2.5 g (1/2 tsp)
Pepper, 1.5 g (1 tsp)
Garlic, 1.0 g (1/3 clove)
Cardamon, 0.3 g (1/5 tsp)

Curing Cure meat, see page 44.

Grinding Pork class I - 13 mm plate.
Pork class II - 8 mm plate.
Beef class I or II - 3 mm plate.
Pork class III - 3 mm plate
Fat - 8 mm plate.

Emulsifying Using food processor emulsify beef class I or II and pork class III adding 15% (30 ml or 1 oz fl) of cold water. Add, Cure #1 and spices during this step.

Mixing Mix everything together.

Stuffing Stuff firmly into large diameter natural or synthetic casings. Form 25-30 cm (12-14") links, tie the ends and make hanging loop.

Conditioning Hang for 60 min at room temperature.

Smoking Apply hot smoke 45-80° C (113-176° F) for 60 min until casings develop brown color.

Cooking Cook in water at 72-75° C (160-167° F) for 30-60 min until sausages reach 68-72° C (154-160° F) internal temperature.

Cooling Cool in cold water for 20 minutes. Keep refrigerated.

Note Blood was added due to shortage of meat. You can use pork meat instead.

Ordinary Sausage

(Kiełbasa zwyczajna)

A typical no frills all pork sausage.

Pork class I, 350 g (0.77 lb)
Pork class II, 400 g (0.88 lb)
Pork class III, 250 g (0.55 lb)

Ingredients per 1 kg (2.2 lb.) of meat

Salt, 18 g (3 tsp)
Pepper, 2.0 g (1 tsp)
Coriander, 0.5 g (1/2 tsp)
Garlic, 3.0 g (1 clove)
Marjoram may be added at 0.5 g (optional).

Curing Cure meat, see page 44.

Grinding Pork class I ground through 13 mm plate. Pork class II ground through 10 mm plate. Pork class III ground through 2 mm plate and emulsified.

Emulsifying Emulsify pork class III in bowl cutter (food processor) adding 35-45% ice or cold water. Add remaining ingredients when emulsifying.

Mixing Mix pork class I and pork class II with emulsified meat.

Stuffing Stuff into 32 mm hog casings. Form 12-14 cm (5-6") links leaving them in a continuous coil.

Conditioning For 30-60 minutes.

Smoking With hot smoke for 100-120 min until casings become light brown.

Cooking In water at 70-72° C (158-161° F) for 20-30 min until the sausages reach 68-70° C (154-158° F) internal temperature.

Cooling Immerse (or shower) in cold water to cool sausages to 12° C (53° F) or lower. Keep refrigerated.

Podlaska

(Kiełbasa podlaska)

Pork class I, 200 g (0.44 lb)
Pork class II, 500 g (1.10 lb)
Beef class I or II with connective tissue, 250 g (0.55 lb)
Pork hard fat trimmings, 50 g (0.11 lb)

Ingredients per 1 kg (2.2 lb) of meat

Salt, 18 g (3 tsp)
Cure #1, 2.5 g (1/2 tsp)
Pepper, 1.5 g (1 tsp)
Garlic, 1.5 g (1/2 clove)

Curing	Cure meat, see page 44.
Grinding	Pork class I - 13 mm plate. Pork class II - 8 mm plate. Beef class I or II - 3 mm plate. Fat - 8 mm plate.
Emulsifying	Using food processor emulsify beef class I or II adding 15% (30 ml or 1 oz fl) of cold water. Add, Cure #1 and spices during this step.
Mixing	Mix everything together.
Stuffing	Stuff firmly into 32-36 mm hog casings. Form 25-30 cm (12-14") links leaving them in a continuous coil.
Conditioning	Hang for 60 min at room temperature.
Smoking	Apply hot smoke 45-80° C (113-176° F) for 80 min until casings develop brown color.
Cooking	Cook in water at 72-75° C (160-167° F) for 30-60 min until sausages reach 68-72° C (154-160° F) internal temperature.
Cooling	Cool in air to 30° C (86° F) internal temperature or immerse sausages in cold water for 20 minutes. Wipe off moisture. Cool to 10° C (50° F) and divide into pairs. Keep refrigerated.

Popular

(Kiełbasa popularna)

Pork class II, 600 g (1.32 lb)
Pork class III, 100 g (0.22 lb)
Beef class II, 300 g (0.66 lb)

Ingredients per 1 kg (2.2 lb) of meat

Salt, 20 g (3-1/3 tsp)
Cure #1, 2.5 g (1/2 tsp)
Pepper, 2.0 g (1 tsp)
Garlic, 1.5 g (1/2 clove)

Curing	Cure meat, see page 44.
Grinding	Pork class II - 8 mm plate. Pork class III - 2-3 mm plate. Beef class II - 2-3 mm plate.
Emulsifying	In food processor emulsify pork class III and beef class II adding 20-25% (90 ml, 3 oz fl) of cold water. Add Cure #1 and spices during this step.
Mixing	Mix pork class II with salt until sticky. Add emulsified meats and mix everything together.
Stuffing	Stuff firmly into beef rounds or 36-40 mm hog casings. Make rings and tie the ends together.
Conditioning	Hang for 60 min at room temperature.
Smoking	Apply hot smoke 45-80° C (113-176° F) for 110-130 minutes.
Cooking	Cook in water at 72-75° C (160-167° F) for 25-35 min.
Cooling	Cool in cold water to 12° C (53° F).
Smoking	Smoke with cold smoke 22° C (71° F) for 12 hours OR with warm smoke 24-32° C (75-90° F) for 6 hours.
Cooling	Cool in air to 8-10° C (46-50° F).

Ring Sausage

(Kiełbasa wiankowa)

Pork class I, 100 g (0.22 lb)
Pork class II, 600 g (1.32 lb)
Beef class I (no connective tissue), 100 g (0.22 lb)
Beef class II with connective tissue, 200 g (0.44 lb)

Ingredients per 1 kg (2.2 lb) of meat

Salt, 20 g (3-1/3 tsp)
Cure #1, 2.5 g (1/2 tsp)
Pepper, 2.0 g (1 tsp)
Paprika, 0.5 g (1/4 tsp)
Marjoram, 0. 5 g (1/4 tsp)
Garlic, 1.5 g (1/2 clove)

Curing	Cut pork class I into 20 mm (3/4") pieces. Mix with 6 g salt and 1/5 Cure #1. Pack tightly in a container, cover with cloth and hold in refrigerator for 2 days.
Grinding	Cut pork class I into 20 mm (3/4") cubes. Pork class II - 10 mm Beef class I without connective tissue - 10 mm plate. Beef class II with connective tissue - 2-3 mm
Emulsifying	In food processor emulsify beef class II adding 15-20% (30 ml, 1 oz fl) of cold water. Add Cure #1 and spices during this step.
Mixing	Mix/knead pork class I and beef class II with remaining salt until sticky. Add emulsified meat and mix everything together.
Stuffing	Stuff firmly into beef runners or 36-40 mm hog casings.
Conditioning	Hang for 60 min at room temperature.
Smoking	Apply hot smoke 45-80° C (113-176° F) for 110-130 minutes until casings become brown with red tint.
Cooking	Cook in water at 80-85° C (176-185° F) for 25-35 min until sausages reach 68-70° C (154-158° F) internal temperature.
Drying	Dry in air for 12 hours at 18° C (64° F) or lower.
Smoking	Apply cold smoke for 48 hours, then warm smoke 24-32° C (75-90° F) for 24 hours.
Cooling	Cool in air to 12° C (53° F) or lower.

Silesian Sausage
(Kiełbasa śląska)

The name comes from Silesia (Śląsk), highly industrial area of Poland.

Pork class I, 350 g
Pork class II, 400 g
Pork class III, 250 g

Ingredients per 1 kg (2.2 lb.) of meat

Salt, 18 g (3 tsp)
Cure #1, 2.5 g (1/2 tsp)
Pepper, 2.0 g (1 tsp)
Coriander, 0.5 g (1/4 tsp)
Garlic, 2.5 g (1 clove)
Marjoram may be added at 0.5 g (optional).

Curing	Cure meat, see page 44.
Grinding	Pork class I ground through 13 mm plate. Pork class II ground through 10 mm plate. Pork class III ground through 2 mm plate and emulsified.
Emulsifying	In a bowl cutter (food processor) emulsify pork class III adding 35-45% ice or cold water. Add spices when emulsifying.
Mixing	Mix pork class I and pork class II with emulsified meat.
Stuffing	Stuff into 32 mm hog casings. Form 12-14 cm (5-6") links leaving them in a continuous coil.
Conditioning	For 30-60 minutes.
Smoking	With hot smoke for 100-120 min until casings develop light brown color.
Cooking	Poach sausages in water at 70-72°C (158-161°F) for 20-30 min until the sausages reaches 68-70° C (154-158° F) temperature inside.
Cooling	Immerse (or shower) in cold water to cool sausages to 12° C (53° F) or lower. Keep refrigerated.

Sluzewiecka

(Kiełbasa służewiecka parzona)

Pork class II, 900 g (1.98 lb)
Beef class II or III, 100 g (0.22 lb)

Ingredients per 1 kg (2.2 lb) of meat

Salt, 18 g (3 tsp)
Cure #1, 2.5 g (1/2 tsp)
Pepper, 1.0 g (1/2 tsp)
Coriander, 0.5 g (1/4 tsp)
Garlic, 1.5 g (1/2 clove)

Curing	Cure meat, see page 44.
Grinding	Pork class II - 13 mm plate. Beef class II or III - 3 mm plate.
Emulsifying	In food processor emulsify adding 50-60% (50 ml, 2 oz fl) of cold water. Add salt, Cure #1 and spices during this step.
Mixing	Mix everything together.
Stuffing	Stuff firmly into beef middles or 65 mm synthetic fibrous casings. Make links 40-45 cm (16-18") long, hanging loop at one end.
Conditioning	Hang for 30-60 min at room temperature.
Smoking	Apply hot smoke for 110-130 minutes.
Cooking	Cook in water at 72-75° C (160-167° F) for 50-70 min until sausages reach 68-70° C (154-158° F) internal temperature.
Cooling	Cool in for 15 minutes in cold water. Wipe off moisture and refrigerate.

Starowiejska

(Kiełbasa starowiejska)

Pork class I, 200 g (0.44 lb)
Pork class II, 600 g (1.32 lb)
Pork class III, 200 g (0.44 lb)

Ingredients per 1 kg (2.2 lb) of meat

Salt, 18 g (3 tsp)
Cure #1, 2.5 g (1/2 tsp)
Pepper, 3.0 g (1-1/2 tsp)
Garlic, 3.5 g (1 clove)
Mustard seeds, ground, 1.0 g (1/2 tsp)
Sugar, 1.0 g (1/5 tsp)

Curing Cure meat, see page 44.

Grinding Pork class I - 12 mm plate.
Pork class II - 12 mm plate.
Pork class III with connective tissue - 2-3 mm plate.

Emulsifying In food processor emulsify pork class III adding 15-20% (30 ml, 1 oz fl) of cold water. Add Cure #1 and spices during this step.

Mixing Mix everything together.

Stuffing Stuff firmly into 32-36 mm hog casings.

Conditioning Hang for 60 min at room temperature.

Smoking Apply hot smoke 45-80° C (113-176° F) for 110-130 minutes until casings become brown with red tint.

Cooking Cook in water at 80-85° C (176-185° F) for 25-35 min until sausages reach 68-70° C (154-158° F) internal temperature.

Cooling Cool in air to 30° C (86° F) internal temperature or immerse sausages in cold water for 20 minutes. Wipe off moisture. Cool to 10° C (50° F). Keep refrigerated.

Suwalska

(Kiełbasa suwalska)

Pork class I, 600 g (0.66 lb)
Pork class II, 210 g (0.46 lb)
Pork class III, 50 g (0.11 lb)
Beef class I with connective tissue, 50 g (0.11 lb)
Blood, 90 g (0.20 lb)

Ingredients per 1 kg (2.2 lb) of meat

Salt, 18 g (3 tsp)
Cure #1, 2.5 g (1/2 tsp)
Pepper, 1.5 g (1 tsp)
Nutmeg, 0.5 g (1/4 tsp)
Sugar, 1.5 g (1/4 tsp)

Curing Cure meat, see page 44.

Grinding Pork class I - 13 mm plate.
Pork class II - 8 mm plate.
Beef class I or II - 3 mm plate.
Pork class III - 3 mm plate.
Fat - 8 mm plate.

Emulsifying Using food processor emulsify beef class I and pork class III adding 15% (30 ml or 1 oz fl) of cold water. Add Cure #1 and spices during this step.

Mixing Mix everything together.

Stuffing Stuff firmly into large diameter natural or synthetic casings. Form 25-30 cm (12-14") links, tie the ends and make hanging loop.

Conditioning Hang for 60 min at room temperature.

Smoking Apply hot smoke 45-80° C (113-176° F) for 60 min until casings develop brown color.

Cooking Cook in water at 72-75° C (160-167° F) for 30-60 min until sausages reach 68-72° C (154-160° F) internal temperature.

Cooling Cool in cold water for 20 minutes. Keep refrigerated.

Note Blood was added due to shortage of meat. You can use pork meat instead.

Tomaszowska Sausage
(Kiełbasa tomaszowska)

The sausage name implies that it originated in the city of Tomaszow.

Pork class II, 150 g (0.33 lb)
Beef class I or II (no connective tissue), 150 g (0.33
Beef class II or III (with connective tissues), 400 g (0.88 lb)
Skinless jowls, 150 g (0.33 lb)
Pork, veal or beef hearts, 150 g (0.33 lb)

I*ngredients per 1 kg (2.2 lb.) of meat*

Salt, 18 g (3 tsp)
Cure # 1, 2.5 g (1/2 tsp)
Pepper, 1.5 g (1 tsp)
Marjoram, 0.5 g (1/2 tsp)
Caraway, 1.0 g (1 tsp)
Garlic, 3.0 g (1 clove)
Maggi *, 1/2 tsp
Maggi® is the internationally famous cooking sauce.

The original recipe allowed replacing the natural pepper with a double amount of herbal pepper (white mustard seed, caraway, marjoram, chili, hot and sweet paprika, bay leaf).

Curing	Cure meat, see page 44.
Grinding	Pork class II, beef class I or II (no connective tissue) and hearts through 10 mm plate. Beef class II or class III (with connective tissue) through 2 mm plate. Jowls through 5 mm plate.
Emulsifying	Using food processor emulsify beef class III or II (with connective tissue) adding 30-40% of ice or cold water. Add ground dewlap and spices at this step.
Mixing	Mix ground hearts with beef class I or II (without connective tissue). Add pork class II, then emulsified mixture and mix everything well together.
Stuffing	Stuff into 60 mm synthetic fibrous casings. Sausage in straight links, 40-45 cm (16-18 ") long. The ends tied with a twine, hanging loop (10-12 cm, 4-5") on one end.
Conditioning	For 2-3 hours.
Smoking	With hot smoke for 80-100 min.
Cooking	In water at 72-75° C (161-167° F) for 50-70 min until the sausages reach 68-70° C (154-158° F) internal temperature.
Cooling	Immerse (or shower) in cold water to cool sausages to 12° C (53° F) or lower. Keep refrigerated.

Vavel Sausage

(Kiełbasa wawelska)

Pork class I, 650 g (1.43 lb)
Beef class I (with connective tissue), 250 g (0.33 lb)
Hard fat trimmings, 100 g (0.22 lb)

Ingredients per 1 kg (2.2 lb) of meat

Salt, 20 g (3-1/3 tsp)
Cure #1, 2.5 g (1/2 tsp)
Pepper, 2.0 g (1 tsp)
Allspice, 0.5 g (1/4 tsp)
Nutmeg, 0.5 g (1/4 tsp)
Garlic, 1.5 g (1/2 clove)

Curing	Cut pork class I into 50 mm (2”) pieces. Mix with 12 g salt and 1/2 Cure #1. Pack tightly in a container, cover with cloth and hold in refrigerator for 3 days. This step ensures solid pink color of a chunk of meat.
Grinding	Cut pork class I into 20 mm (3/4”) cubes. Beef class I with connective tissue - 2-3 mm plate. Fat trimmings - 8 mm plate.
Emulsifying	In food processor emulsify beef class I adding 20-25% (60 ml, 2 oz fl) of cold water. Add remaining salt, Cure #1 and spices during this step.
Mixing	Mix/knead pork class I until sticky. Add emulsified meat and mix everything together.
Stuffing	Stuff firmly into beef middles or 50-65 mm synthetic fibrous casings.
Conditioning	Hang for 60 min at room temperature.
Smoking	Apply hot smoke 45-80° C (113-176° F) for 110-120 minutes. Bake in smokehouse at 80-90° C (176-194° F) for 40-60 min (thin smoke allowed) until sausages develop brown color and reach 68-70° C (154-158° F) internal temperature.
Cooling	Cool in air to 18° C (64° F).
Smoking	Apply warm smoke 24-32 C (75-90 F) for 2-3 hours.
Cooling	Cool in air to 12° C (53° F) or lower.

Warsaw Sausage

(Kiełbasa warszawska)

Pork class I, 650 g (1.43 lb)
Beef class I (with connective tissue), 100 g (0.22 lb)
Pork class III, 100 g (0.22 lb)
Hard fat trimmings, 150 g (0.33 lb)

Ingredients per 1 kg (2.2 lb) of meat

Salt, 18 g (3 tsp)
Pepper, 2.5 g (1 tsp)
Sweet paprika, 0.5 g (1/4 tsp)
Coriander, 0.5 g (1/4 tsp)

Curing Cut pork class I into 50 mm (2") pieces. Mix with 12 g salt and 1/2 Cure #1. Pack tightly in a container, cover with cloth and hold in refrigerator for 3 days. This step ensures solid pink color of a chunk of meat.

Grinding Cut pork class I into 20 mm (3/4") cubes.
Pork class III - 2-3 mm plate.
Beef class II - 2-3 mm plate.
Fat trimmings - 8 mm plate.

Emulsifying In food processor emulsify pork class III and beef class I adding 40% (80 ml, 2.5 oz fl) of cold water. Add remaining salt, Cure #1 and spices during this step.

Mixing Mix everything together.

Stuffing Stuff firmly into beef middles or 75-80 mm synthetic fibrous casings.

Conditioning Hang for 30 min at room temperature.

Smoking Apply hot smoke 45-60° C (113-140° F) for 110-130 minutes.

Cooking Cook in water at 80-85° C (176-185° F) for 25-35 min until sausages reach 68-70° C (154-158° F) internal temperature.

Cooling Cool in cold water for 20 min. Dry in air and keep refrigerated.

Chapter 8

Hot Smoked Sausages, Finely Ground (Emulsified), With Limited Shelf Life

Meats are either ground and then emulsified in bowl cutters, or the entire operation is performed in a bowl cutter until a fine paste is obtained. Although the speed of the rotating bowl and the speed of rotating knives are adjustable, this operation generates a significant amount of heat. This heat will dull the knives and will start cooking the meat. To eliminate this danger about 30% of crushed ice or cold water is added into the meat.

The cuts are clean and the protein structure opens which permits the introduction of large amounts of water. Commercially prepared water binding solutions which contain phosphates are introduced in order to hold this water inside of the meat. This results in much higher profits for the manufacturer as the customer is buying a significant amount of water. There is no sense in complaining as this is legal. The final product has a consistency of a paste and will effectively hide any ingredient that was added. Products like bologna, hot dogs, frankfurters and wieners are all made by emulsifying the meat.

It is unlikely that an average home sausage maker will invest in an expensive bowl cutter. He can, however, emulsify meat in a kitchen food processor adding as little water or meat stock as possible. It is strongly recommended to grind the meat first through a fine plate.

- Grind meat through 2 mm (1/8”) plate.
- Emulsify in a food processor adding crushed ice or cold water (follow recipe).

You can emulsify meats using a grinder, after all not every butcher owns a meat cutter. Grind meat with a 2-3 mm (1/16”) plate, refrigerate or place in a freezer for 30 minutes then grind again. This can be done 2-3 times. The advantage of this method is that it can be done without adding crushed ice or cold water so the meat’s flavor is not diluted.

Emulsified sausages are ground and emulsified until a fine paste is obtained. Then they are processed in the same way as other sausages. Hot dog, frankfurter, mortadela or bologna are examples of sausages that belong to this group.
It may come as a surprise to many but a hot dog or frankfurter is a lightly smoked product. In order to keep costs down, commercial manufacturers spray sausages with atomized liquid smoke. You may say that sausages go into the shower room. After smoking and poaching a sausage in hot water the meat hardens and holds its shape even after removing the cellulose casing. Of course there is no need to do it when using a sheep casing.

There was no way to predict what went into those sausages before, but now with better government control we get a better product and certain parts like brains or lungs are not permitted anymore.

Photo 8.1 Emulsified meat on top of ground meat that has already been mixed with spices.

Photo by Szczepan

Bacon Sausage

(Kiełbasa boczkowa)

Pork belly gives the sausage its name. When cured and smoked it becomes bacon and imparts a delicious flavor to the sausage.

Beef class II or I, 250 g (0.55 lb)
Beef class I or II, (no connective tissue), 150 g (0.33 lb)
Pork class III, 250 g (0.55 lb)
Pork belly, 250 g (0.55 lb)
Skinless jowls, 100 g (0.22 lb)

Ingredients per 1 kg (2.2 lb.) of meat

Salt, 18 g (3 tsp)
Cure # 1, 2.0 g (3/8 tsp)
Pepper, 2.0 g (1 tsp)
Paprika, 1.0 kg (1/2 tsp)
Coriander, 0.5 g (1/4 tsp)
Ginger, 0.5 g (1/4 tsp)
Garlic, 3.5 g (1 clove)
Sugar, 1.0 g (1/5 tsp)

Curing Cure meat, see page 44.

Grinding Grind beef class II or I, pork class III and jowls through 2 mm plate and then emulsify. Beef class I or II (without connective tissue) ground through 5 mm plate. Belly meat diced into 15 mm (½") cubes.

Emulsifying Using bowl cutter (food processor) emulsify beef class I or II (with connective tissue) and pork class III adding 30% of ice or cold water. Add ground jowls and spices. Continue emulsifying until thoroughly mixed.

Mixing Mix beef class I or II (without sinews) with emulsified mixture, then add diced belly, spices and mix everything together.

Stuffing Stuff into 70 mm synthetic fibrous or cellulose casings and tie the ends with twine. Straight sausage links 35-40 cm (14-16") long, 10 cm (4-5") hanging loop on one end.

Conditioning Hang for 2-3 hours at room temperature.

Smoking With hot smoke for 100 min.

Cooking Cook in water at 72-75° C (161-167° F) for 80 min until sausages reach 68-70° C (154-158° F) internal temperature.

Cooling Immerse (or shower) in cold water to cool sausages to 12° C (53° F) or lower. Keep refrigerated.

Bytomska Sausage

(Kiełbasa bytomska)

This sausage recipe originates in the city of Bytom which lies in the southern part of Poland.

Beef class I (connective tissue allowed), 750 g (1.65 lb)
Beef class III, 150 g (0.33 lb)
Hard fat trimmings, 100 g (0.22 lb)

Ingredients per 1 kg (2.2 lb) of meat

Salt, 18 g (3 tsp)
Cure #1, 2.5 g (1/2 tsp)
Pepper, 1.5 g (1-1/2 tsp)
Coriander, 0.5 g (1/4 tsp)
Garlic, 1.5 g (1/2 clove)

Curing	Cure meat, see page 44.
Grinding	Beef class I and fat ground through 6 mm plate. Keep separate.
Emulsifying	Using food processor emulsify beef class III adding 50 ml (3 tablespoons) of cold water. Add spices during this step.
Mixing	Mix ground beef until sticky. Add emulsified mixture and ground fat and mix everything well together.
Stuffing	Stuff into 36 mm hog casings.
Conditioning	Hang at room temperature for 1-2 hours.
Smoking	With hot smoke for 1-2 hours.
Cooking	Immerse in water at 80° C (176° F) and cook until sausages reach 68-70° C (154-158° F) internal temperature.
Cooling	Cool sausages for 15 minutes in cold water and pat dry. Keep refrigerated.

Mortadella

(Mortadela)

Mortadela has its roots in the Italian city of Bologna. The sausage was made popular by Italian immigrants settling in many parts of the world and it became known in Spanish countries as "Mortadela", in the USA as "Bologna", Iran as "Martadella" and in Poland as "Mortadela". Polish Mortadela like Italian original and Spanish versions is made with visible cubes of fat inside.
It is often served by dipping it in egg, then covering both sides with bread crumbs and frying in oil or butter on a frying pan.

Pork class III, 550 g (1.21 lb)
Beef class II or I, 250 g (0.55 lb)
Back fat, 100 g (0.22 lb)
Fat trimmings or skinless jowls, 100 g (0.22 lb)

I*ngredients per 1 kg (2.2 lb.) of meat*

Salt, 18 g (3 tsp)
Cure # 1, 2.5 g (1/2 tsp)
Pepper, 1.5 g (1 tsp)
Nutmeg or mace, 0.5 g (1/2 tsp)
White mustard seeds, whole, 1.0 g (1/2 tsp)
Sugar, 2.0 g (1/2 tsp)

The original recipe allowed substituting the natural pepper with a double amount of herbal pepper (white mustard seed, caraway, marjoram, chili, hot and sweet paprika, bay leaf). Nutmeg may be substituted with white mustard seed. Garlic is optional at 1.5 g (1/2 clove).

Curing Cure meat, see page 44.

Grinding Pork, beef, pieces of fat or jowl, all ground through 2 mm plate and then emulsified. *Dice back fat into 6 mm (¼ ") cubes.*

Emulsifying Emulsify beef class I or II and pork class III adding 30-40% of ice or cold water. Add spices, fat trimmings and jowls. Continue emulsifying until thoroughly mixed.

Mixing Mix diced pieces of fatback with emulsified mixture until fat cubes are evenly distributed.

Stuffing Stuff into 100-120 mm synthetic fibrous or cellulose casings. firmly and tie the ends with twine. Straight sausage links 35-40 cm (14-16"). Laced up with twine: twice lengthwise and every 4-5 cm (1.5-2") across. Both ends tied together with a twine.

Conditioning Hang at room temperature for 30-60 min.

Smoking	With hot smoke for 100-135 min.
Cooking	Cook in water at 72-75° C (161-167° F) for 90-120 min until sausages reach 68-70° C (154-158° F) internal temperature.
Cooling	Immerse (or shower) in cold water to cool sausages to 12° C (53° F) or lower. Keep refrigerated.

Sausage Links

(Kiełbaski porcjowe)

If this sausage were stuffed into smaller diameter casings it would look like an American hot dog. The only other difference is that American hot dog is a skinless sausage. Served hot by boiling briefly in hot water.

Pork class III, 200 g (0.44 lb)
Beef class II or I, 500 g (1.10 lb)
Fat trimmings, 300 g (0.66 lb)

Ingredients per 1 kg (2.2 lb.) of meat

Salt, 18 g (3 tsp)
Cure # 1, 2.0 g (3/8 tsp)
Pepper, 1.5 g (3/4 tsp)
Paprika, 1.0 g (1/2 tsp)
Coriander, 0.5 g (1/4 tsp)
White mustard seeds, whole, 1.0 g (1/2 tsp)
Garlic, 1.5 g (1/2 clove)

The natural pepper may be substituted with a double amount of herbal pepper (white mustard seed, caraway, marjoram, chili, hot and sweet paprika, bay leaf).

Photo 8.2 Sausage links.

Photo by Marcin Klessa vel Oli

Curing Use 2/3 salt for curing meat and 1/3 for salting fat.

Grinding Pork class III, beef class II or I and 2/3 of fat ground through 2 mm plate. Remaining 1/3 of fat diced into 5 mm (¼") cubes.

Emulsifying Emulsify beef class I or II and pork class III adding 30-40% of ice or cold water. Add spices and ground fat. Continue emulsifying until thoroughly mixed.

Mixing Mix diced fat pieces with emulsified mixture.

Stuffing Stuff into 32 mm hog casings. Twist casings to make links about 100 g each. Leave them in a continuous coil.

Conditioning Hang for 15-30 minutes at room temperature.

Smoking With hot smoke for about 90 min until casings develop light brown color.

Cooking In water at 72-75° C (161-167° F) for 20-30 min until sausages reach 68-70° C (154-158° F) internal temperature.

Cooling Immerse (or shower) in cold water to cool sausages 12° C (53° F) or lower. Keep refrigerated.

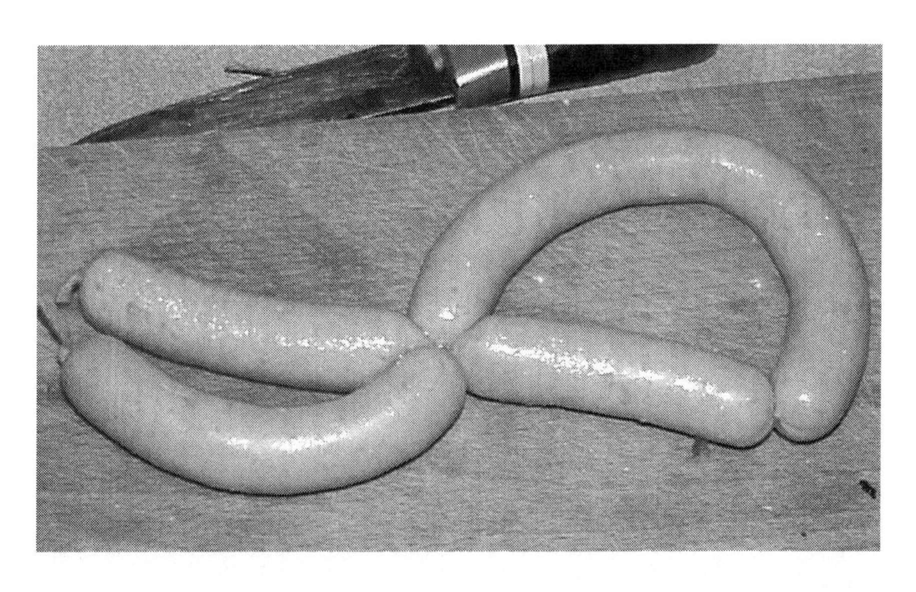

Photo 8.3 Steamed sausage links.

Photo by Marcin Klessa vel Oli

Serdelki
(Serdelki)

Wonderful kind of a large wiener sausage. It is boiled briefly and served hot.

Pork class II, 500 g (1.10 lb)
Beef class II or I, 250 g (0.55 lb)
Fat trimmings, 250 g (0.55 lb)

Ingredients per 1 kg (2.2 lb.) of meat

Salt, 18 g (3 tsp)
Cure # 1, 9 g (1/2 tsp)
Pepper, 1.5 g (1 tsp)
Nutmeg, 0.5 g (1/4 tsp)
Optionally, garlic may be added at 1.0 g (1/3 clove)

Curing Cure meat, see page 44.

Grinding Grind pork class II and fat pieces through 3 mm plate. Grind beef class I or II through 2 mm plate.

Emulsifying Emulsify beef class II or I adding 65-70% ice or cold water. Add spices during this step.

Mixing Mix pork with fat and then add emulsified meat and mix everything well together.

Stuffing Stuff into 36 mm beef rounds or 32-36 mm hog casings. Sausage links 6-7 cm (2¼-2¾") separated with a twine and left in continuous coil.

Conditioning For 15-30 min.

Smoking With hot smoke for 65-85 min until casings will develop light brown color.

Cooking In water at 70-72° C (158-161° F) for 20-35 min until the sausages reach 68-70° C (154-158° F) internal temperature.

Cooling Immerse (or shower) in cold water to cool sausages to 12° C (53° F) or lower. Keep refrigerated.

Serdelowa Sausage
(Kiełbasa serdelowa)

Wiener type sausage but larger. Served hot by poaching briefly in hot water.

Pork class II, 100 g (0.22 lb)
Pork class III, 250 g (0.55 lb)
Beef class I, II or III, 400 g (0.88 lb)
Fat trimmings or skinless jowls, 250 g (0.55 lb)

Ingredients per 1 kg (2.2 lb.) of meat

Salt, 18 g (3 tsp)
Cure # 1, 2.5 g (1/2 tsp)
Pepper, 1.5 g (1 tsp)
Nutmeg or mace, 0.5 g (1/2 tsp)

The natural pepper may be substituted with a double amount of herbal pepper (white mustard seed, caraway, marjoram, chili, hot and sweet paprika, bay leaf). Nutmeg may be substituted with white mustard seed.
1.5 g (1/2 clove) of garlic may be added.

Curing	Cure meat, see page 44.
Grinding	All meats ground through 2 mm plate.
Emulsifying	Using bowl cutter (food processor) emulsify all meats adding a little amount of cold water. Add spices at this stage.
Mixing	*Performed this step if meats were not emulsified.* Mix all meats and spices together. You may add a small amount of ice or cold water.
Stuffing	Stuff into beef rounds of all sizes or 36 mm or larger hog casings forming rings. Sausages formed into 50-70 cm (20-28") rings (outside diameter) and shaped by the beef middle twist characteristics. Both ends tied together with a twine.
Conditioning	Hang at room temperature for 15-30 min.
Smoking	With hot smoke for 75-100 min until casings develop light brown color.
Cooking	In water at 70-72° C (158-161° F) for 25-40 min until sausages reach 68-70° C (154-158° F) internal temperature.
Cooling	Immerse (or shower) in cold water to cool sausages to 12° C (53° F) or lower. Keep refrigerated.

Serdelowa Veal Sausage

(Kiełbasa serdelowa cielęca)

High quality wiener type sausage but much larger. Served hot by poaching briefly in hot water.

Veal class II, 700 g (1.54 lb)
Fat trimmings or skinless jowls, 300 g (0.66 lb)

Ingredients per 1 kg (2.2 lb.) of meat

Salt, 18 g (3 tsp)
Cure # 1, 2.0 g (1/2 tsp)
Pepper, 2.0 g (1 tsp)
Paprika, 2.0 g (1 tsp)
Allspice, 0.5 g (1/4 tsp)

The natural pepper may be substituted with a double amount of herbal pepper (white mustard seed, caraway, marjoram, chili, hot and sweet paprika, bay leaf). 1.5 g (1/2 clove) of garlic may be added.

Curing	Meat curing, see page 44.
Grinding	All meats ground through 2 mm plate.
Emulsifying	Using bowl cutter (food processor) emulsify veal class II adding 35% ice or cold water. Add spices, then fat and continue until thoroughly emulsified.
Stuffing	Stuff into 36 mm hog or 34-40 mm cellulose casings. Hog casings linked every 25-30 cm (10-12") and left in a continuous coil. Cellulose casings - straight links.
Conditioning	Hang for 15-30 minutes at room temperature.
Smoking	With hot smoke for 75-100 min until casings will develop light pink color with a yellow tint.
Cooking	In water at 70-72° C (158-161° F) for 20-30 min until sausages reach 68-70° C (154-158° F) internal temperature.
Cooling	Immerse (or shower) in cold water to cool sausages to 12° C (53° F) or lower. Divide sausage links into pairs. Keep refrigerated.

Steamed Sausage

(Kiełbasa parówkowa)

Those fully cooked small sausages are often served hot for breakfast by boiling them shortly in hot water. Then when placed on a plate they are known to emit steam ("para" in Polish) and hence the name parówka.

Pork class III, 600 g (1.32 lb)
Jowls, skinless 400 g (0.88 lb)

Ingredients per 1 kg (2.2 lb.) of meat

Salt, 18 g (3 tsp)
Cure # 1, 2.0 g (1/2 tsp)
Pepper, 1.0 g (1/2 tsp)
Paprika, 1.0 g (1/2 tsp)
Nutmeg, 0.5 g (1/4 tsp)
Garlic, 1.5 g (1/2 clove)

Curing Cure meat, see page 44.

Grinding Grind all meats through 3 mm plate.

Emulsifying Using food processor emulsify pork class III adding 35-40% ice or cold water. Add spices and ground jowls and emulsify thoroughly.

Stuffing Stuff into 32 mm hog casings. Sausages linked every 12-14 cm (4-5") and left in continuous coil.

Conditioning For 15-30 min.

Smoking With hot smoke for 65-85 min until casings will develop light brown color.

Cooking In water at 70-72° C (158-161° F) for 70 min until the sausages reach 68-70° C (154-158° F) internal temperature.

Cooling Immerse (or shower) in cold water to cool sausages to 12° C (53° F) or lower. Keep refrigerated.

The original recipe allowed replacing the natural pepper with a double amount of herbal pepper (white mustard seed, caraway, marjoram, chili, hot and sweet paprika, bay leaf). Nutmeg may be substituted with white mustard seed.

Steamed Sausage Links
(Parówki)

Those fully cooked small sausages are often served hot for breakfast by boiling them shortly in hot water. Then when placed on a plate they are known to emit steam ("para" in Polish) and since the name parówka.

Pork class I, 200 g (0.44 lb)
Pork class III, 200 g (0.44 lb)
Beef class I, 300 g (0.66 lb)
Jowls, skinless, 300 (0.66 lb)

Ingredients per 1 kg (2.2 lb.) of meat

Salt, 18 g (3 tsp)
Cure # 1, 2.0 g (1/2 tsp)
Pepper, 1.5 g (3/4 tsp)
Paprika, 1.0 g (1/2 tsp)
Nutmeg, 0.5 g (1/4 tsp)
Garlic, 1.5 g (1/2 clove)

Nutmeg nay be substituted with white mustard seed.
Beef class I may be substitutes entirely or in part by veal class II.

Curing Cure meat, see page 44.

Grinding All meats ground through 2 mm plate.

Emulsifying Using food processor emulsify pork class III and beef class I adding 40-50% ice or cold water. Add spices, then fat and continue until thoroughly emulsified.

Stuffing Stuff into 20-22 mm sheep casings. Sausages linked every 12-14 cm (4-5") and left in continuous coil.

Conditioning For 15-30 min.

Smoking With hot smoke for 60 min until casings will develop light brown color.

Cooking In water at 70-72° C (158-161° F) for 10 min until sausages reach 68-70° C (154-158° F) internal temperature.

Cooling Immerse (or shower) in cold water to cool sausages to 12° C (53° F) or lower. Keep refrigerated.

Veal Mortadella

(Mortadela cielęca)

Mortadela has its roots in the Italian city of Bologna. The sausage was made popular by Italian immigrants settling in many parts of the world and it became known in Spanish countries as "Mortadela", in the USA as "Bologna", Iran as "Martadella" and in Poland as "Mortadela". Polish Mortadela like Italian original and Spanish versions is made with visible cubes of fat inside.

Polish Veal Mortadela like American Bologna look different from its Italian original as they exclude fat cubes from the recipe. The fat and veal are emulsified to the consistency of a fine paste and stuffed into a large diameter casing. It is often served by dipping in egg, then covering both sides with bread crumbs and frying in oil or butter on a frying pan.

Veal class II, 800 g (1.76 lb)
Fat trimmings or skinless jowls, 200 g (0.44 lb)

Ingredients per 1 kg (2.2 lb.) of meat

Salt, 18 g (3 tsp)
Cure # 1, 2.5 g (1/2 tsp)
Pepper, 1.5 g (3/4 tsp)
Nutmeg, 0.5 g (1/4 tsp)
White mustard seeds, whole, 1.0 g (1/2 tsp)
Sugar, 2.0 g (1/2 tsp)

The natural pepper may be substituted with a double amount of herbal pepper (white mustard seed, caraway, marjoram, chili, hot and sweet paprika, bay leaf).

Curing	Cure meat, see page 44.
Grinding	Veal and fat ground through 2 mm plate.
Emulsifying	Using bowl cutter (food processor) emulsify veal class II adding 30-40% of ice or cold water. Add spices and fat trimmings or jowls. Continue emulsifying until thoroughly mixed.
Stuffing	Stuff into 100-120 mm synthetic fibrous or cellulose casings. firmly and tie the ends with twine. Straight sausage links 35-40 cm (14-16"). Laced up with twine: twice lengthwise and every 4-5 cm (1.5-2") across. Both ends tied together with a twine.
Conditioning	Hang at room temperature for 30-60 min.
Smoking	With hot smoke for 90-120 min.

Cooking	In water at 72-75° C (161-167° F) for 60-75 min until sausages reach 68-70° C (154-158° F) internal temperature.
Cooling	Immerse (or shower) in cold water to cool sausages to 12° C (53° F) or lower. Keep refrigerated.

Photo 9.1 White sausages.

Chapter 9

Fresh Sausages

Fresh sausages are very easy to make as normally no curing, smoking or cooking is involved. They are kept in a refrigerator and cooked just before consumption. If you study the official list of Polish sausages you will notice that there is only one fresh sausage called "White Sausage." In the USA most sausages are of fresh variety as they will be either fried for breakfast or grilled outside. In Poland sausages were invariably smoked and processed in such a way that they will last long time at room temperature.

Fresh sausages are the easiest to make and you can make any sausage presented in the book (except head cheeses, liver and blood sausages) by stuffing ground meat into casings and storing it in a refrigerator. Then cook the sausage before consumption. Of course the sausage will have a useful life of just a few days. If you look at the recipe for White Sausage you will find out that Polish Smoked Sausage and White Sausage are composed of the same meats and spices and what separates them is a different manufacturing process.

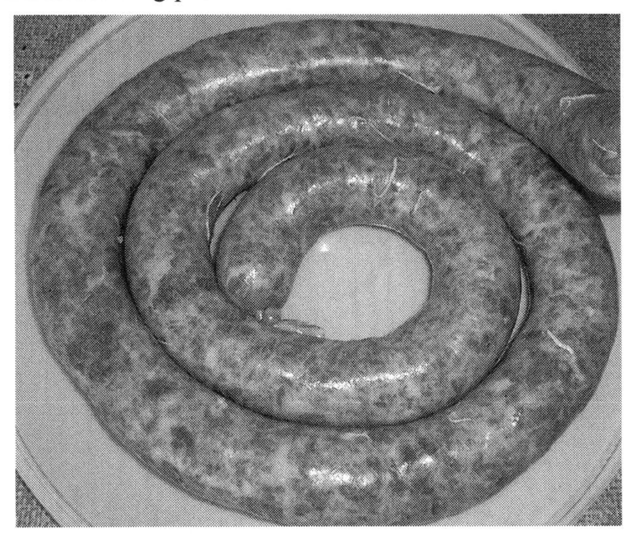

Photo 9.2 White sausage.

White Sausage

(Kiełbasa biała surowa)

During Easter Holiday White Sausage can be found on every dining table and is traditionally served with soup called "zurek". It is also a great sausage for grilling.

Pork class I, 200 g (0.44 lb)
Pork class II, 700 g (1.54 lb)
Beef class I or II, 100 g (0.22 lb)

Ingredients per 1 kg (2.2 lb.) of meat

Salt, 18 g (3 tsp)
Pepper, 2.0 g (1 tsp)
Crushed marjoram, 1.5 g (1 tsp)
Garlic, 3.0 g (1 clove)

Grinding Pork class I ground through 13 mm plate. Pork class II ground through 10 mm plate. Beef class I or II ground through 2 mm plate and then emulsified.

Emulsifying Emulsify beef class I or II adding 45% ice or cold water. Add spices during the process.

Mixing Mix pork class I with pork class II adding 6% of cold water in relation to the weight of meat (pork class I and II) until water is fully absorbed. Add emulsified mixture and mix all well together.

Stuffing Stuff into 32-36 mm hog casings leaving sausage in a continuous coil. The ends tied with butcher's twine.

Conditioning For 15-30 min.

Note This is a fresh variety sausage and perishable. Keep refrigerated.

The natural pepper may be substituted with a double amount of herbal pepper (white mustard seed, caraway, marjoram, chili, hot and sweet paprika, bay leaf).

Chapter 10

Head Cheeses

Head cheese was one of the first meat products to be made after pig slaughtering as it incorporates highly perishable organ meats and often blood as well. Those ingredients must be processed without delay. Meats selected for its manufacture may be considered to be inferior by many people, the truth is that those meats are lean and rich in vitamins. The meats normally selected are: head meat, heart, tongue, organ meat (liver, kidneys, lungs, brains, spleen), bladder, stomach, tripe. For different reasons many people object to blood consumption and a white head cheese (without blood and often filled with rice) has become quite popular. To make head cheese in a traditional way you need meats that are very rich in collagen (connective tissues). Those meats (hocks, skins) will produce gelatin which will bind everything together. Most Polish head cheeses have names related to the names of areas or cities that were once German or are located close to the German border. It will be very logical and almost correct to conclude that head cheese was the most popular among the German and Polish border towns.

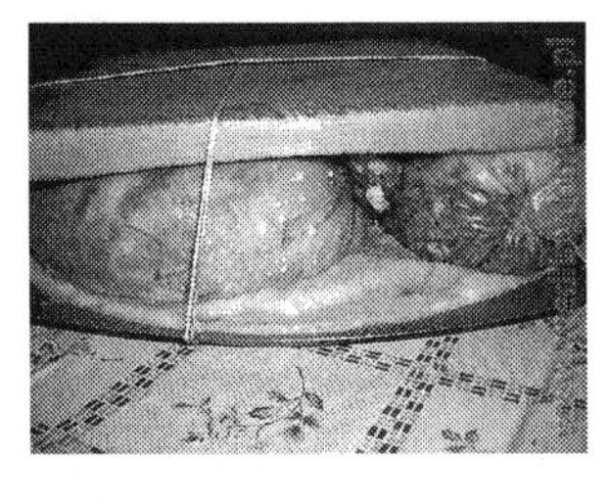

Photo 10.1 *courtesy Bunia.*

*The original Polish name for a head cheese is **"salceson"** which has its origin in German name "pressen" - to press.*

Photo 10.2 *courtesy Kruszynka.*

In older technology books head cheese was often referred to as "brawn." Jelled pork trimmings, chopped and pickled in vinegar were traditionally called "souse." You may find in a supermarket a factory made head cheese bearing that name.

Head Cheese Color

Meat color is discussed in detail in the curing section. Not cured cooked meat develops a grey color, cured meat becomes pink. It is easy to cure small cuts of meat using the dry method of curing meat for sausages, however, traditional cheeses are made from pork head meat and less often from cow head meat. The head is a large part of an animal and is usually split into halves. It is possible to trim the meat off the head and cure it for 2-3 days with salt and sodium nitrite, however, some meat will remain attached to the bones. This meat transfers into a loss of money for a meat plant. It is more practical to cure the split head in curing solution for 4 days. After that the head will be cooked and the meat will be easily separated from bones with fingers. After cooking such meat will be pink.

In many head cheeses meats are grey, so there was no curing at all. Some head cheeses are even called White Head Cheese, so the curing step does not take place. You may cure tongues only and leave other meats uncured. As a result, the solid chunks of red tongue will contrast with the grey meat and white skins and will become "show pieces" of the head cheese. In other words it is basically up to you how to influence the looks of the product.

You can add Cure #1 to hot water, let's say 1 tsp of Cure #1 per 2 cups of water when you cook meats and this will *paint* the meat pink. However, they will not be really cured and the pink layer will only be 1-2 mm (1/16") deep. The inside of the meat will still be grey. This might not look well in a thick meat cut, however, the difference will be hardly noticeable if the thickness of the meat is less than 10 mm (1/2"). What is interesting is that you can place a fully *cooked* grey meat in boiling water with Cure # 1 and the meat will acquire a pink color, however, on the outside only. Commercially produced head cheeses were made from split pork and beef heads which were cured in a solution of salt, nitrate and water. After that, they were rinsed and cooked. Such meats developed a pink color. The majority of head cheeses are made from uncured meat, even if the split pork heads are used. The meats are just boiled without being cured with sodium nitrite (Cure #1).

If you want a solid chunk of meat to stand out and become "show meat", cure it for 3 days with salt and sodium nitrite (Cure #1). Weigh the meat and apply 1.8% salt (18 g per 1 kg of meat). Estimate the amount of Cure #1 using the guideline of 2.5 g of Cure #1 per 1 kg (2.2 lb) of meat.

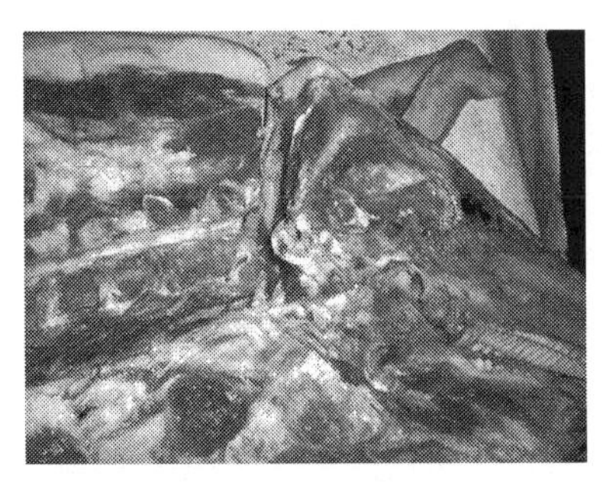

Photo 10.3 Meat selection.

Photo 10.4 Poached meats.

Photo 10.5 Cutting and grinding.

Photo 10.6 Mixing with groats.

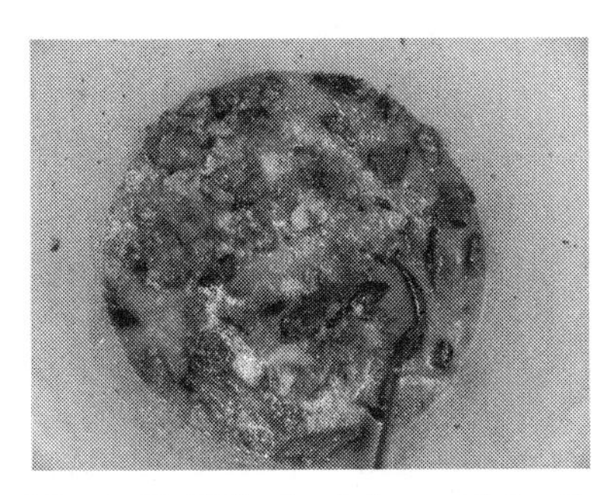

Photo 10.7 Final mixing with broth.

Photo 10.8 Stuffing.

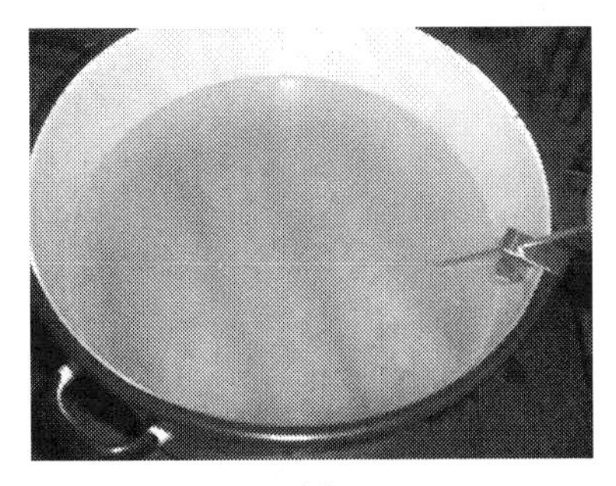

Photo 10.9 Poaching.

Photo 10.10 Cooling.

Many people object to eating head cheese because of its name. In other languages the name for headcheese does not mention "head" at all. The fact is that head cheese contains pork head meat, skin, snout, the parts that do not have much visual appeal. People do not realize that they consume those parts eating hot dogs and bologna where they are are hidden in the form of an emulsified paste. Yes, the American favorite sausage is made from offal meat, bone scrapped meat, plenty of water and chemicals.

Photo 10.11 Meats for head cheese.

Photo 10.12 Cooking meats.

Photo 10.13 Draining and cooling.

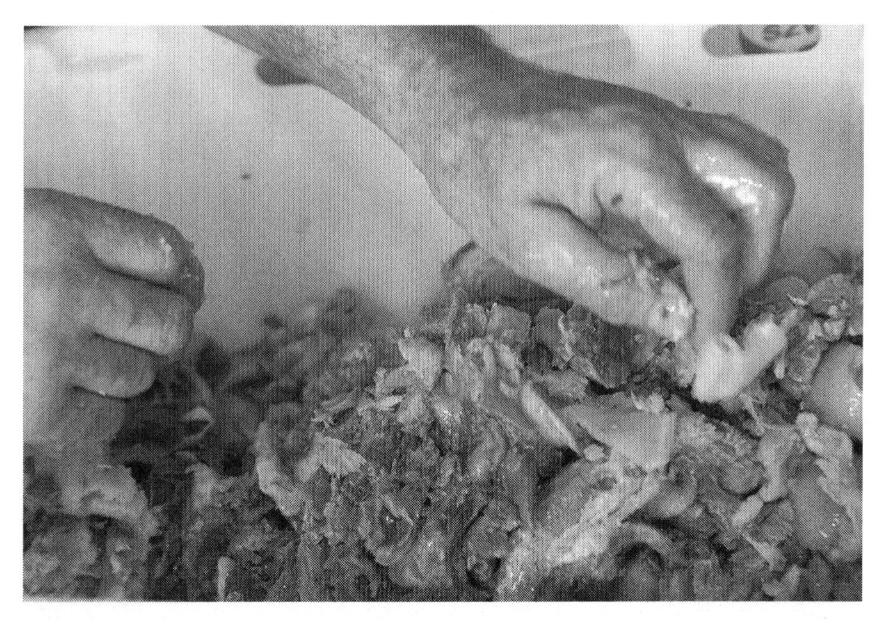

Photo 10.14 Separating meat from bones is easier when the meat is still warm.

Photo 10.15 Cooked head cheeses. Pork stomachs have been traditionally used for centuries.

All Trimmings Head Cheese

(Salceson podrobowy)

All unused organ meat and blood are utilized in this head cheese.

Lungs, spleens, udders, pork tripe, veal casings, veal pork stomachs, beef, veal or lamb head meat, bone meat, beef and veal lips, pork skins, pork class IV and beef class V, pork, beef, veal or lamb brains, 750 g (1.65 lb)
Blood, 100 g (0.22 lb)
Jowls/dewlap, 150 g (0.33 lb)
Lips and skins weight total not to exceed 30% total weight. Lamb meat total not to exceed 10 % total weight.

Ingredients per 1 kg (2.2 lb) of meat

Salt, 18 g (3 tsp)
Pepper, 7.5 g
Marjoram, 8.5 g
Allspice, 1.5 g
Onion, fresh, 125 g
The natural pepper may be substituted with a double amount of herbal pepper (white mustard seed, caraway, marjoram, chili, hot and sweet paprika, bay leaf).

Cooking Except spleen, brains and blood, cook other meats in small amount of water:

- lungs, tripe and bloody meats at 85° C (185° F) until soft.
- heads, skins, lips, udders, tripe and pork stomachs at 95° C (203° F) until soft.
- jowls/dewlap at 85° C (185° F) until semi-soft

Remove gristle from lungs and meat from heads when still warm. Spread meats apart on a flat surface to cool.

Grinding Cut dewlap into 8-10 mm (3-4") cubes. Grind: udders and lungs through 5 mm, raw spleen and other meats through 3 mm plate.

Mixing Mix meats thoroughly with salt, spices and blood.

Stuffing Stuff loosely into veal bladders or 60 mm synthetic casings. Sew the bladder ends with twine. Tie the synthetic casings ends with twine.

Cooking Cook bladders in water at 82° C (180° F) for 78-80 min (depending on size) and synthetic casings at 78-80° C (172-176° F) until meat reaches 68-70° C (154-158° F) internal temperature.

Cooling Spread head cheeses on a flat surface and let the steam out. Flatten stomachs with weight and cool to 6° C (43° F) or lower.

Finishing Clean head cheeses of any fat and aspic that accumulated on the surface, even them out and cut off excess twine.

Black Head Cheese

(Salceson czarny)

Dark colored head cheese due to the large amount of blood used.

Pork jowls/dewlap, 400 g (0.88 lb)
Hearts and kidneys, 100 g (0.22 lb)
Pork or veal lungs, beef, veal or lamb head meat, bone meat, pork class IV and V, 100 g (0.22 lb)
Skins, pork or veal leg meat, 100 g (0.22 lb)
Blood, 250 g (0.55 lb)
Semolina, bread crumbs or bread crust, 50 g (0.11 lb)

Ingredients per 1 kg (2.2 lb) of materials

Salt, 20 g (3-1/3 tsp)
Cure # 1, 2.0 g (1/2 tsp)
Pepper, 2.0 g
Marjoram, 1.0 g (1/2 tsp)
Garlic, 1.5 g (1/2 clove)
Allspice at 0.5 g (1/4 tsp) may be added.

Cooking Cook meats in small amount of water:

- hearts, kidneys, lungs at 85° C (185° F) until soft.
- skins, heads and legs at 95° C (203° F) until soft.
- jowls at 85° C (185° F) until semi-soft.

Remove gristle from lungs and meat from heads and legs when still warm. Spread apart on a flat surface to cool.

Grinding Cut jowls/dewlap into 10-12 mm (3/8-1/2") cubes. Grind skins through 3 mm plate. Grind other through 3 mm plate.

Mixing Add salt, Cure #1, spices and semolina or bread crumbs to ground meats and mix thoroughly with blood.

Stuffing Stuff loosely into pork middles, stomachs or 100 mm synthetic strong casings. Final shape will depend on individual characteristics of a casing used. Approximated sizes (length x width x height in centimeters):

- pork- middles (25 x 12 x 7), bladders (2 x 20 x 7), stomachs (25 x 15 x 7).
- veal or lamb: bungs (18-25) x 12 x 7.
- beef bungs (40-45) x (8-14) x (5-9).

Cooking	Cook in water at 82° C (180° F) for 90-120 min (depending on size) until meat reaches 68-70° C (154-158° F) internal temperature. Remove air with a needle from pieces that swim up to the surface.
Cooling	Spread head cheeses on a flat surface and let the steam out. Flatten stomachs with weight and cool to 6° C (43° F) or lower.
Finishing	Clean head cheeses of any fat and aspic that accumulated on the surface, even them out and cut off excess twine.

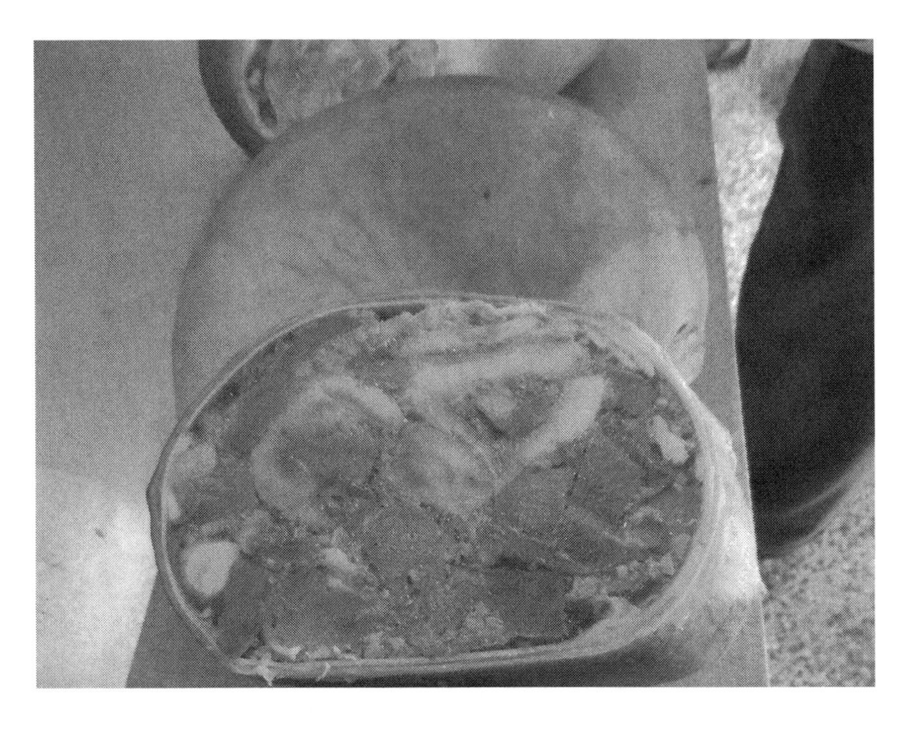

Photo 10.16 Head cheese stuffed in pork stomach.

Brunszwicki Head Cheese

(Salceson brunszwicki)

Head cheeses are very popular in Poland and Germany and the origins of this one are leading to a German town of Brunszwik.

Pork heads without ears, 600 g (1.32 lb)
Fat pieces, 100 g (0.22 lb)
Pork or veal liver, 150 g (0.33 lb)
Pork or veal lungs, boiled beef or veal head meat, 100 g (0.22 lb)
Pork skins, 0.50 g (0.11 lb)

Ingredients per 1 kg (2.2 lb) of meat

Salt, 18 g (3 tsp)
Cure # 1, 2.0 g (1/2 tsp)
Pepper, 2.0 g (1 tsp)
Marjoram, 2.0 g (1 tsp)
Onion, 30 g (1/2 small onion)

Cooking Cook meats (except liver) in small amount of water until soft:

- snouts, lungs, jowls at 85°C (185°F).
- skins and heads at 95°C (203°F).
- fat at 85°C (185°F) until semi-soft.

Remove gristle from lungs and meat from heads when still warm. Spread apart on a flat surface to cool.

Grinding Cut jowls and snouts into cubes 10-12 mm (3/8 -1/2"). Remaining meats ground through 2 mm plate.

Mixing Mix all meats, salt, Cure #1 and spices well together.

Stuffing Stuff loosely into stomach, bladder, pork middles or 100 mm synthetic strong casings. Flattened pork or beef bladders in a shape of irregular disk up to 25 cm (10") diameter and 8 cm (3 ") thick. Flattened pork middles, 18-25 cm (7-10") long, about 15 cm (6") wide and 7 cm (3") high.

Cooking Cook in water at 82° C (180° F) for 90-150 min (depending on size) until meat reaches 68-70° C (154-158° F) internal temperature. Remove air with a needle from pieces that swim up to the surface.

Cooling Spread head cheeses on a flat surface and let the steam out. Flatten stomachs with weight and cool to 6°C (43°F) or less.

Finishing Clean head cheeses of any fat and aspic that accumulated on the surface, even them out and cut off excess twine.

Farmer Head Cheese

(Salceson wiejski)

A bare bone farmer's head cheese.

Pork heads, 820 g (1.80 lb)
Pork legs, 160 g (0.35 lb)
Blood, 20 g (0.70 oz)

Ingredients per 1 kg (2.2 lb) of materials

Salt, 15 g (2-1/2 tsp)
Pepper, 1.5 g (5/8 tsp)
Allspice, 0.5 g (1/4 tsp)

Cooking In separate containers cook heads and legs in water at 85° C (185° F) until soft. The meat should not be cooked but should start separating from the bone. Save meat stock. Spread all pieces on a flat surface to cool.

Grinding Cut head meat into 12 mm (½") cubes. Grind leg meat through 3 mm plate.

Mixing Mix all meats with salt, spices and blood together. Add some of the meat stock.

Stuffing Stuff loosely into pork stomachs or large diameter synthetic casings.

Cooking Cook in water at 82° C (180° F) for 90-120 min (depending on size) until meat reaches 68-70° C (154-158° F) internal temperature.

Cooling Spread head cheeses on a flat surface and let the steam out. Flatten with weight and cool to 6° C (43° F) or lower.

Finishing Clean head cheeses of any fat and aspic that accumulated on the surface and cut off excess twine.

Photo 10.17 Flattened head cheese *by Dziadek.*

Italian Head Cheese

(Salceson włoski)

Although carrying Italian name, this has been always a very popular head cheese in Poland.

Pork heads, 750 g (1.65 lb)
Meat from beef heads, 130 g (0.28 lb)
Pork skins, 120 g (0.26 lb)

Ingredients per 1 kg (2.2 lb.) of meat

Salt, 18 g (3 tsp)
Cure # 1, 2.5 g (1/2 tsp)
Pepper, 2.0 g (1 tsp)
Caraway, 1.0 g (1/2 tsp)
Garlic, 3.0 g (1 clove)

Garlic may be replaced with the double amount of onion. Meat from beef heads may be replaced with beef meat or boned cured pork picnics.

Rinsing Soak cured pork heads, cured beef meat and skins in running cold water for 15 minutes.

Cooking Cook meats in a small amount of water: pork heads at 85° C (185° F), beef head meat and pork skins at 95° C (203° F). Remove meat from heads and spread all meats apart on a flat surface to cool. Save meat stock.

Grinding

- cut pork head meat into strips 1.5 x 2 cm (⅝ x ¾") by 7-10 cm (2 x 4")
- cut beef head meat into strips 1 x 5 cm (⅜ x 2")
- grind other meats with 3 mm (⅛") plate.

Mixing Mix meats with salt, Cure # 1, spices and 10% of the meat stock (in relation to the weight of the meat).

Stuffing Stuff *loosely* into pork stomachs, bladders or 100 mm synthetic strong casings. Flattened pork stomachs, 30 cm (12") long, about 20 cm (8") wide and 8 cm (3") high.

Cooking Cook in water at 82 °C (180° F) for 90-150 min (depending on size) until meat reaches 68-70° C (154-158° F) internal temperature. Remove air with a needle from pieces that swim up to the surface.

Cooling Spread head cheeses on a flat surface and let the steam out. Flatten stomachs with weight and cool to 6° C (43° F).

Finishing Clean head cheeses of any fat and aspic that accumulated on the surface, even them out and cut off excess twine. Keep refrigerated.

Mazowiecki Head Cheese
(Salceson mazowiecki)

A typical head cheese of the Mazowsze region.

Skwarki, * 300 g (66 lb)
Pork skins, 150 g (0.33 lb)
Dewlaps/jowls, 150 g (0.33 lb)
Kidneys, lungs, beef and veal head meat, pork class IV, beef class V, veal casings, beef tripe, udders, brains, spleen, 250 g (0.55 lb)
Blood, 150 g (0.33 lb)

Ingredients per 1 kg (2.2 lb) of meat

Salt, 20 g (3-1/3 tsp)
Herbal pepper, ** 4.0 g (2 tsp)
Marjoram, 2.0 g (1 tsp)
Allspice, 0.5 g (1/4 tsp)
Onion, fresh, 15 g (1 tablespoon)

**Skwarki, see page 78.*

***Herbal pepper (white mustard seed, caraway, marjoram, chili, hot and sweet paprika, bay leaf) can be substituted with ½ amount of black pepper.*

Cooking Except spleen, brains, blood and skwarki, * cook other meats in small amount of water:

- lungs, kidneys, veal heads, veal casings and pork class IV at 85° C (185° F) for about 90 min.
- beef class V, skins, heads, tripe, and udders at 95° C (203° F) for about 2 hours until semi-soft.
- dewlap/jowls at 85° C (185° F) until semi-soft.

Remove gristle from lungs and meat from heads. Spread meats apart on a flat surface to cool. Soak skwarki * in meat stock taking 400 ml of stock for 1 kg of skwarki.

Grinding Cut dewlap/jowl into 8-10 mm (3/8") cubes. Meats, spleen, tripe kidneys, udders, sheep casings and veal head meat ground through 5 mm plate. Skwarki * and skins ground through 3 mm plate.

Mixing Mix all meats with salt, spices and blood together.

Stuffing Stuff loosely into beef middles, beef bungs or large synthetic casings.

Cooking Cook in water at 85° C (185° F) for 90-120 min (depending on size) until meat reaches 68-70° C (154-158° F) internal temperature.

Cooling Spread head cheeses on a flat surface and let the steam out. Flatten with weight and cool to 6° C (43° F) or lower. Clean head cheeses of any fat and aspic that accumulated on the surface.

Pomorski Black Head Cheese
(Salceson czarny pomorski)

Dark colored head cheese due to the large amount of blood used. Popular in the Northern, located by the sea regions.

Pork head meat, 300 g (0.66 lb)
Jowls/dewlap, 250 g (0.55 lb)
Skins, pork or veal leg meat, 100 g
Lungs, boiled beef, veal, lamb or sheep head meat, boiled bone meat, pork class IV, beef class V, skwarki, * 150 g, (0.33 lb)
Blood, 200 g (0.44 lb)

Ingredients per 1 kg (2.2 lb) of materials

Salt, 21 g (3-1/2 tsp)
Cure # 1, 2.0 g (1/2 tsp)
Pepper, 2.0 g (1 tsp)
Marjoram, 1.0 g (1/2 tsp)
Garlic, 1.5 g (1/2 clove)

** Skwarki, sere page 78.*
The natural pepper may be substituted with a double amount of herbal pepper (white mustard seed, caraway, marjoram, chili, hot and sweet paprika, bay leaf).

Cooking Cook meats until soft in small amount of water:
- pork heads, snouts, jowls, lungs and pork class IV at 85°C (185° F).
- skins, beef, veal or sheep heads and legs at 95°C (203° F).
- dewlap at 85°C (185° F) until semi-soft.

Remove gristle from lungs and meat from heads and legs when still warm. Spread apart on a flat surface to cool.

Grinding Cut snouts. jowls, dewlaps into 15 mm (5/8") cubes. Except skwarki * grind all meats 3 mm plate.

Mixing Add salt, Cure #1 and spices to cut and ground meats and mix thoroughly with blood.

Stuffing Stuff loosely into pork middles, stomachs, bladders or 100 mm synthetic strong casings. Final shape will depend on individual characteristics of a casing used.

Cooking Cook in water at 82° C (180° F) for 90-120 min (depending on size) until meat reaches 68-70° C (154-158° F) internal temperature. Remove air with a needle from pieces that swim up to the surface.

Cooling Spread head cheeses on a flat surface and let the steam out. Flatten stomachs with weight and cool to 6° C (43° F) or lower. Clean head cheeses of any fat and aspic that accumulated on the surface, even them out and cut off excess twine.

Silesian Head Cheese

(Salceson śląski)

As the name implies this head cheese was popular in the South Western industrial area of Poland known as Silesia (Śląsk in Polish).

Pork heads with bone, 900 g (1.98 lb)
Pork skins, 100 g (0.22 lb)

Ingredients per 1 kg (2.2 lb) meat

Salt, 18 g (3 tsp)
Cure # 1, 2.0 g (1/2 tsp)
Pepper, 1.0 g (1/ tsp)
Caraway, 0.5 g (1/2 tsp)
Garlic, 1.5 g (1/2 clove)

The natural pepper may be substituted with a double amount of herbal pepper (white mustard seed, caraway, marjoram, chili, hot and sweet paprika, bay leaf). Garlic may be replaced with to 10 g onion (per 1 kg of meat).

Cooking Cook until soft in small amount of water:

- heads at 85° C (185° F). Save stock.
- skins at 95° C (203° F).

Remove warm meat from heads and spread it apart on a flat surface to cool. Spread skins and let them cool.

Grinding Cut pork head meat into strips (7-10 cm, 3-4") x (1-1.5 cm, ½-¾"). Grind skins through 3 mm plate.

Mixing Add salt, cure #1, spices and 10% of the meat stock (in relation to the weight of the meat). Mix everything well together.

Stuffing Stuff *loosely* into pork stomachs, bladders or 100 mm synthetic strong casings. Flattened pork stomachs, 30 cm (12") long, about 20 cm (8") wide and 8 cm (3") high.

Cooking Cook in water at 82° C (180° F) for 90-150 min (depending on size) until the meat reaches 68-70° C (154-158° F) internal temperature. Remove air with a needle from pieces that swim up to the surface.

Cooling Spread head cheeses on a flat surface and let the steam out. Flatten stomachs with weight and cool them to 6° C (43° F) or lower.

Finishing Clean head cheeses of any fat and aspic that accumulated on the surface, even them out and cut off excess twine. Keep refrigerated.

Tongue Head Cheese
(Salceson ozorkowy)

Classical type of head cheese made with blood and tongues ("ozorek" denotes tongue in Polish).

Pork or veal tongues, 350 g (0.77 lb)
Skinless jowls/dewlap, 400 g (0.88 lb)
Skins, 50 g (0.11 lb)
Pork liver, 100 g (0.22 lb)
Blood, 100 g (0.22 lb)

Ingredients per 1 kg (2.2 lb) of materials

Salt, 20 g (3-1/3 tsp)
Cure # 1, 2 g (1/2 tsp)
Pepper, 2.0 g (1 tsp)
Marjoram, 1.0 g (1/2 tsp)
Cloves, 0.5 g (1/4 tsp)
Garlic, 1.5 g (1/2 clove)

Curing Blanch tongues with hot water and remove the skin before submitting them for curing. Cut pork or veal tongues into 5 cm (2") cubes. Mix with 10 g salt and 1 g Cure #1, pack tightly in a container and place in refrigerator for 3 days.

Cooking Cook meats (except liver) in small amount of water until soft:
- tongues at 85° C (185° F).
- skins at 95° C (203° F).
- jowls/dewlap at 85° C (185° F) until semi-soft

Grinding Cut jowls/ dewlap into 5 mm (¼ ") cubes. Dice tongues into 2.5 cm (1") cubes. Grind boiled skins through 2-3 mm plate. Grind raw pork liver through 2-3 mm plate.

Mixing Add remaining salt, Cure #1 and spices to ground meats and mix thoroughly with blood.

Stuffing Stuff loosely into pork middles or bladders, 100 mm synthetic strong casings. Flattened pork middles, 18-25 cm (7-10") long, about 15 cm (6") wide and 7 cm (3") high. Flattened pork bladders in a shape of irregular disk up to 20 cm (8") diameter and 7 cm (3 ") thick.

Cooking Cook in water at 82° C (180° F) for 90-120 min (depending on size) until meat reaches 68-70° C (154-158° F) internal temperature. Remove air with a needle from pieces that swim up to the surface.

Cooling Spread head cheeses on a flat surface and let the steam out. Flatten stomachs with weight and cool to 6° C (43° F) or less.

Finishing Clean head cheeses of any fat and aspic that accumulated on the surface, even them out and cut off excess twine.

Photo 10.18 Although the traditional look of a head cheese is gone, the waterproof plastic casings do the job quite nicely.

Photo courtesy Bunia.

Photo 10.19 Mr. Kruszynka starts making head cheese.

White Head Cheese Supreme

(Salceson biały wyborowy)

A very popular head cheese made without blood.

Pork heads, 750 g (1.65 lb)
Beef head meat, 130 g (0.28 lb)
Pork skins, salted, 120 g (0.26 lb)

Ingredients per 1 kg (2.2 lb) of meat

Salt, 18 g (3 tsp)
Cure # 1, 2.0 g (1/2 tsp)
Pepper, 1.0 g (1/2 tsp)
Caraway, 0.5 g (1/4 tsp)
Garlic, 1.5 g (1/2 clove)

Photo 10.20 Head cheese by Bunia.

Cooking Cook until soft in small amount of water:

- heads at 85° C (185° F)
- skins at 95° C (203° F)

Remove warm meat from heads and spread apart on a flat surface to cool. Spread skins and let them cool.

Grinding Cut pork head meat into strips (7-10 cm, 3-4") x (1-1.5 cm, ½-¾"). Cut beef head meat into strips 1 cm (½") wide and 5 cm (2") long. Grind skins and any meat with sinews through 3 mm plate.

Mixing Mix meat with salt, cure #1, spices and 10% of the meat stock (in relation to the weight of the meat).

Stuffing Stuff loosely into stomach, bladder or 100 mm synthetic strong casings. Flattened pork or beef bladders in a shape of irregular disk up to 25 cm (10") diameter and 8 cm (3 ") thick.

Cooking Cook in water at 82° C (180° F) for 90-150 min (depending on size) until the internal temperature of the meat reaches 68-70° C (154-158° F). Remove air with a needle from pieces that swim up to the surface.

Cooling Spread head cheeses on a flat surface and let the steam out. Flatten stomachs with weight and cool to 6°C (43°F) or less.

Finishing Clean head cheeses of any fat and aspic that accumulated on the surface, even them out and cut off excess twine.

Wolsztynski Head Cheese

(Salceson wolsztyński)

Wolsztyn was the city famous for its head cheeses and recently for the annual parade of steam locomotives.

Head meat, snouts, jowls, 150 g (0.33 lb)
Pork, beef or veal hearts, 150 g (0.33 lb)
Pork skins, 400 g (0.88 lb)
Pork or veal blood, 300 g (0.66 lb)

Ingredients per 1 kg (2.2 lb) of meat

Salt, 20 g (3-1/3 tsp)
Pepper, 2.0 g (1 tsp)
Marjoram, 1.0 g (1/2 tsp)
Allspice, 1.0 g (1/2 tsp)
Onion, 25 g (1/2 small onion)
Garlic, 3.0 g (1 clove)

Cooking Cook all meats in water at 90° C (194° F) until semi-soft. Skins should be cooked until soft. Spread on a flat surface to cool.

Grinding Cut head meat and hearts into 1.5 cm (5/8") strips. Take ¼ (100 g) of the skins and grind with onion through 3 mm plate. Cut remaining ¾ (300 g) skins into 5-6 mm strips about 5-6 cm (2-3") long.

Mixing Mix spices thoroughly with all meats and blood.

Stuffing Stuff loosely into stomachs, bladders or 100 mm synthetic casings. Sew or tie the ends with twine.

Cooking Cook in water at 85°C (185°F) for 90-180 min (depending on size) until meat reaches 68-70°C (154-158°F) internal temperature. Remove air with a needle from pieces that swim up to the surface.

Cooling Spread head cheeses on a flat surface and let the steam out. Flatten stomachs with weight and cool to 6° C (43° F) or lower.

Finishing Clean head cheeses of any fat and aspic that accumulated on the surface, even them out and cut off excess twine.

Photo 10.21 Filling pork stomachs with head cheese.

Chapter 11

Liver Sausages

(Kiszki pasztetowe i wątrobianki)

Liver sausages belong to a group of sausages known as "kiszki."'The word "kiszka" usually described a blood or a liver sausage, but occasionally a sausage made from offal meat (meat organs) and meat trimmings was called "kiszka" as well, for example Jowl Sausage *(Kiszka podgardlana).* These sausages had a distinctive shape as they were stuffed into large irregular natural casings so they were easy to distinguish.

Photo 11.1 Traditionally stuffed kiszka - liver sausage.

You may divide liver sausages into:

- Pâté type liver sausages: liver, higher meat grades, fat. A lot of pâtés are made without stuffing them into casings. Both types are high quality spreadable products.
- Regular liver sausages: liver, lower meat grades, other organs, fats. A high quality spreadable product.

Most good liver sausages will contain pork liver, some recipes call for veal liver which is a great choice though expensive. Beef liver makes sausages darker and it should not be added in amounts larger than 25% of the total meat mass. Liver is the only meat that must not be boiled as it will lose its binding properties. To remove any remaining traces of blood it is acceptable to poach liver for about 5 minutes or soak it for 15 min in cold water.

You can customize the recipe by introducing meats from other animals, just remember that meat from younger animals will make a better sausage. Also the best meats for liver sausages are: veal, pork, and poultry (goose, turkey, or duck). For making liver sausages those birds provide meats and livers that are superior to chicken. Beef, lamb and goat meats can be used sparingly. Rabbit meat and liver is great, venison can be used as well.

Photo 11.2 An assortment of liver sausages in a store. Some liver pâtés are not stuffed into casings but baked in forms.

Photo 11.3 Basic meats in liver sausages are liver, fat and meat.
Photo 11.4 When emulsified, ingredients become a paste.

Photo 11.5 Making sausages can be a lot of fun.

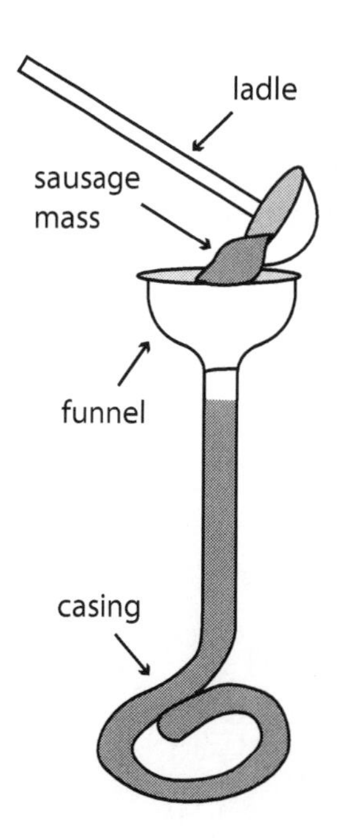

Fig. 11.1 Emulsified liver paste can be stuffed with a stuffer or with a ladle and a funnel.

Liver Sausage

(Kiszka wątrobiana)

Liver sausage.

Pork, beef or lamb liver, 300 g
Brains, tongues, hearts, kidneys, 100 g
Lungs, beef or lamb tripe, stomachs, not salted veal casings, beef, veal or lamb boiled head meat, boiled bones meat, pork class IV, 300 g
Fat trimmings, 300 g

Ingredients per 1 kg (2.2 lb) of meat

Salt, 20 g (3-1/3 tsp)
Pepper, 1.0 g (1/2 tsp)
Marjoram, 1.0 g (1/2 tsp)
Onion, 20 g (1/2 small onion)

0.5 g allspice may be added. The natural pepper may be substituted with a double amount of herbal pepper (white mustard seed, caraway, marjoram, chili, hot and sweet paprika, bay leaf).

Washing Soak meats and liver in cold water for about 2 hours. Remove sinews, cut into slices and immerse into water.

Cooking Poach meats *(except liver and brains)* in small amount of water:

- kidneys and lungs at 80-85° C (176-185° F).
- other meats (except fat) at 95° C (203° F) until soft. Save stock.
- fat trimmings at 85° C (185° F) until medium-soft.

Grinding Liver, brains and all meats and fat ground through 2 mm plate.

Emulsifying Using food processor emulsify liver until feels spreadable. Then add salt, spices, all other meats, lastly fat pieces and keep on emulsifying everything together. During emulsifying add about 10% of the stock (in relation to the weight of cooked meats) that remained after poaching.

Stuffing Stuff loosely into beef middles or large hog casings. Sausages about: 25-35 cm (10-14") long, 4-8 cm (1¾-3") thick. The ends tied with a twine. hanging loop 10-12 cm (4-5") at one end.

Cooking Immerse sausages in boiling water and cook at 80-85° C (176-185° F) for 50-90 min until sausages reach 68-70° C (154-158° F) internal temperature.

Cooling Cool sausages for about 15 min in cold water, then hang them and cool down to 6° C (43° F) or lower. Keep refrigerated.

Liver Pátė Sausage

(Kiszka pasztetowa)

A fine liver sausage.

Pork class I or veal class I, 150 g (0.33 lb)
Pork class II, 150 g (0.33 lb)
Pork or veal liver, 250 g (0.55 lb)
Fat trimmings, 400 g (0.88 lb)
Back fat, 50 g (0.11 lb)

Ingredients per 1 kg (2.2 lb) of meat

Salt, 20 g (3-1/3 tsp)
Pepper, 2.0 g (1 tsp)
Marjoram, 0.5 g (1/4 tsp)
Onion, 30 g (1/2 small onion)

Cutting	Cut back fat into 5-6 mm (¼") cubes and then poach them.
Washing & Poaching	Soak liver in cold running water for 1 hour, remove sinews, cut into slices and cover with water of 90° C (194° F). Poach 8-10 min stirring frequently. Do the same with previously diced back fat but poach for 5 min. Cool liver and back fat pieces in cold water for about 5 min and leave to drain water away.
Grinding	Grind previously poached liver through 2 mm plate and emulsify. Grind pork, veal, brains (if used) and fat pieces through 2 mm plate and emulsify.
Emulsifying	Emulsify liver until feels spreadable. Add salt, spices, pork class I, veal class I or II, pork class II and brains (if used), lastly add fat pieces and keep on emulsifying everything together.
Mixing	Mix emulsified mixture with back fat pieces until uniformly distributed.
Stuffing	Stuff loosely into pork bungs, pork middles, 65 mm synthetic cellulose casings, make 16-18" long links. Tie the ends with twine and make hanging loop.
Cooking	Immerse sausages in boiling water and poach at 80-85° C (176-185° F) for 50-90 min until internal meat temperature reaches 68-70° C (154-158° F).

Cooling Cool sausages in cold running water for about 10 min, then hang them up and cool down to below 6° C (43° F). If no cooling facilities are available, the sausage must be air dried to 12° C (53° F) or less.

Smoking (Optional) If smoky flavor is desired, the sausages may be cold smoked for 5-6 hours and then cooled down again.

Finishing After cooling clean head cheeses of any fat and aspic that accumulated on the surface and cut off excess twine.

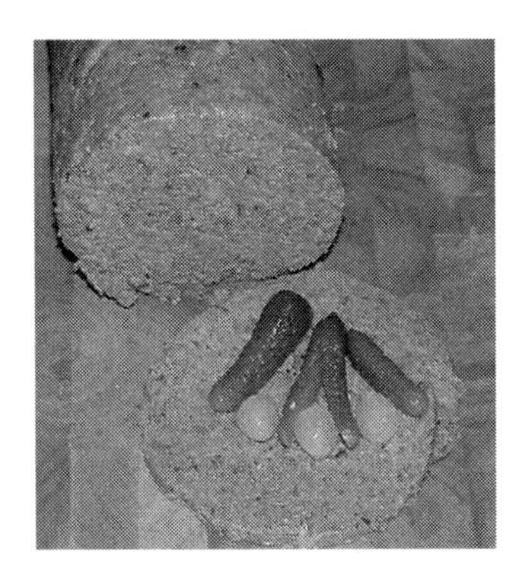

Photo 11.6 *by Marcin Klessa vel Oli.*

Liver Pâté Sausage with Semolina
(Kiszka pasztetowa z manną)

Liver sausage with semolina.

Pork class II, 200 g
Pork or veal liver, 250 g
Fat trimmings, 400 g
Back fat, 50 g
Semolina flour, 100 g

Ingredients per 1 kg (2.2 lb) material

Salt, 18 g (3 tsp)
Pepper, 2.0 g (1 tsp)
Marjoram, 1.0 g (1/2 tsp)
Onion, 25 g (1/2 small onion)

The amount of marjoram may be increased or removed from the recipe. Fresh onion may be substituted with dehydrated onion: 0.15 kg of dry onion replaces 1 kg fresh onion.

Cutting	Cut back fat into 5-6 mm (¼") cubes.
Washing & Cooking	Soak liver in cold running water for 1 hour, remove any glands or sinews, cut into slices and cover with 90°C (194°F) water. Poach 8-10 min stirring frequently. Do the same with previously diced back fat but poach for 5 min. Then cool liver and back fat pieces in cold water for about 5 min and drain.
Grinding	Grind poached liver through 2 mm plate. Grind pork, brains (if used) and fat trimmings through 2 mm plate.
Emulsifying	Using food processor emulsify semolina adding equal amount of water. Emulsify liver until it feels spreadable. Then add already emulsified semolina, salt, spices, pork type II and brains (if used), lastly fat trimmings and emulsify everything together.
Mixing	Mix emulsified mixture with cubes of back fat until uniformly distributed.
Stuffing	Stuff loosely into pork bungs, beef middles or 65 mm cellulose casings. Bungs and middles: 36-50 cm (14-20") long, 4-8 cm (1¾-3") thick. Synthetic casings: 40-45 cm (16-18") long, 65 mm dia. The ends tied with a twine. hanging loop 10-12 cm (4-5") at one end.

Cooking Immerse sausages into boiling water and cook at 80-85° C (176-185° F) for 50-90 min until sausages reach 68-70° C (154-158° F) internal temperature.

Cooling Place sausages for 15 minutes in cold water, then hang them up and cool to 6°C (43°F) or lower. Keep refrigerated.

Photo 11.7 *courtesy Dziadek*

Obornicka Liver Sausage

(Kiszka wątrobiana obornicka)

The name of this sausage comes from the city called Oborniki located in Poznan region.

Pork, beef or lamb liver, 250 g (0.55 lb)
Boiled pork leg meat, pork, beef or veal brains, pork class IV, pork, beef or veal lungs, spleen, 500 g (1.10 lb)
Fat trimmings, 250 g (0.55 lb)

Ingredients per 1 kg (2.2 lb) of meat

Salt, 18 g (3 tsp)
Herbal pepper * 2.5 g (1 tsp)
Marjoram, 1.0 g (1/2 tsp)
Onion, 20 g (1/2 small onion)

* *Herbal pepper may be substituted with ½ regular pepper.* *See page 77.*

Washing Wash meat organs (except brains). Soak lungs and any bloody meat briefly in cold water. Drain.

Cooking Cook meats (except liver and brains) in small amount of water:

- lungs and bloody meat at 80-85° C (176-185° F).
- legs at 95° C (203° F) until soft. Save stock.
- fat at 85°C (185° F), until semi-soft.
- spleen at 80-85° C (176-185° F).

After poaching remove gristle from lungs and meat from legs. Spread meats apart on a flat surface to cool.

Grinding All meats ground through 2 mm plate.

Emulsifying Using food processor emulsify leg meat adding 25-30% meat stock . Add salt, spices, all other meats, fat pieces and emulsify everything together.

Stuffing Stuff loosely into large hog, cellulose or fibrous casings. Straight links 25-30 cm (10-12"). Tie the ends with twine. Make hanging loop.

Cooking Immerse sausages into boiling water and cook at 80-82° C (176-180° F) for 45-60 min until sausages reach 74° C (165° F) internal temperature.

Cooling	Cool sausages in cold water, then hang them to dry. Their internal temperature should be less than 12° C (53° F).
Smoking	With cold smoke for about 6 hours until sausages develop light yellow color.
Cooling	Hang sausages and cool down to 6° C (43° F) or less. Keep refrigerated.

Photo 11.8 Liver sausage made *by Dziadek.*

Photo 12.1 Stuffing and linking blood sausages.

Chapter 12

Blood Sausages

(Kiszki Krwiste)

Blood sausages are one of the oldest sausages that man has been making and every country has its own variety. Well, almost every country. It is impossible to come up with an American version of a blood sausage. One doesn't even see them in a typical supermarket unless one goes to some ethnic meat stores, be them Polish, German, Russian, Serb, Slovak or Spanish. I've asked for a blood sausage in a large supermarket and the sales people did not even know what it was. And it has nothing to do with the English language, the best proof is that blood sausages (called black puddings) are consumed everywhere in England. When you eat medium rare steak, what you see on the plate is fresh blood. So what is wrong with fully cooked blood inside the sausage?

English black pudding normally consists of blood, cubed pork fat, cooked barley and rusk. In other countries cooked rice and barley will be used. The majority of blood sausages employ fresh and finely diced onions as an ingredient though they will be poached or fried for a short time first. Polish blood sausages use bread crumbs, rice and buckwheat or barley groats and of course pork blood, liver and other meats commonly used in liver sausages and head cheeses. Although some people eat them cold, the majority fry them on a frying pan until crispy brown. Then they are served with fried onions, potatoes and pickles or mustard.

More About Blood

Pig blood has a nicer, lighter color than blood from cattle which is much darker, commonly brown and sometimes almost black. This can be attributed to the age of the animal at the time of slaughter, the pigs are much younger. Blood has a natural tendency to coagulate (form solids) so commercial producers add anticoagulation agents to it. In home conditions salting blood or curing blood with salt and nitrite will bring a similar effect. Mixing blood and adding about 5% salt (re-adjust recipe for salt content) will result in a stabilized blood.

Blood Sausage Making Process

P 12.2 Cooking groats.

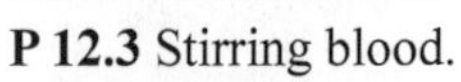

P 12.3 Stirring blood.

Photos by Dziadek

P 12.4 Boiled and ground meat.

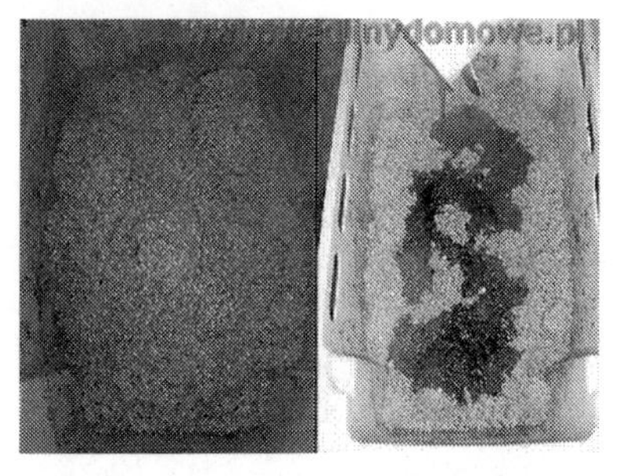

P12.5 Groats on meat/Blood on groats.

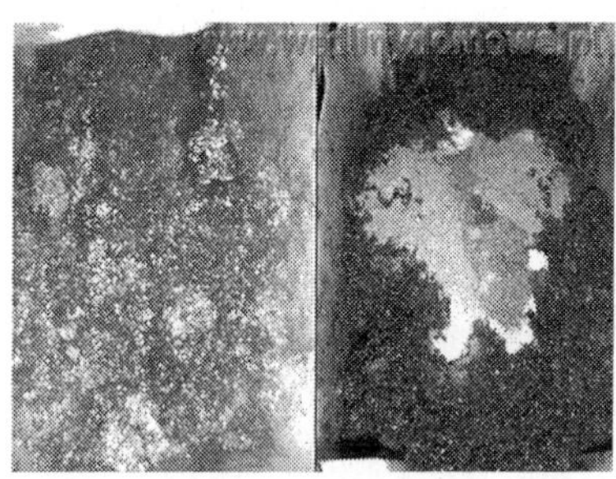

P 12.6 Blood, groats and meats together.

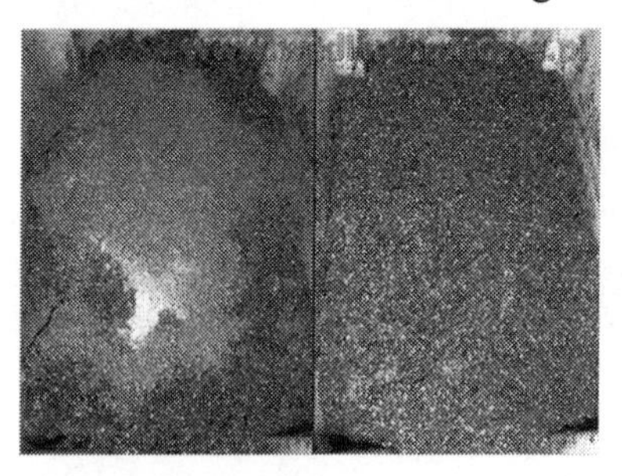

P 12.7 Fried onions, salt and spices.

P12.8 Linked sausages.

P 12.9 Cooked sausages.

Blood Sausage

(Kiszka krwista)

Blood sausage with bread crumbs or semolina.

Dewlap/jowls, 300 g (0.66 lb)
Pork beef or lamb liver, 50 g (0.11 lb)
Pork, beef or veal lungs, boiled bone meat, beef class V, veal class III, 300 g (0.66 lb)
Blood, 250 g (0.55 lb)
Bread crumbs, dry rolls or semolina flour, 100 g (0.22 lb)
No more than 10% of skins is permitted.

Ingredients per 1 kg (2.2 lb) of materials

Salt, 20 g (3-1/3 tsp)
Pepper, 1.0 g (1 tsp)
Marjoram, 1.0 g (1 tsp)
Allspice, 0.5 g (1/4 tsp)

The natural pepper may be substituted with a double amount of herbal pepper (white mustard seed, caraway, marjoram, chili, hot and sweet paprika, bay leaf).

Cooking Cook meats (except liver) in a small amount of water:

- dewlap/jowls at 80-85° C (176-185° F) until semi-soft.
- lungs at 85° C (185° F).
- skins, heads at 95° C (203° F) until soft.

After cooking remove gristle from lungs and meat from heads. Spread meats apart on a flat surface to cool.

Grinding Cut dewlap/jowls into 10-12 mm (4-5") cubes. Grind all other meats through 2 mm plate. Soak rolls or bread crumbs in left over stock, using 75% of stock in relation to bread crumbs.

Emulsifying If semolina is used, emulsify it in a food processor with 75% of meat stock (in relation to semolina).

Mixing Add salt and spices to ground meats and bread crumbs (or semolina flour), add blood and mix everything well together.

Stuffing Stuff loosely into pork middles or beef rounds. Pork middles or beef rounds, 40 cm (16") each. The ends tied with twine. Hanging loop 10-12 cm (4-5") on one end.

Cooking Immerse sausages in boiling water and cook at 80-85° C (176-185° F) for about 45 min until sausages reach 68-70° C (154-158° F) internal temperature.

Cooling Immerse sausages for 15 min in cold water, then hang and cool to 6° C (43° F) or lower. Keep refrigerated.

Blood Sausage with Bread Crumbs
(Kiszka bułczana krwista)

Pork head meat, 100 g (0.22 lb)
Jowls/dewlaps, 150 g (0.33 lb)
Pork skins, pork class IV, pork lungs, 350 g (0.77 lb)
Pork blood, 200 g (0.44 lb)
Bread crumbs or dry rolls, 200 g (0.44 lb)
Limit the amount of skins to no more than 50 g (2 oz).

Ingredients per 1 kg (2.2 lb) materials

Salt, 18 g (3 tsp)
Herbal pepper * 4.0 g (2 tsp)
Marjoram, 2.0 g (1 tsp)
Allspice, 0.5 g (1/4 tsp)
Onion, 20 g (1/3 of small onion)

** The herbal pepper (white mustard seed, caraway, marjoram, chili, hot and sweet paprika, bay leaf) may be substituted with a ½ amount of regular pepper).*

Washing Wash meats well in water.

Cooking Cook meats in a small amount of water:

- heads, lungs, other meats at 80-85° C (176-185° F). Save stock.
- skins at 95°C (203° F) until soft.

After cooking remove gristle from lungs and meat from heads. Spread meats apart on a flat surface to cool.

Grinding Grind all meats through 2 mm plate. Soak bread crumbs or dry rolls in 30% (in relation to the weight of the rolls) of left over stock.

Mixing Add salt and spices to ground meats and then process in food processor together with blood and soaked rolls.

Stuffing Stuff into hog casings loosely and form links. Twisted links 8-12 cm (3-5") each. Form pairs.

Cooking Immerse sausages in a boiling water and cook at 80-82° C (176-180° F) for 25-30 min until internal meat temperature reaches 68-70° C (154-158° F).

Cooling Place sausages in cold, then hang and cool to 6° C (43° F) or lower.

Blood Sausage with Rice
(Kiszka krwista z ryżem)

Blood sausages made with rice are very popular not only in Poland but in other countries as well.

Pork head meat, jowls, snouts, 350 g (0.77 lb)
Pork or veal lungs, 200 g (0.44 lb)
Pork skins, 100 g (0.22 lb)
Blood, 150 g (0.33 lb)
Rice, 200 g (0.44 lb)

Ingredients per 1 kg (2.2 lb) materials

Salt, 20 g (3-1/3 tsp)
Pepper, 2.0 g (1 tsp)
Marjoram, 2.0 g (1 tsp)
Allspice, 1.0 g (1/2 tsp)
Garlic or cinnamon, 1.0 g (1/2 tsp)

Cooking Cook meats in small amount of water:

- skins at 95° C (203° F) until soft.
- other meats at 80-85° C (176-185° F) until soft. Save stock.

After cooking remove gristle from lungs and meat from heads. Spread meats apart on a flat surface to cool. Don't cool by rinsing with water.
Boil rice until semi-soft taking 200-250 liters of meat stock or water for each 100 kg of rice (200-250 g of broth/water per 100 g of rice). Add rice to boiling stock/water and cook for 30 minutes stirring frequently. After boiling leave for 1 hr covered.

Grinding Head meat, jowls, snouts ground through 8 mm plate. Other meats ground with 3 mm plate.

Mixing Add salt and spices to ground meats, then mix with blood and rice well together.

Stuffing Stuff loosely into large hog casings, after ends, or 80 mm synthetic casings. Make links 15-30 cm (6-12" long).

Cooking Immerse sausages in a boiling water and cook at 80-85° C (176-185° F) for about 60-90 min until sausages reach 68-70° C (154-158° F) internal temperature.

Cooling Place sausages in cold water for 15 minutes and then spread them on a flat surface to cool to 6° C (43° F) or lower.

Lodzka Blood Sausage

(Kiszka łódzka)

Blood sausage with bread crumbs popular in Lodz, the second biggest city in Poland.

Dewlap/jowls, 250 g, (0.55 lb)
Pork skins, 100 g, (0.22 lb)
Cooking vessel fat, * 50 g (0.11 lb)
Blood, 350 g, (0.77 lb)
Dry rolls or bread crumbs, 250 g (0.55 lb)
* *Cooking vessel fat is the fat that remains after boiling meats.*

Ingredients per 1 kg (2.2 lb) materials

Salt, 18 g (3 tsp)
Herbal pepper, * 2.0 g (1 tsp)
Marjoram, 2.0 g (1 tsp)
Allspice, 0.5 g (1/4 tsp)
Cinnamon, 0.5 g (1/4 tsp)

* *The herbal pepper (white mustard seed, caraway,marjoram, chili, hot and sweet paprika, bay leaf) may be substituted with a ½ amount of regular pepper).*

Cooking Cook in a small amount of water:
- dewlaps/jowls at 80-85° C (176-185° F) until semi-soft.
- skins at 95° C (203° F) until soft.

Spread meats apart on a flat surface to cool.

Grinding Cut dewlap/jowls into 5-8 mm (2-3”) cubes, grind skins through 3 mm plate. Cut rolls, soak in blood for 20-30 min and grind through 8 mm plate.

Mixing Add salt and spices to ground meats, add ground rolls, blood and melted vessel fat and mix everything well together.

Stuffing Stuff loosely into 36 mm or larger hog casings or beef middles up to 40 mm. Form rings. Tie the ends with twine.

Cooking Immerse in a boiling water and cook at 80-82° C (176-180° F) for 30-35 min until sausages reach 68-70° C (154-158° F) internal temperature.

Cooling Immerse sausages for 15 min in cold water, then hang and cool to 6° C (43° F) or lower. Keep refrigerated.

Popular Blood Sausage

(Kiszka kaszana popularna)

A popular blood sausage.

Beef class V, beef and veal lips, skins, spleens, lungs, beef and lamb liver, udders, beef and lamb tripe, veal casings, pork stomachs, skwarki *, boiled beef, veal and lamb head meat, boiled bone meat, 600 g (0.66 lb)
Fat (stock fat from cooking meats), 200 g (0.44 lb)
Blood, 300 g (0.66 lb)
Barley or buckwheat groats, 200 g (0.44 lb)

Use 50-100 g skins. Save meat stock.
** Skwarki, see page 78.*

Ingredients per 1 kg (2.2 lb) of material

Salt, 20 g (3-1/3 tsp)
Pepper, 2.0 g (1 tsp)
Marjoram, 2.0 g (1 tsp)
Onion, 30 g (1/2 small onion)

The natural pepper may be substituted with double amount of herbal pepper (white mustard seed, caraway,marjoram, chili, hot and sweet paprika, bay leaf).

Cooking Cook meats (except liver, spleen and skwarki *) in small amount of water:

- lungs at 80-85° C (176-185° F) until soft.
- skins, beef class V, lips, udders, tripe and heads at 95° C (203° F).
- veal casings at 80-85° C (176-185° F) until semi-soft.

After cooking remove gristle from lungs and meat from heads when still warm. Spread meats apart on a flat surface to cool. Boil barley grouts (200 g) in 400-440 ml of left over meat stock or water until semi-soft. Boil buckwheat grouts (200 kg) in 360-400 ml of left over stock or water. Boil grouts for ½ hr stirring continuously. After boiling leave for ½-1 hr covered.

Grinding Beef type V, skins, beef and veal lips, lungs, udders, veal casings, pork stomachs-all boiled and ground through 3 mm plate. Grind boiled head and bone meat through 3 mm plate. Grind beef and lamb liver, raw spleen and skwarki * through 3 mm plate.

Mixing	Add salt and spices to ground meats, mix barley or buckwheat groats with blood, add stock fat and then mix everything well together.
Stuffing	Stuff loosely into 50 mm cellulose or fibrous synthetic casings. Straight links 40-45 cm (16-18") long. The ends tied up with twine. Hanging loop 10-12 cm (4-5") at one end.
Cooking	Immerse sausages into boiling water and cook at 75-78° C (167-172° F) for about 80-100 min until sausages reach 68-70° C (154-158° F) internal temperature.
Cooling	Immerse sausages for 15 min in cold water, then hang and cool to 6° C (43° F) or lower. Keep refrigerated.

Due to its high water content (85%) and many nutrients blood is a highly perishable product attracting bacteria. It must be immediately collected and cooled quickly to about 37° F (3° C) and stored for up to 2 days at about 32° F (0° C) or in a refrigerator. Then it must be processed. After cooking blood will be black even if cured with nitrite. To extend its life, blood can be frozen.

Silesian Krupnioki

(Krupnioki śląskie)

Krupnioki borrows its name from the silesian word "krup" which in pure Polish means "kasza" (buckwheat or barley grouts). Basically a different, regional name for a blood sausage.

Pork head meat, jowls, snouts, 200 g (0.44 lb)
Pork liver, 50 g (0.11 lb)
Pork lungs, 150 g (0.33 lb)
Pork skins, 50 g (0.11 lb)
Pork jowls/dewlaps, 50 g (0.11 lb)
Skwarki, * 50 g (0.11 lb)
Stock fat (from boiling meats), 100 g (0.22 lb)
Pork blood, 200 g (0.44 lb)
Buckwheat groats, 150 g (0.33 lb)

Ingredients per 1 kg (2.2 lb) of material

Salt, 20 g (3-1/3 tsp)
Pepper, 2.0 g (1 tsp)
Marjoram, 1.0 g (1/2 tsp)
Allspice, 0.5 g (1/4 tsp)
Onion, 30 g (1/2 small onion)

* *Skwarki see page 78.*

Cooking Cook meats (except liver and skwarki *) in small amount of water:

- skins at 95° C (203° F).
- dewlap at 80-85° C (176-185° F) until semi-soft.
- other meats at 80-85° C (176-185° F) until soft.

Remove gristle from lungs and meat from heads when still warm. Spread meats apart on a flat surface to cool.
Boil buckwheat grouts (150 g) in 270-300 ml of left over meat stock or water. One cup holds 250 ml of water. Boil grouts for ½ hr stirring continuously. After boiling leave for ½-1 hr covered.

Grinding Grind the following meats through 3 mm plate:

- boiled: head meat, jowls, snouts, dewlap, lungs.
- raw liver, fresh onion.
- skwarki * (soaked in meat stock).

Mixing Add salt and spices to ground meats, mix buckwheat grouts with blood, add stock fat and then mix everything well together.

Stuffing Stuff loosely into 32-36 mm hog casings. Form paired links 18-20 cm (17-18") long. Approximate weight each link 250 g. Tie the ends with twine.

Cooking Immerse sausages in boiling water and cook at 85° C (185° F) for about 30 minutes.

Cooling Immerse sausages for 15 min in cold water, then hang and cool to 6° C (43° F) or lower. Keep refrigerated.

Simple Blood Sausage

(Kiszka krwista zwyczajna)

A simple blood sausage.

Pork blood, 570 g (1.25 lb)
Pork or veal lungs, skwarki *, pork skins, 250 g (0.55 lb)
Groin, 70 g (0.15 lb)
Bread crumbs or dry rolls, 110 g (0.24 lb)
No more than total of 10 % of skins and skwarki is permitted.*

Ingredients per 1 kg (2.2 lb) of material

Salt, 20 g (3-1/3 tsp)
Herbal pepper, ** 2.0 g
Marjoram, 3.0 g (1.5 tsp)
Cinnamon, 0.5 g (1/4 tsp)
Allspice, 0.5 g (1/4 tsp)
Onion, 5.0 g (1 tablespoon)

* *Skwarki, see page 78.*
** *The herbal pepper (white mustard seed, caraway,marjoram, chili, hot and sweet paprika, bay leaf) may be substituted with a ½ amount of regular pepper).*

Cooking Cook meats in small amount of water:

- lungs and groin at 80-85° C (176-185° F) until semi-soft. Save stock.
- skins at 95° C (203° F) until soft. Remove gristle from lungs and meat from heads when still warm. Spread meats apart on a flat surface to cool.

Soaking Cover rolls with an equal amount of meat stock and soak for about ½ hr. Soak skwarki * in stock using 25% of stock in relation to the weight of skwarki.

Grinding Grind soaked in stock rolls through 2 mm plate. Grind all meats through 2 mm plate.

Mixing Mix all ground ingredients with blood, adding salt and spices.

Stuffing Stuff loosely into pork middles or beef rounds 40 cm (16”) each.

Cooking Immerse sausages in boiling water and cook at 80-85 ° C (176-185° F) for about 50-80 min until sausages reach 68-70° C (154-158° F) internal temperature.

Cooling Immerse sausages for 15 min in cold water, then hang and cool to 6° C (43° F) or lower. Keep refrigerated.

Supreme Blood Sausage

(Kiszka kaszana wyborowa)

Blood sausage with buckwheat or barley grouts.

Pork head meat, jowls, snouts, 200 g (0.44 lb)
Jowls, 200 g (0.44 lb)
Pork liver, 50 g (0.11 lb)
Pork or veal lungs, 100 g (0.22 lb)
Pork skins, 50 g (0.11 lb)
Blood, 200 g (0.44 lb)
Buckwheat or barley groats, 200 g (0.44 lb)

Ingredients per 1 kg (2.2 lb) of materials

Salt, 20 g (3-1/3 tsp)
Pepper, 2.0 g (1 tsp)
Marjoram, 2.0 g (1 tsp)
Allspice, 0.5 g (1/4 tsp)
Onion, 30 g (1/2 small onion)

The natural pepper may be substituted with equal amount of herbal pepper (white mustard seed, caraway,marjoram, chili, hot and sweet paprika, bay leaf).

Boiling Cook meats (except liver) in small amount of water:

- skins at 95° C (203° F) until soft.
- jowls at 85° C (185° F) until semi-soft.
- other meats at 80-85° C (176-185° F) until soft.

Remove gristle from lungs and meat from heads when still warm. Spread meats apart on a flat surface to cool.
Boil barley grouts (200 g) in 400-440 ml of left over meat stock or water until semi-soft. Boil buckwheat grouts (200 g) in 360-400 ml of left over meat stock or water. One cup holds 250 ml of water. Boil grouts for ½ hr continuously stirring. After boiling leave for ½-1 hr covered.

Grinding Head meat, jowls, snouts and ¼ (50 g) dewlap ground through 10 mm plate. Grind lungs and remaining ¾ (150 g) jowls through 5 mm plate. Grind boiled skins through 3 mm plate. Grind raw liver through 3 mm plate.

Mixing Add salt and spices to ground meats, mix barley or buckwheat grouts with blood and then mix everything together.

Stuffing Stuff loosely into pork middles or beef rounds. Pork middles or beef rounds, 15-30 cm (6-12") each. About 8 cm (3") thick. The ends tied up with twine.

Cooking Immerse sausages in boiling water and cook at 80-85° C (176-185° F) for about 60-90 min until sausages reach 68-70° C (154-158° F) internal temperature.

Cooling Immerse sausages for 15 min in cold water, then hang and cool to 6° C (43° F) or lower. Keep refrigerated.

Photo 12.10 Blood sausage.

Photo courtesy Dziadek

Other Kiszki

The following two sausages are classified as kiszki, however they do not fit into liver or blood sausage group.

Brain Sausage

(Kiszka mózgowa)

A sausage where the principal ingredient are brains.

Pork, beef. veal or lamb brains, 500 g
Fat trimmings, 250 g
Pork skins, 100 g
Pork class IV, 50 g
Semolina flour, 100 g

Ingredients per 1 kg (2.2 lb) materials

Salt, 18 g (3 tsp)
Pepper, 2.0 g (1 tsp)
Ginger, 0.5 g (1/4 tsp)
Allspice, 0.5 g (1/4 tsp)
Onion, 30 g (1/2 small onion)

Cooking In a small amount of water cook the following::

- pork type IV for 10-15 min at 80-85° C (176-185° F).
- pork skins for 2-3 hours at 85° C (185° F) and then they are drained..Save stock.

Grinding Brains, fat trimmings, precooked pork class IV, *cooked* skins and onion, all ground through 2 mm plate.

Emulsifying Using food processor emulsify semolina with the equivalent amount of stock left after poaching skins for about 10 minutes. Then add salt, spices and skins and emulsify for additional 5-10 min. Add pork class IV, fat trimmings, brains and emulsify everything together until an uniform paste is obtained.

Stuffing Stuff into 55-60 mm cellulose or synthetic fibrous casings. casings. Make straight links 35-40 cm (14-16"), about 5 cm (2") diameter. Tie the ends and make hanging loop.

Cooking Immerse sausages in boiling water and poach at 80-85° C (176-185° F) for 50-90 min until sausages reach 68-70° C (154-158° F) internal temperature.

Cooling Cool sausages in cold water for 15 minutes, then hang them and in a drafty area to 6° C (43° F) or lower.

Jowl Sausage
(Kiszka podgardlana)

All trimmings sausage with significant amount of jowls.

Pork, beef, veal or lamb liver, 100 g (0.22 lb)
Beef or lamb lungs, tripe, pork stomachs, veal casings, boiled beef, veal and lamb head meat, boiled bone meat, brains, pork class IV, skwarki *, skins, boiled pork or veal leg meat, 500 g (1.10 lb)
Fat trimmings, skinless jowls and dewlaps, 200 g (0.44 lb)
Semolina flour or dry rolls or bread crumbs, 200 g (0.44 lb)

Ingredients per 1 kg (2.2 lb) of materials

Salt, 20 g (3-1/3 tsp)
Pepper, 2.0 g (1 tsp)
Marjoram, 2.0 g (1 tsp)
Allspice, 0.5 g (1/4 tsp)
Onion, 30 g (1/2 small onion)

** Skwarki see page 78.*
The natural pepper may be substituted with a double amount of herbal pepper (white mustard seed, caraway, marjoram, chili, hot and sweet paprika, bay leaf).

Cooking Poach meats (except liver, brains and skwarki *) in small amount of water:

- lungs and veal casings at 80-85° C (176-185° F).
- other meats (except fat) at 95° C (203° F) until soft. Save stock.
- fat at 85° C (185° F) until semi-soft.

After poaching remove gristle from lungs and meat from heads and legs. Spread meats apart on a flat surface to cool.

Grinding Fat, pork class IV and lungs ground through 3 mm plate. All other meats ground through 3 mm plate. Soak bread crumbs or dry rolls in 75% (in relation to the weight of the rolls) of left over stock.

Emulsifying In food processor emulsify semolina flour (if used) with 75% of left over stock after poaching. Emulsify separately tripe, stomachs and veal casings adding 10-15% of left over stock. When emulsifying tripe, add salt and spices.

Mixing Mix either emulsified semolina or soaked in stock rolls (bread crumbs) with emulsified meats.

Stuffing	Stuff loosely into pork middles or synthetic casings. Straight links 25-35 cm (10-14"), diameter random. The ends tied with twine.
Cooking	Immerse sausages into boiling water at 80-85° C (176-185° F) for 50-90 min until sausages reach 68-70° C (154-158° F) internal temperature.
Cooling	Spread sausages on flat surface and cool to 6° C (43° F) or less.

Photo 12.11 Polish Kabanosy sausage is without a doubt the finest meat stick in the world. Kabanosy are shown in a big pile on the left and Wiktor Minkiewicz has to make quite a lot of them to meet the demand.

Chapter 13

Old Sausage Recipes

In the past sausages were made using the same processing steps as today. Meat was chopped with a knife and manually stuffed with any device that would be suitable. Back fat was normally cut into long and narrow strips. Wood for smoking was often wet and the final product was very dark. Sometimes after smoking the sausages were over baked or sometimes still raw and needed to be cooked in water. In many cases sausages were not smoked at all but dried for a few hours over a hot stove plate and then kept in a cool place. Then the sausage was boiled in water before serving.

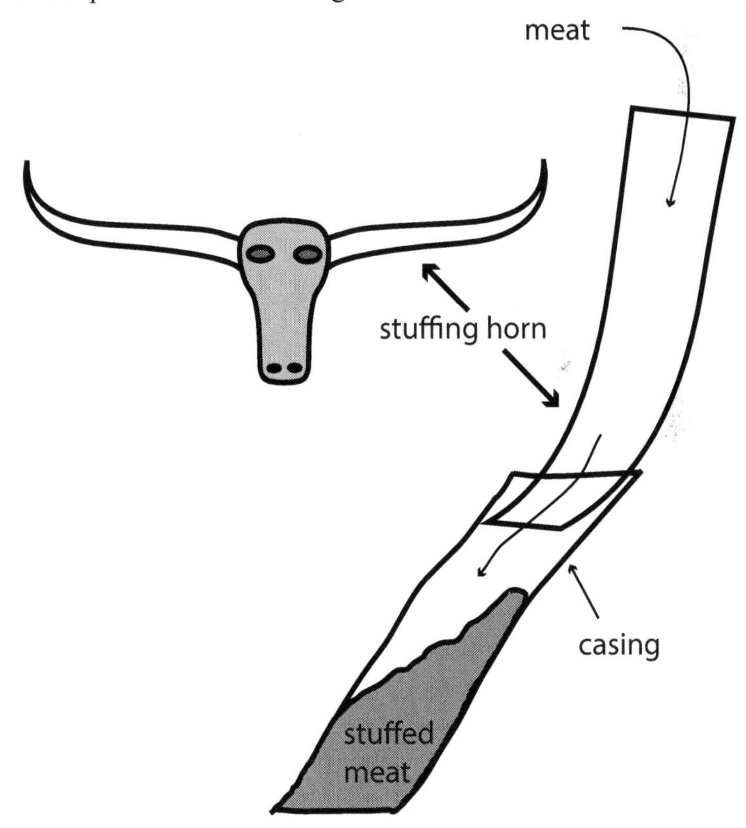

Fig. 13.1 To stuff sausage casings with manually cut meat any suitable device was used: a section of pipe, a funnel or an animal stuffing horn.

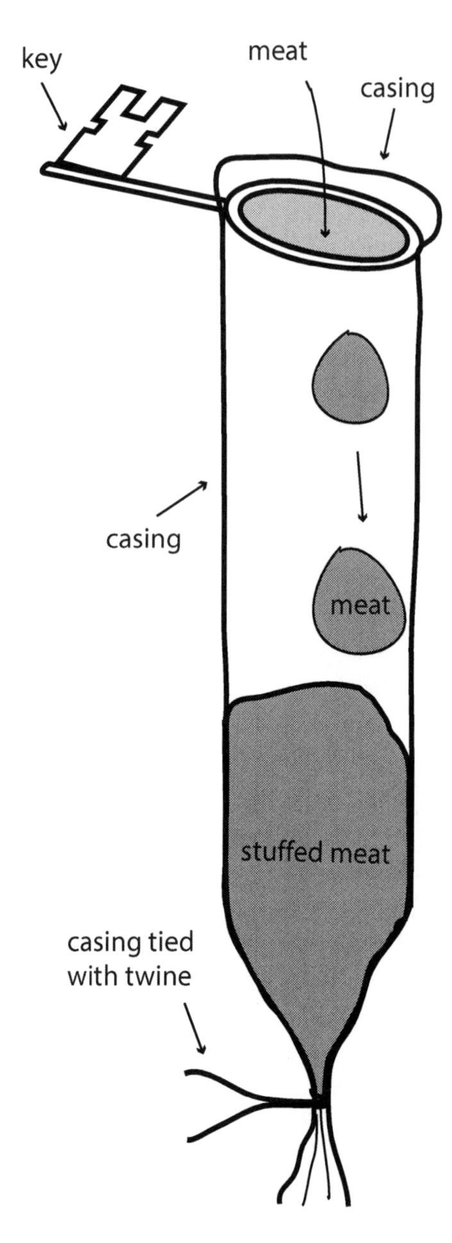

Old keys were massive pieces of metal and the loop of the key would be inserted into the end of the casing. The casing would be held around the key loop with fingers. The other end of the casing would be tied with butcher's twine.

Meat would be pushed down through the loop of the key and from time to time the casing would be removed and meat would be pushed down further by squeezing the casing on the outside. The process would eliminate most of the air which was important as most sausages were smoked and air dried. This operation would be repeated until the casing would be full.

Then the open end of the casing would be tied with twine and the sausage would be rolled over on a flat surface to make it straight. Any air pockets would be removed by pricking them with a needle.

Fig. 13.2 Key method of stuffing a sausage.

Finger Sausage
(Palcówka)

One of the oldest known sausages that gets its name from the method used to fill the casing. The casings were stuffed with fingers (palce) by means of any suitable device like a pipe, funnel or a horn (stuffing horn). Needless to say a meat grinder was either not invented yet, or only a few lucky ones happened to own it. The majority of people had to chop meat manually with a knife.

That required careful meat selection and removal of all inedible parts like sinews, gristle, parts of tendon, etc. Today a grinder will cut and mechanically tenderize meat at the same time but in those times meat was cut into little chunks. The product was definitely juicy and first class.

Pork butt, 400 g (0.88 lb)
Lean pork (ham) or lean beef, 400 g (0.88 lb)
Belly or back fat, 200 g (0.44 lb)

Ingredients per 1 kg (2.2 lb) of meat

Salt, 21 g (3-1/2 tsp)
Cure #1, 2.5 g (1/2 tsp)
Pepper, 2.0 g (1 tsp)
Sugar, 3.0 g (1/2 tsp)
Garlic, 1.5 g (1/2 clove)
Coriander, 1.0 g (1/2 tsp)
White mustard seeds, 1.0 g (1/2 tsp)
Marjoram, 1.0 g (1/2 tsp)
Allspice, 1.0 g (1/2 tsp)

Curing	Cut meat into ½-¾" (1-2 cm) pieces. Cur belly into smaller pieces. Mix meat pieces with salt, Cure #1 and sugar. Pack tight in container and leave in refrigerator for 24 hours.
Mixing	Mix meat with spices. Add an extra 6 g (1 tsp) of salt if *cold smoked* sausage will be made.
Stuffing	Stuff through a funnel into hog casings.
Cold Smoking	Apply *cold* smoke for 2 days. Hang at 11° C (52° F) for 2 weeks to dry. *Do not cook.*
***OR* Hot Smoking**	Apply hot smoke for 2 hours.
Cooking	Cook *hot smoked* sausages in water at 80° C (176° C) until the sausages reach 72° C (160° F) internal temperature.

Kindziuk

(Kindziuk)

Lithuania was the region that developed a reputation for making wonderful and long lasting products. One of the most famous products was known as "Kindziuk" ("Skilandis" in Lithuanian).

Lean pork *(ham, butt)*, 850 g (1.87 lb)
Lean beef (chuck), 150 g (0.33 lb)

Ingredients per 1 kg (2.2 lb) of meat

Salt, 30 g (5 tsp)
Cure #2, 5.0 g (1 tsp)
Sugar, 0.5 g (1/5 tsp)
Black pepper, 2.0 g (1 tsp)
Garlic, 3.0 g (1 clove)

Curing Cut meat into 1.5" (300-400 g) pieces. Rub in salt, Cure # 2 and sugar and leave on a screen for 3-4 days at 3-4° (37-40° F) to drain the moisture away.

Grinding Cut pork into 20-30 mm (3/4-11/4") by 10-15 mm (3/8-5/8") pieces. Grind beef through 2-3 mm (1/8") plate.

Mixing Mix meats with spices.

Stuffing Stuff firmly into pork stomach, bladder, 60 mm hog middles or large fibrous casing (60 mm). Avoid creating air pockets. Reinforce with butcher's twine: two loops lengthwise and loops across the casings every 5 cm (2 inches). Form 10-12 cm (4-5") hanging loop on one end.

Drying/ Smoking Hang for 2 months at 2-4° C (35-40° F).
Apply cold smoke 18-22° C (64-72° F) for 8 hours.
Hang in a cool place for 2 weeks.
Apply cold smoke 18-22° C (64-72° F) for 8 hours (2nd time).
Dry for 2 months at 8° C (46° F) and 75% humidity. The sausage should loose about 35% of its original weight.

Storing Store in a dark, cool and dry place.

Notes Meat should come from mature animals.
Traditional Kindziuk was smoked with alder wood.

Nobility Sausage
(Kiełbasa szlachecka)

The Polish term "szlachta" designated the "gentle" or "noble class." It encompassed the idea of gentility or nobility of blood, and was roughly equivalent to the English "gentry" and "nobility." A specific nobleman was called a "szlachcic," and a noblewoman, a "szlachcianka". This particular sausage had to be good if it was nicknamed the nobility sausage.

Old records indicate that this sausage was already produced at the beginning of the XVII century when everything was made by hand and the word meat technology was not invented yet. Many say that this is The Sausage of all of them and that nothing else comes close. All we can say that this recipe is quite original if only for the fact that it calls for sea salt. Sea salt which contains many minerals was often added when bone in hams were made in a traditional way. The reason was that sea salt having coarse grain would keep on eliminating moisture much longer than regular salt. It also had a milder flavor.

You may also wonder why eggs were used. Well, lean meat class I has no connective tissue and is ill suited for binding sliced meats together. Eggs have been traditionally used in the kitchen to bind ingredients together and in this case they bind the meat.

Lean pork, *(ham, butt)*, 1000 g (2.2 lb)

Ingredients per 1 kg (2.2 lb) of meat

Sea salt, 18 g (3 tsp)
Pepper, 3.0 g (1-1/2 tsp)
Garlic, 1.5 g (1/2 clove)
Basil, 1.0 g (1/2 tsp)
Oregano, 1.0 g (1/2 tsp)
Honey, 25 ml (1 oz)
Egg, 1
Water, 50 ml (2 oz)

Cutting Cut meat into ½" slices.

Pounding/ Grinding Mix meats with salt and spices. Place meats in a suitable container and pound them with a wooden pestle until squashed.

Curing Leave in a cool place for 12 hours.

Mixing Add egg and mix for about 15 minutes until there is no trace of egg.

Stuffing	Stuff into beef bungs, pork middles. pork bladder or synthetic fibrous casings. Stuff firmly through a funnel using your hands and make sure there are no air pockets. Sausage in beef bungs 35-50 cm (14-20") lengths and laced up with twine. Two loops lengthwise and loops across the bung every 4-6 cm (1.5-2 1/4"). Fibrous casings: 35-40 cm (14-16") lengths and laced up with twine. Two loops lengthwise and loops across the casings every 4-5 cm (1.5-2"). The ends tied up with twine, hanging loop 10-12 cm (4-5") on one end.
Smoking	Smoke with warm smoke until dark brown color is obtained.
Baking	Bake in oven at 180° C (350° F) for 1.5 hours. Originally the sausages were baked in adobe bread ovens.
Cooling	Leave for at least 5 hours at room temperature.

Photo 13.1 Nobility *(szlachecka)* sausage.

Photo courtesy Szczepan

Staropolska Sausage

(Kiełbasa staropolska)

Recipe provided by: "Szczepan

One of the oldest Polish sausages made by monks in a monastery that was originally stuffed with a key.

Lean pork, *(ham, butt)*, 700 g (1.54 lb)
Fat pork (*butt*), 100 g (0.22 lb)
Fat pork (*picnic*), 200 g (0.44 lb)

Ingredients per 1 kg (2.2 lb) of meat

Salt, 18 g (3 tsp)
Cure # 1, 2.5 g (1/2 tsp)
Sugar, 1.0 g (1/2 tsp)
Pepper, 3.0 g (1-1/2 tsp)
Garlic, 1.5 g (1/2 clove)
Nutmeg, 0.5 g (1/4 tsp)

Photo 13.2 Staropolska sausage.

Grinding Cut lean pork into 1.5 cm x 2 cm (5/8 x 3/4") squares. Grind fat pork (butt) through 6 mm plate. Grind fat pork (picnic) through 3 mm plate.

Mixing Smash garlic and add with sugar to 50 ml (2 oz) of water. Bring to a boil then remove from heat and let cool at room temperature. Mix garlic solution with ground meats.

Stuffing Stuff firmly into 28-30 mm hog casings forming 40 cm (16") pairs.

Conditioning Hang sausages for 2 hours, preferably in a drafty area.

Smoking With warm smoke for 4 hours until light brown color is obtained.

Baking Increase smokehouse temperature to 80-85° C (176-185° F) and maintain for 1 hour.

Cooling Remove sausages from the smokehouse and cool in the air.

Smoking Cold smoke for 4 hours.

Storing Store at 12° C (53° F) or lower.

Wooden Pick Method of Tying Sausages

The original recipes that were listed in government manuals asked for butcher's twine or wooden picks as materials used to tie the ends of sausage casings. In this book we mention only butcher's twine but we explain below how the picks were employed. To begin with they have one big advantage over butcher's twine: all you need is a knife and a tree branch to make them. And that was very important when the war ended in Poland as often there was no twine available but people were making sausages all the same. *The round wooden picks that are used for holding meats on sandwiches will be a perfect material.* This is a very simple and quite ingenious method and people still use it today. It is not used when poaching sausages in water as they move and the picks might puncture the casings.

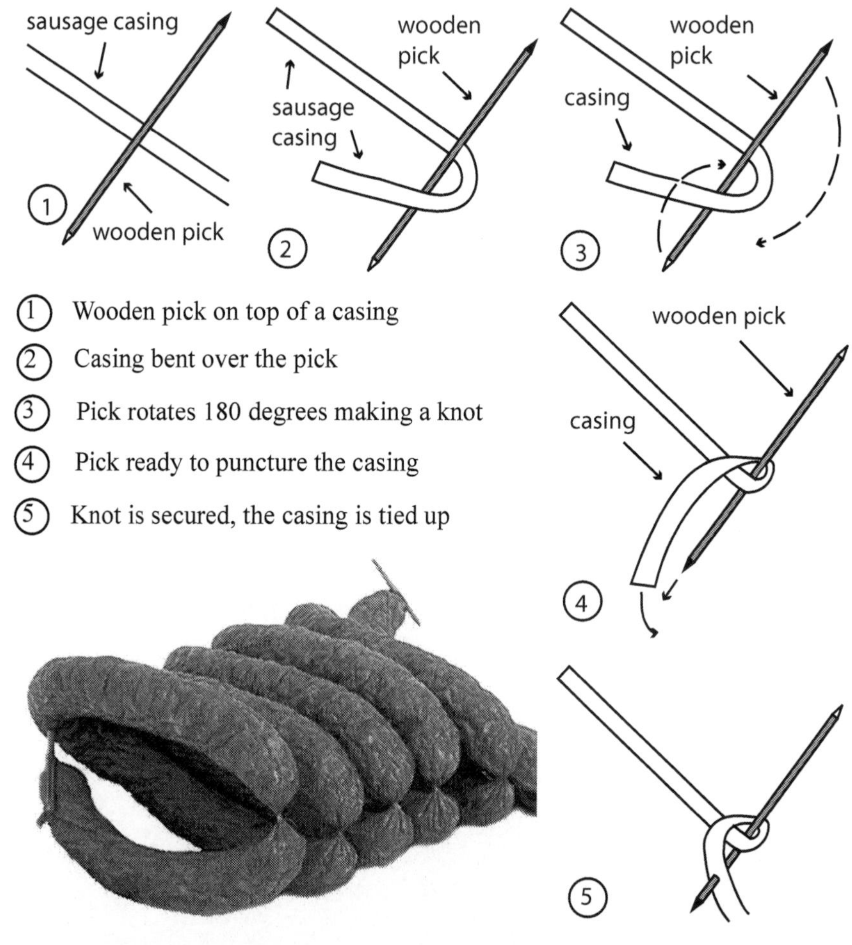

1. Wooden pick on top of a casing
2. Casing bent over the pick
3. Pick rotates 180 degrees making a knot
4. Pick ready to puncture the casing
5. Knot is secured, the casing is tied up

Photo 13.3 Mysliwska Sausage tied with wooden picks.

You can make more than one rotation with a pick and the knot will be even stronger.

Chapter 14

Other Sausages of Merit

Grandpa's Pork and Turkey Sausage
(Kiełbasa Dziadka wieprzowo-indycza)

Recipe by "Dziadek"

Great sausage recipe created by Master Butcher and sausage Maker "Dziadek". What makes it more interesting is that it uses a combination of pork and turkey and it could be modified to accommodate any wild game bird.

Lean pork butt, 200 g
Fat pork butt, 200 g
Pork type III (with connective tissue), 100 g
Turkey leg meat, 400 g
Jowls/dewlap, 50 g
Fat trimmings, 50 g

Ingredients per 1 kg (2.2 lb) of meat

Salt, 18 g (3 tsp)
Cure #1, 2.5 g` (1/2 tsp)
Pepper, 1.0 g (1/2 tsp)
White mustard, 1.0 g (1/2 tsp)
Coriander, 1.0 g (1/2 tsp)
Caraway, 1.0 g (1/2 tsp)
Marjoram, 1.0 g (1/2 tsp)
Sugar, 1.0 g (1/5 tsp)
Garlic, 3.0 g (1 clove)
Water, 30 ml (1 oz)

Photo 14.1 Pork and turkey sausage.
Photo courtesy Dziadek

Grinding Grind:

- lean pork and turkey through 12 mm plate.
- fat pork through 8 mm plate.
- jowls and fat trimmings through 6 mm plate.
- pork type III through 3 mm plate.

Mixing Mix pork type III with 30 ml of water until sticky. Add lean pork, turkey meat, pork type III, salt, Cure # 1, spices, and mix until sticky. Add jowls, fat pork, and ground fat trimmings and mix everything together.

Stuffing Stuff into 32-36 mm hog casings forming 25-26 cm (10") links. Leave in a continuous coil.

Conditioning Hang for 1 hour at room temperature.

Drying Dry sausages in a smoker (no smoke applied) at 40-60° C (104-140° F) until casings feel dry. Leave draft controls or top of your smoker fully open.

Smoking Smoke with hot smoke 45-60° C (113-140° F) for 80-100 min until brown. Total time of drying and smoking about 3 hours.

Cooking **Baking**: at 85° C (185° F) for 30 min until sausages reach 68-72° C (154-161° F) internal temperature ***OR***
Poaching: in water at 72-75° C (161-167° F) until sausages reach 68-72° C (154-161° F) internal temperature.

Cooling Cool baked sausages in air, poached sausages in cold water. Keep refrigerated.

Grill Sausage with Cheese

(Kiełbasa grillowa z żółtym serem)
Recipe by: "Szczepan

Tasty fully cooked sausage that can be grilled or fried. Very popular with kids

Lean pork, *(ham, butt)*, 400 g (0.88 lb)
Pork belly, 350 g (0.77 lb)
Pork class III (*picnic*) or beef, 200 g (0.44 lb)
Hard yellow cheese, 50 g (0.11 lb)

Photo 14.2 Grill sausage.

Ingredients per 1 kg (2.2 lb) of materials

Salt, 18 g (3 tsp)
Cure # 1, 2.5 g (1/2 tsp)
Sugar, 1.0 g (1/5 tsp)
Pepper, 1.0 g (1/2 tsp)
Paprika, 1.5 g (3/4 tsp)
Garlic, 1.5 g (1/2 clove)
Nutmeg, 0.5 g (1/4 tsp)
Basil, 1.0 g (1/2 tsp)

Grinding Grind lean pork through 8 mm plate. Grind belly through 3 mm plate. Grind pork class III or beef 2-3 times through 3 mm plate. Dice yellow cheese into 10 mm (3/8") cubes.

Mixing Knead pork class III (*picnic*) or beef until gluey. Add remaining meats, spices and 100 mm (3/8 cup) of water and mix well together. At the end add diced cheese and mix until evenly distributed.

Stuffing Stuff firmly into 26-28 mm hog casings forming 18-20 cm (7-8") links.

Smoking With hot smoke until light brown in color.

Cooking In water at 75° C (167° F) for 20 minutes.

Cooling Shower with cold water to 15° C (60° F) or less. Keep refrigerated.

Notes Use a hard yellow cheese with 45% fat or less. During smoking and cooking a softer cheese will not hold its shape and will melt down.

Pork And Beef Sausage
(Kiełbasa wieprzowo-wołowa)

Recipe by Jacek Woś "Ligawa"

Just two spices are used and the quality of this sausage depends primarily on proper meat selection. Brisket fat is what gives this sausage a specific pleasant taste.

Lean pork *(ham)*, 500 g (1.10 lb)
Beef (*brisket*), 150 g (0.33 lb)
Fat trimmings from *ham or butt* (40/60 % fat/lean), 200 g (0.44 lb)
Back fat or jowls, 150 g (0.33 lb)

Beef brisket should not be overly fat. Absolutely, no beef fat or suet is allowed to be added.

Ingredients per 1 kg of meat

Salt, 18 g (3 tsp)
Cure # 1, 2.0 g (1/2 tsp)
Pepper, 1.5 g (3/4 tsp)
Garlic, 3.0 g (1 clove)
Water, 75 mm (1/3 cup)

Grinding Grind pork through 12 mm plate. Grind beef through 6 mm plate. Grind jowls and fat trimmings through 3 mm plate.

Mixing Mix all ground meats with salt, Cure #1, spices and water until the mixture feels sticky. Add ground fat and mix again.

Stuffing Stuff into 38-40 mm hog casings forming 60 cm (24") rings.

Conditioning Hang for 60 minutes at room temperature.

Drying Dry sausages in a smoker (no smoke applied) at 40-60° C (104-140° F) until casings feel dry. Leave draft controls or top of your smoker fully open.

Smoking With hot smoke for 4 hours.

Cooking **Baking**: at 85° C (185° F) for 30 min until sausages reach 68-72° C (154-161° F) internal temperature ***OR***
Cooking in water at 72-75° C (161-167° F) until sausages reach 68-72° C (154-161° F) internal temperature.

Cooling Cool baked sausages in air, poached sausages in cold water. Keep refrigerated.

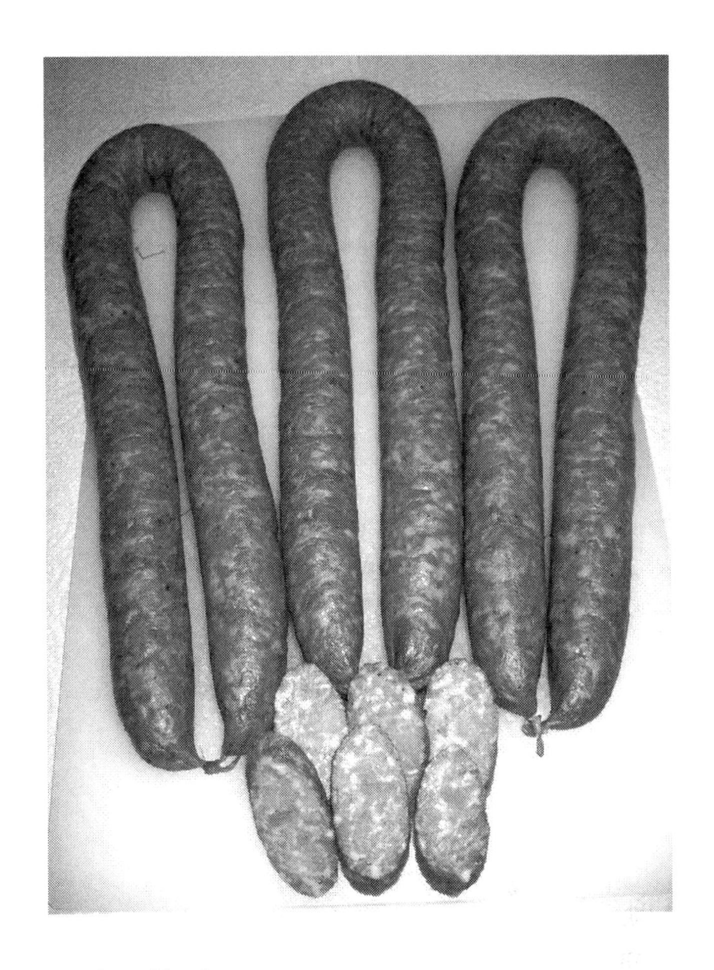

Photo 14.3 Pork and beef sausage.

Photo courtesy Jacek Woś Ligawa.

Index

T

V

W

Other Books by Stanley and Adam Marianski

Home Production of Quality Meats and Sausages bridges the gap that exists between highly technical textbooks and the requirements of the typical hobbyist. The book covers topics such as curing and making brines, smoking meats and sausages, making special sausages such as head cheeses, blood and liver sausages, hams, bacon, butts, loins, safety and more...

ISBN: 978-0-9824267-3-9

Meat Smoking And Smokehouse Design explains differences between grilling, barbecuing and smoking. There are extensive discussions of curing as well as the particulars about smoking sausages, meat, fish, poultry and wild game.

ISBN: 978-0-9824267-0-8

The Art Of Making Fermented Sausages shows readers how to control meat acidity and removal of moisture, choose proper temperatures for fermenting, smoking and drying, understand and control fermentation process, choose proper starter cultures and make traditional or fast-fermented products, choose proper equipment, and much more...

ISBN: 978-0-9824267-1-5

Home Canning Meat, Poultry, Fish and Vegetables explains in simple language the science of canning low-acid foods such as meat, poultry, fish ans vegetables and reveals the procedures that are used by the canning industry. The material is based on the U.S. government requirements as specified in the Code of Federal Regulations and the relevant links are listed. After studying the book, a newcomer to the art of canning will be able to safely process foods at home in both glass and metal containers.

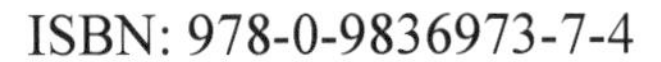
ISBN: 978-0-9836973-7-4

Home Production of Vodkas, Infusions & Liqueurs is a guide for making quality alcohol beverages at home. The book adopts factory methods of making spirits but without the need for any specialized equipment. A different type of alcohol beverage can be produced from the same fruit and the authors explain in simple terms all necessary rules.

ISBN: 978-0-9836973-4-3

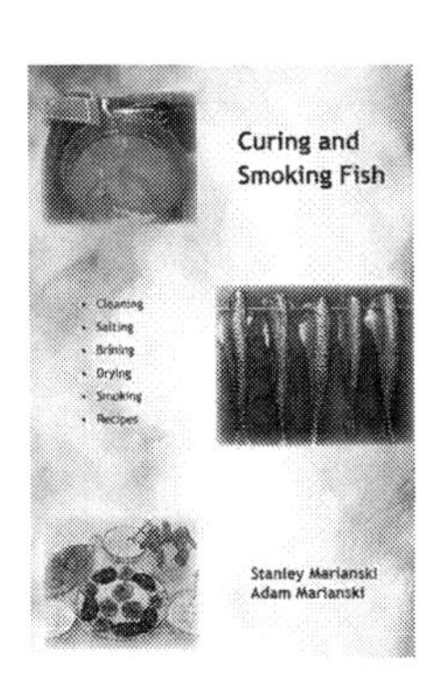

Curing and Smoking Fish provides all the information needed to understand the entire process of preparing and smoking fish, shellfish such as clams, mussels, oysters and shrimp. The subject of making brines is covered in detail and simplified by advocating the use of brine tables and testers. A collection of recipes for smoking fish, making fish spreads and preparing sauces for serving fish is included.

ISBN: 978-0-9836973-9-8

Sauerkraut, Kimchi, Pickles & Relishes teaches you how to lead a healthier and longer life. Most commercially produced foods are heated and that step eliminates many of the beneficial bacteria, vitamins and nutrients. However, most of the healthiest vegetables can be fermented without thermal processing. The book explains in simple terms the fermentation process, making brine, pickling and canning.

ISBN: 978-0-9836973-2-9

Making Healthy Sausages reinvents traditional sausage making by introducing a completely new way of thinking. The reader will learn how to make a product that is nutritional and healthy, yet delicious to eat. The collection of 80 recipes provides a valuable reference on the structure of reduced fat products.

ISBN: 978-0-9836973-0-5

The Amazing Mullet offers information that has been gathered through time and experience. Successful methods of catching, smoking and cooking fish are covered in great depth and numerous filleting, cleaning, cooking and smoking practices are reviewed thoroughly. In addition to mullet recipes, detailed information on making fish cakes, ceviche, spreads and sauces are also included.

ISBN: 978-0-9824267-8-4

Learn more at: **www.bookmagic.com**

Printed in Great Britain
by Amazon